'This book is an exciting, thoughtful and wide-ranging collection of papers from some of the leaders in the area of DDL. It is an understatement to say that it is long overdue! Amazingly, almost three decades have passed since DDL emerged as a pedagogical approach in language teaching and, in all of that time, this is the first edited volume to curate work on the use of DDL specifically in the context of young learners. While the volume is very forward-looking in the context of ever-improving technology and availability of corpus data and tools, contributors do not shy away from the challenges that have prevailed over the years to limit the mainstreaming of DDL as a pedagogical practice. Authors, exploring primary and secondary school learning contexts, showcase the potential of DDL for young learners but they consistently point to the need for more research, better teacher development and more equitable access to technology in primary and secondary schools. This book is a fanfare to what DDL has to offer in the context of language teaching in primary and secondary schools and, for sure, it will inspire teachers and researchers to open up to the opportunities of DDL for young learners.'

—**Dr Anne O'Keeffe**, *MIC, University of Limerick, Ireland*

'This is a very timely collection of papers that showcase recent research on pedagogical corpus use in primary and secondary school settings. The book will no doubt serve as an invaluable resource for anyone who is curious about whether and how DDL can work with younger learners, and for anyone who is ready to be inspired by some of the leading teacher-researchers in the field. Highly recommended!'

—**Ute Römer**, *Associate Professor of Applied Linguistics, Georgia State University, USA*

'This interesting and timely collection of studies is an essential reading for anyone conducting research on Data-Driven Learning (DDL) or considering using this approach with young learners. Together, the authors of the chapters present an in-depth review of the relevant literature on DDL, explain its strengths and weaknesses, and discuss the conceptual barriers and technical difficulties that might need to be overcome before the approach can be successfully adopted in the classroom. The book also describes some innovative uses of mainstream and custom DDL tools as well as offering many practical suggestions for designing useful DDL activities. In short, it is an extremely valuable resource.'

—**Laurence Anthony**, *Professor, Faculty of Science and Engineering, Waseda University, Japan*

DATA-DRIVEN LEARNING FOR THE NEXT GENERATION

Despite advancements in and availability of corpus software in language classrooms facilitating data-driven learning (DDL), the use of such methods with pre-tertiary learners remains rare. This book specifically explores the affordances of DDL for younger learners, testing its viability with teachers and students at the primary and secondary years of schooling. It features both eminent and up-and-coming researchers from Europe, Asia, and Australasia who seek to address best practice in implementing DDL with younger learners, while providing a wealth of empirical findings and practical DDL activities ready for use in the pre-tertiary classroom.

Divided into three parts, this volume's first section focuses on overcoming emerging challenges for DDL with younger learners, including where and how DDL can be integrated into pre-tertiary curricula, as well as potential barriers to this integration. It then considers new, cutting-edge innovations in corpora and corpus software for use with younger learners in the second section, before reporting on actual DDL studies performed with younger learners (and/or their teachers) at the primary and secondary levels of education.

This book will appeal to post-graduate students, academics, and researchers with interests in corpus linguistics, second language acquisition, primary and secondary literacy education, and language and educational technologies.

Peter Crosthwaite is Lecturer in Applied Linguistics at the School of Languages and Cultures, University of Queensland, Australia.

DATA-DRIVEN LEARNING FOR THE NEXT GENERATION

Corpora and DDL for
Pre-tertiary Learners

Edited by Peter Crosthwaite

LONDON AND NEW YORK

First published 2020
by Routledge
2 Park Square, Milton Park, Abingdon, Oxon OX14 4RN

and by Routledge
52 Vanderbilt Avenue, New York, NY 10017

Routledge is an imprint of the Taylor & Francis Group, an informa business

© 2020 selection and editorial matter, Peter Crosthwaite; individual chapters, the contributors

The right of Peter Crosthwaite to be identified as the author of the editorial material, and of the authors for their individual chapters, has been asserted in accordance with sections 77 and 78 of the Copyright, Designs and Patents Act 1988.

All rights reserved. No part of this book may be reprinted or reproduced or utilised in any form or by any electronic, mechanical, or other means, now known or hereafter invented, including photocopying and recording, or in any information storage or retrieval system, without permission in writing from the publishers.

Trademark notice: Product or corporate names may be trademarks or registered trademarks, and are used only for identification and explanation without intent to infringe.

British Library Cataloguing-in-Publication Data
A catalogue record for this book is available from the British Library

Library of Congress Cataloging-in-Publication Data
Names: Crosthwaite, Peter, editor.
Title: Data-driven learning for the next generation : corpora and DDL for pre-tertiary learners / edited by Peter Crosthwaite.
Description: London ; New York, NY : Routledge, 2020. | Includes bibliographical references and index.
Identifiers: LCCN 2019031345 (print) | LCCN 2019031346 (ebook) | ISBN 9781138388000 (Hardback) | ISBN 9781138388017 (Paperback) | ISBN 9780429425899 (eBook)
Subjects: LCSH: Corpora (Linguistics)—Data processing. | Computational linguistics. | Language and languages—Computer-assisted instruction. | Second language acquisition.
Classification: LCC P128.C68 D38 2020 (print) | LCC P128.C68 (ebook) DDC 372.6—dc23
LC record available at https://lccn.loc.gov/2019031345
LC ebook record available at https://lccn.loc.gov/2019031346

ISBN: 978-1-138-38800-0 (hbk)
ISBN: 978-1-138-38801-7 (pbk)
ISBN: 978-0-429-42589-9 (ebk)

Typeset in Bembo
by Apex CoVantage, LLC

Printed and bound by CPI Group (UK) Ltd, Croydon, CR0 4YY

CONTENTS

Editor's acknowledgements   ix
List of Contributors   xi
Foreword   xiv
Alex Boulton

1 Data-driven learning and younger learners: introduction to the volume   1
 Peter Crosthwaite

PART I
Overcoming emerging challenges for DDL with younger learners   **11**

2 A case for constructive alignment in DDL: rethinking outcomes, practices, and assessment in (data-driven) language learning   13
 Fanny Meunier

3 Data-driven learning in the secondary classroom: a critical evaluation from the perspective of foreign language didactics   31
 Oliver Wicher

4 Barriers to trainee teachers' corpus use   47
 Eva Schaeffer-Lacroix

PART II
Applying new DDL methods for younger learners   65

5 The pedagogic advantage of teenage corpora for secondary school learners   67
Pascual Pérez-Paredes

6 The development of a multimodal corpus tool for young EFL learners: a case study on the integration of DDL in teacher education   88
Eri Hirata

7 Query complexity and query refinement: using Web search from a corpus perspective with digital natives   106
Maristella Gatto

PART III
Infusing DDL into practice – new empirical findings from younger learners   131

8 Effects of data-driven learning on enhancing the phraseological knowledge of secondary school learners of L2 English   133
Paweł Szudarski

9 "It helps me get ideas on how to use my words": primary school students' initial reactions to corpus use in a private tutoring setting   150
Peter Crosthwaite and Annita Stell

10 Teaching French to young learners through DDL   171
Sonia Di Vito

11 Data-driven learning in a Greek secondary education setting: the implementation of a blended approach   187
Vasiliki Papaioannou, Marina Mattheoudakis, and Eleni Agathopoulou

12 The effect of data-driven learning activities on young EFL learners' processing of English idioms   208
Trisevgeni Liontou

Afterword   228
Peter Crosthwaite

Index   *230*

EDITOR'S ACKNOWLEDGEMENTS

As with any edited volume, this work would not be possible without the wonderful contributions produced by the team of researchers who answered the original call for chapters. As DDL with younger learners is such an under-researched area of applied linguistics, I have to confess that I had almost given up on the volume shortly after the call for chapters went out, as I received very few proposals initially. However, shortly before the deadline, the proposals started to arrive in earnest, and it finally looked as if we had a volume, much to my relief! I extend my sincere thanks not only to those whose chapters made it into the volume but also to those who showed initial interest. I hope the contributors continue to "spread the word" and produce more excellent studies in this area in the near future.

I would also like to extend my sincere thanks to Alex Boulton, who graciously agreed to provide the excellent foreword to this volume, and for his ongoing support for DDL research at the highest level. A huge thanks also to Ute Römer, Laurence Anthony, and Anne O'Keefe for providing excellent endorsements for the volume – thanks so much for your kindness!

A huge shout goes out to Katie Peace and the team at Routledge for their support in getting this volume into print – from the very first meeting about this volume back at the 2017 Applied Linguistics Association of Australia conference, held in Auckland. I have to confess I almost didn't make the meeting, having overslept, and I literally ran from my hotel to the venue. I'm very glad I made it in time!

I'd also like to sincerely thank Annita Stell, who stepped in to save my own chapter for this volume from failure when I didn't secure the funding I needed to do DDL research in schools. An informal conference chat about private tutoring led to the chapter we have produced for this volume, but it almost wasn't to be. Many thanks for stepping up and for being a great researcher.

Finally, I'd like to thank Yunmi Cho and Erin and William Crosthwaite for the support and quiet times needed at home to put the volume together. A good editor needs a good support team, and you are one of the best.

CONTRIBUTORS

Eleni Agathopoulou is Associate Professor at the Department of Theoretical and Applied Linguistics, School of English, Aristotle University of Thessaloniki. She is a graduate of the School of English and holds an MA in applied linguistics (University of Reading, UK) and holds a Ph.D. in linguistics from the School of English, Aristotle University of Thessaloniki. Her main research interests concern foreign language learning and teaching, bilingualism, and language for academic purposes.

Peter Crosthwaite is Lecturer in Applied Linguistics at the School of Languages and Cultures, University of Queensland, Australia. His research interests cover English for specific/general academic purposes, corpus linguistics, and the intersection of both in the form of data-driven learning. He is the co-author (with Lisa Cheung) of "Learning the Language of Dentistry: Disciplinary corpora in the teaching of English for Specific Academic Purposes", part of *Studies in Corpus Linguistics, 93*. He has also published in most leading applied linguistics journals that focus on SLA, EAP, and ESP.

Sonia Di Vito is a research fellow in French language and translation (L-LIN 04) at the University of Tuscia (Italy). She mainly deals with corpus linguistics as applied to contrastive analysis (Fr, It), the teaching of French, and intercomprehension between Romance languages. She has participated in numerous national and international research projects.

Maristella Gatto is Associate Professor of English Linguistics and Translation at the University of Bari (Italy), where she teaches in undergraduate and postgraduate programmes. She is the author of *Web As Corpus: Theory and Practice* (Bloomsbury

Academic, 2014) and has published articles and book chapters on corpus linguistics, translation, and specialized discourse.

Eri Hirata is Associate Professor in the Department of English at Fukuoka Jo Gakuin University, Japan. She gained her MA and PhD from the University of Birmingham, UK. Her main interests include primary EFL education, EFL literacy instruction for young learners, and the application of corpora in teaching and teacher education.

Trisevgeni Liontou is Assistant Professor of Applied Linguistics at the Department of Language and Linguistics, Faculty of English Language and Literature, University of Athens. She has been an EFL teacher educator with several years' teaching experience in a range of school settings and is particularly interested in bringing together theoretical and practical aspects of EFL pedagogy.

Marina Mattheoudakis is Professor of Applied Linguistics at the School of English, Faculty of Philosophy, Aristotle University of Thessaloniki. She is a graduate of the School of English and holds an MA in teaching English as a second/foreign language (University of Birmingham, U.K.) and a PhD in applied linguistics from the School of English, Aristotle University of Thessaloniki. Her research interests lie in the areas of instructed second language acquisition, bilingual education, and corpus linguistics.

Fanny Meunier is Professor of English language, linguistics, and didactics at UCLouvain (Belgium). She is the director of the Center for English Corpus Linguistics (CECL) and the head of the teacher training unit in modern languages. Her main research interest is second language acquisition research and language pedagogy nexus.

Vasiliki Papaioannou is a state school EFL teacher. She is a graduate of the School of English and holds an MSc in machine translation (UMIST, UK), an MA in language and communication studies (AUTh Greece), and a PhD in applied corpus linguistics from the School of English, Aristotle University. Her research interests concern foreign language learning, corpus linguistics, educational technology, and case-based reasoning.

Pascual Pérez-Paredes is Lecturer in Research in Second Language Education at the Faculty of Education, University of Cambridge. His main research interests are learner language variation, the use of corpora in language education, and corpus-assisted discourse analysis. He has published research in journals such as *Computer Assisted Language Learning, Discourse & Society, English for Specific Purposes, Journal of Pragmatics, Language, Learning & Technology, System, ReCALL*, and *International Journal of Corpus Linguistics*. He is also the Overall Coordinator of the MEd Research Methods Strand, Faculty of Education, University of Cambridge.

Eva Schaeffer-Lacroix is a senior lecturer at the Department of Education of Sorbonne Université in Paris, where she teaches applied linguistics, technology-enhanced language learning, and German as a foreign language. Her main research interests are corpus linguistics, language awareness, and writing in a foreign language.

Annita Stell is a PhD student in applied linguistics at the University of Queensland, Australia. Her research interests include writing development, peer interaction, mediation, and collaborative writing in second language classrooms. She currently teaches academic and creative writing to both L1 and L2 learners in Australia.

Paweł Szudarski teaches at the School of English, University of Nottingham. His research interests centre on second language acquisition and corpus linguistics, with a particular focus on vocabulary learning. He is also interested in the status of English as a global language, linguistic creativity, and digital pedagogy.

Oliver Wicher is a PhD student at the Department of Romance Studies, University of Cologne, with a dissertation on a corpus-based multifactorial analysis of tense and aspect in French. His main research interests are corpus linguistics and foreign language teaching, vocabulary and grammar teaching, and tense and aspect. He teaches French and geography at a German secondary school and is responsible for the compilation of the French component of the International Comparable Corpus (ICC).

FOREWORD

Data-driven learning for younger learners: obstacles and optimism

Although I've been researching data-driven learning for many years now, I know virtually nothing about DDL with younger learners. The simple fact is that probably no one really does. An ongoing but certainly not exhaustive collection of research in the area currently brings up 378 separate publications featuring empirical study of DDL.[1] Of these, only 19 explicitly state that the participants are in high school and none in a primary school context. The overwhelming majority are conducted in university contexts for a variety of reasons. But before we explore these, perhaps we need to define what we mean by DDL. This is no easy task, and I often read published papers or listen to conference presentations where the authors explicitly situate their work as DDL, only to hear colleagues respond, "But that's not data-driven learning!"

That DDL means different things to different people is not new. The approach is closely associated with work by Tim Johns, who coined the term in 1990; in his various publications, he gave examples of open-ended serendipitous corpus exploration; one-to-one writing correction, class use of hands-on concordancing on pre-determined language points; reusable paper-based materials for remedial grammar; and even "blackboard concordancing" whereby each learner is given a page of a text, directed to find examples of a particular feature, and then directed to write them on the blackboard in concordance-like format. So it should come as no surprise that there are many definitions of DDL. At the narrow end, we might adopt a prototype definition, i.e. a kind of core which everyone can agree on. I once suggested this might be something like "the hands-on use of authentic corpus data (concordances) by advanced, sophisticated foreign or second language learners in higher education for inductive, self-directed language learning of advanced usage" (Boulton, 2011, p. 572). With a prototype definition like this,

> the further an activity is from the central, prototypical core, the less DDL-like it is, but any cut-off point beyond which we might like to say "this is no longer DDL" seems likely to be arbitrary rather than empirically grounded or based on a coherent, hermetic definition
>
> (p. 563)

While a prototype definition has its uses, in many cases a more general definition is preferable, such as that proposed by Gilquin and Granger: "Data-driven learning (DDL) consists in using the tools and techniques of corpus linguistics for pedagogical purposes" (2010, p. 359).

DDL is not a theory of language or language learning, though it can be argued that corpus linguistics has radically changed our understanding of language, giving rise to a number of theories, such as the idiom principle (Sinclair, 1991), lexical priming (Hoey, 2005), the mental corpus (Taylor, 2012), and norms and exploitations (Hanks, 2013). Further, it aligns with several important principles and theories in current thinking, such as authenticity, autonomy, chunking, consciousness-raising, constructivism, critical thinking, complexity and dynamic systems theory, discovery learning, focus on form, individualisation, induction, learner-centredness, (meta-)cognitive skills, noticing, salience, task-based learning, usage-based learning, etc. It is beyond the scope of this short text to discuss these alleged advantages in detail; various aspects are raised in the papers present here (see also Flowerdew, 2015). But if DDL is so wonderful, why isn't it more widespread? And in particular, why has it been comparatively under-researched in the case of younger learners?

First, it could be simply that the majority of researchers in the field are themselves university academics using DDL in their own teaching (cf. Chambers, 2019). This certainly includes me, but the case is not exclusive to DDL, with university students being by far the most extensively studied population in second language acquisition (SLA) and applied linguistics as a whole. Although languages are of course widely taught to younger learners, research in that context tends to be more the domain of education rather than applied linguistics, each field having its own journals and cultures. Unfortunately, the two do not talk to each other very much, with the result that DDL work in applied linguistics remains relatively unknown in educational circles. The consequence of this is not only that DDL is understudied with younger learners but also that DDL and corpus linguistics tend not to form a major part of teacher training programmes (see Hirata, this volume). Consequently, trainee teachers (outside applied linguistics programmes) are rarely introduced to DDL and cannot themselves use its tools or techniques in their own teaching. As Conrad (2000, p. 556) notes, "the strongest force for change could be a new generation of ESL teachers who were introduced to corpus-based research in their training programs"; until such time as researchers in applied linguistics talk to researchers and decision-makers in education, the current situation is unlikely to change much, and DDL will remain on the margins, rarely integrated (Wicher, this volume) and never "normalised" (Chambers, 2019). Of course, the same can be said of the students themselves: School exams and teaching practices need to be constructively aligned for any innovation to have the opportunity to penetrate (Meunier, this volume), and it is understandable that language students (just like student teachers) might resent time spent on practices that do not directly help with exam results (Szudarski, this volume).

A second reason why DDL is less studied among younger learners might be that researchers and practitioners expect it not to work very well in the first place (see also Schaeffer-Lacroix, this volume). This could be because their young age is taken to be synonymous with insufficient levels of language proficiency, an issue much debated even in university contexts, where few projects have explored DDL among lower-level learners. One solution is to use prepared materials of appropriately selected items, and even for hands-on work the texts can be selected to be appropriate for the target users or graded for level (e.g. Hadley & Charles, 2017). But it is certainly true that there is a lack of appropriate corpora and tools beyond academic corpus linguistics, as argued by Pérez-Paredes (this volume), who looks at uses of SACODEYL, a corpus of teenage interviews. If existing corpora tend to be geared to older users (or linguists), it is still possible for teachers to create their own corpora that are specifically relevant to younger learners, as shown in several other papers in this volume: corpora of children's news in Di Vito; corpora of the learners' textbooks in Papaioannou *et al.*, and multimodal corpora in Hirata.

The language points discussed in DDL also tend to be relatively advanced, but this is not in itself an indication that DDL is inaccessible for other features appropriate to lower levels. Liontou (this volume) for example provides successful results in the "notoriously difficult" area of idiomatic phrases. Indeed, most of the studies with lower levels have found promising results, although two recent meta-analyses of DDL come to slightly differing conclusions. For DDL as a whole, Boulton and Cobb (2017) analysed 88 unique samples from 64 studies and found that proficiency did not systematically correlate with effect sizes, suggesting that it is open to all levels. Lee, Warschauer, and Lee (2019) focused on DDL just for vocabulary in 38 samples from 29 studies and did find a medium difference between advanced and low-level learners, but there was still a significant effect in all cases. Caution should always be a watchword in dealing with such findings since proficiency is not only difficult to assess but also reported in so many ways that what is "advanced" in one study might be considered "intermediate" or even "low" in another context. Of studies apparently with advanced learners in major CALL journals, Burston and Arispe (2016) found that fully 50% were at best B1 level on the Common European Framework of Reference for Languages, which is commonly thought of as lower intermediate. But coming back to the main point: "DDL works pretty well in almost any context where it has been extensively tried" (Boulton & Cobb, 2017, p. 386).

Another explanation might be that children lack the cognitive development necessary for sophisticated language work. A number of studies have addressed DDL with children in exploring their mother tongue (L1); some of these are mentioned in Crosthwaite and Stell (this volume). Over ten years ago, John Sinclair, often considered the father of modern corpus linguistics with the COBUILD project, planned the wide-ranging introduction of corpora to primary schools in Scotland via a tool known as PhraseBox:

> PhraseBox . . . is like giving each pupil real-time access to a huge memory of all the different ways in which thousands of people have expressed themselves over several years, all instantly available in a highly organised presentation. Gradually, students are expected to internalise what they need of the resource and gather confidence in their ability to express themselves publicly; but the resource will always be available when it is needed.
>
> (Sinclair, 2006)

Sadly, the resource never did become available, as Sinclair died in 2007 and the project along with him. I was fortunate to see him demonstrate it with Ana Mauranen at the IVACS conference in Nottingham in 2006, but he wrote little about it (see also Stubbs, 2011). Nonetheless, the very fact that he and people in a national education system believed in it is revealing in itself: there is no a priori reason to assume that younger learners are unable to use the technology and analyse language in ways compatible with DDL.

This brings us specifically to the issue of ICT (information and communication technology) and whether younger learners have the skills necessary for DDL. To counter that, it might be pointed out that DDL can be conducted using prepared, paper-based printouts which still give medium effect sizes (Boulton & Cobb, 2017). Further, younger learners who have grown up with ICT may actually be more relaxed about it than older learners, as discussed by Gatto (this volume). A case in point: Some of my students in an English master's degree program have difficulty with the wildcard function which so impressed a 10-year-old in Crosthwaite and Stell (this volume).

Finally, the fact that there are few published studies of DDL for children does not necessarily mean that it is absent from common classroom practice. Johns and King (1991, p. iii) situated DDL "within the overall aim of developing students' ability to puzzle things out for themselves". For our purposes, this has to involve language data in one form or another, but otherwise that leaves the field very open. So in particular, while the Internet is not a "corpus" and Google is not a "concordancer", it is quite possible that teachers are encouraging their learners to explore language without ever having heard of DDL. As McCarthy (2008, p. 566) puts it, "We are, all of us, corpus users, because we use the internet". And if we are using the Internet as a source of repeated language examples, we are all doing DDL (Gatto, this volume; see also Boulton, 2015). As one student remarked of COCA in the study by Papaioannou et al. (this volume): "This is just another tool the internet offers us to learn new words". And of course it is possible that learners are doing this without their teachers' knowledge or even against their recommendations. Meunier (this volume) discusses several tools that provide opportunities for very DDL-like activities, using accessible corpora (e.g. TV series such as *Breaking Bad* or *Game of Thrones* in PlayPhrase.me) with no mention of "corpus" or "concordance" or other problematic terms.

Research can be based on actual practice and can certainly inform it, but it should never be "applied". The main consumers of research are other researchers rather than teachers or decision-makers (e.g. Borg, 2009), but when teachers do read research, it is essential that they interpret and adapt research findings to their own local contexts and needs: Existing reports of DDL aimed at students and adults should not be simply transformed into a "corpus approach for kids". If the search for a single "best method" has been largely abandoned in recognition of the diversity of teaching goals, contexts, needs, and profiles of the individuals involved (Brown et al. 2007), it cannot be desirable to impose DDL as the sole form of language instruction. Researchers thus also need to remain open to a variety of approaches and not be dogmatic about what is or is not DDL and how it should be implemented across the board. As Meunier (this volume) argues, we need to think outside the box and go off the beaten path to promote creativity in DDL. It is refreshing that some of the examples given in this volume (e.g. Liontou; Papaioannou *et al.*) are quite different from usual expectations of DDL. What we have is a host of variants under the umbrella term of DDL, which have their place alongside others for some learners in some contexts and for some language questions.

I hope this short foreword has shown that the common assumption that DDL is not suitable for younger learners is just an assumption – an absence of research evidence merely means that it has not been widely tested, not that it is not or cannot be effective. DDL might even be more appropriate for children than for older learners as their expectations are less fixed and the approach lends itself to the inquisitive; the children in Di Vito (this volume) remembered the methodology well because they felt involved and valued and encouraged to think for themselves. There certainly are obstacles, and we should not be blasé about them (Schaeffer-Lacroix, this volume), but there are any number of reasons to think that DDL, appropriately implemented, can bring something to the table in a variety of contexts. The present volume thus addresses a genuine need for DDL research among younger learners, with the various papers examining relevant arguments, describing potential uses, and evaluating experimental or ecological examples.

Alex Boulton

Note

1 "Empirical" here is defined as studies that "subject some aspect of DDL to observation or experimentation with some kind of externally validated evaluation other than the researchers' own intuition" (Boulton, 2010, p. 130).

References

Borg, S. (2009). English language teachers' conceptions of research. *Applied Linguistics, 30*(3), 358–388. doi: 10.1093/applin/amp007.

Boulton, A. (2010). Learning outcomes from corpus consultation. In M. Moreno Jaén, F. Serrano Valverde, & M. Calzada Pérez (Eds.), *Exploring new paths in language pedagogy: Lexis and corpus-based language teaching* (pp. 129-144). London: Equinox.

Boulton, A. (2011). Data-driven learning: The perpetual enigma. In S. Goźdź-Roszkowski (Ed.), *Explorations across languages and corpora* (pp. 563-580). Frankfurt: Peter Lang.

Boulton, A. (2015). Applying data-driven learning to the web. In A. Leńko-Szymańska & A. Boulton (Eds.), *Multiple affordances of language corpora for data-driven learning* (pp. 267–295). Amsterdam: John Benjamins. doi: 10.1075/scl.69.13bou.

Boulton, A., & Cobb, T. (2017). Corpus use in language learning: A meta-analysis. *Language Learning, 67*(2), 348–393. doi: 10.1111/lang.12224.

Brown, H., Tarone, E., Swan, M., Ellis, R., Prodromou, L., Jung, U. . . . Savignon, S. (2007). Forty years of language teaching. *Language Teaching, 40*, 1–15. doi: 10.1017/S0261444806003934.

Burston, J., & Arispe, K. (2016). The contribution of CALL to advanced-level foreign/second language instruction. In S. Papadima-Sophocleous, L. Bradley, & S. Thouësny (eds.), *CALL communities and culture* (pp. 69–73). Dublin: Research-Publishing.net. doi: 10.14705/rpnet.2016.eurocall2016.539.

Chambers, A. (2019). Towards the corpus revolution? Bridging the research – practice gap. *Language Teaching*, FirstView. doi: 10.1017/S0261444819000089.

Conrad, S. (2000). Will corpus linguistics revolutionize grammar teaching in the 21st century? *TESOL Quarterly, 34*, 548–560. doi: 10.2307/3587743.

Flowerdew, L. (2015). Data-driven learning and language learning theories: Whither the twain shall meet. In A. Leńko-Szymańska & A. Boulton (Eds.), *Multiple affordances of language corpora for data-driven learning* (pp. 15–36). Amsterdam: John Benjamins. doi: 10.1075/scl.69.

Gilquin, G., & Granger, S. (2010). How can data-driven learning be used in language teaching? In A. O'Keeffe & M. McCarthy (Eds.), *The Routledge handbook of corpus linguistics* (pp. 359–370). London: Routledge.

Hadley, G., & Charles, M. (2017). Enhancing extensive reading with data-driven learning. *Language Learning & Technology, 21*(3), 131–152. http://llt.msu.edu/issues/october2017/hadleycharles.pdf

Hanks, P. (2013). *Lexical analysis: Norms and exploitations*. Cambridge, MA: MIT Press. doi: 10.1017/S1351324913000302.

Hoey, M. (2005). *Lexical priming: A new theory of words and language*. London: Routledge. doi: 10.4324/9780203327630.

Johns, T. (1990). From printout to handout: Grammar and vocabulary teaching in the context of data-driven learning. *CALL Austria, 10*, 14–34.

Johns, T., & King, P. (Eds.). (1991). Classroom concordancing. *English Language Research Journal, 4*.

Lee, H., Warschauer, M., & Lee, J. H. (2019). The effects of corpus use on second language vocabulary learning: A multilevel meta-analysis. *Applied Linguistics*, Advance Article. doi: 10.1093/applin/amy012.

McCarthy, M. (2008). Accessing and interpreting corpus information in the teacher education context. *Language Teaching, 41*(4), 563–574. doi: 10.1017/S0261444808005247.

Sinclair, J. (1991). *Corpus, concordance, collocation*. Oxford: Oxford University Press.

Sinclair, J. (2006, January). A language landscape. *West Word.* www.westword.org.uk/jan2006.html

Stubbs, M. (2011). A tribute to John McHardy Sinclair (14 June 1933–13 March 2007). In T. Herbst, S. Faulhaber, & P. Uhrig (Eds.), *The phraseological view of language: A tribute to John Sinclair* (pp. 1–16). Berlin: De Gruyter Mouton. doi: 10.1515/9783110257014.

Taylor, J. (2012). *The mental corpus: How language is represented in the mind.* Oxford: Oxford University Press. 10.1093/acprof:oso/9780199290802.001.0001.

1

DATA-DRIVEN LEARNING AND YOUNGER LEARNERS

Introduction to the volume

Peter Crosthwaite

If you are reading this volume, the chances are that you have some interest in the use of technology for language learning. You are likely to be in tertiary education as a lecturer or research student, or you may be involved in preparing language teaching materials or language teacher training for pre-tertiary education. You are likely to at least have heard of corpora, or "[electronic] bodies of texts assembled in a principled way" (Johansson, 1995, p. 19), and have probably been exposed to or have previously used corpus software to learn about language or to teach language to others. If that is true, we can also be fairly certain that you have previously graduated from high school and that a fair few years may have passed since you did so.

In order to appropriately explain the purpose of this volume, you may need to cast your mind back to the educational technologies available during your high school days. My own personal experience with such technology was limited to programming in BASIC on primitive BBC microcomputers, learning to type on 386- and 486-based PCs, drawing cartoons in MS Paint with a mouse on the first Pentium PCs, and copying my homework from the *Microsoft Encarta* encyclopedia once the first CD-ROMs became available. Dial-up 56k modems were largely available only during my undergraduate days (so, no Internet). As for technology in the language learning classroom, we had cassette tapes accompanying our L2 German textbooks. Teachers spent more time rewinding or fast-forwarding these tapes to get to the right spot than they spent on the actual lesson. In terms of reference resources, a paper English-to-German dictionary was essential, although this weighed down your backpack considerably. For the record, I was never very good at German. And while I must confess I remember very little of my primary school days, I can safely say that educational technology was not a major factor in the primary curriculum of the time.

Now, fast-forward 25 years to the era of the (so-called) *digital natives* (Prensky, 2001, see also Gatto, this volume). In the vast majority of educational contexts, technology is now the medium through which knowledge is transferred, stored, and evaluated, in some cases replacing the teacher entirely. Capability in information and communications technology (ICT) is embedded as a key learning objective in pre-tertiary curricula the world over and has transformed the way we view literacy in first language learning contexts. The Internet has allowed for real-time communication between young second language learners and native speakers of target languages anywhere at any time, with access to a wealth of video and Web 2.0 multimodal resources that have forever changed the nature of materials preparation, learning, and teaching. We are now long past Bax's (2003) state of *normalisation* for computer-assisted language learning (CALL) technologies in pre-tertiary classrooms, where

> computers ... are used every day by language students and teachers as an integral part of every lesson, like a pen or a book ... without fear or inhibition, and equally without an exaggerated respect for what they can do. They will not be the centre of any lesson, but they will play a part in almost all. They will be completely integrated into all other aspects of classroom life, alongside coursebooks, teachers and notepads. They will go almost unnoticed.
>
> (Bax, 2003, p. 23)

In fact, a 2016 paper by Stickler and Shi outlining the 12 most-cited CALL-focused papers between 2004 and 2015 in the journal *System* suggests

> The "classroom" of the future might not look anything like classrooms even as recently as 2003: mobile learning (MALL) seems to be an ongoing and unstoppable trend; an increasing recognition of multilingualism as the norm might influence the way we use online resources; and the democratisation of research might show effects in the language classrooms of the future, as well, with teachers going well beyond the methods of action research *and learners becoming involved in the production of research rather than being regarded as passive "participants" or "subjects"*.
>
> (Stickler & Shi, 2016, p. 125, emphasis mine)

The idea that language learners may be able to use technology to play a more active role in their own language learning process is one that has not escaped applied linguists, and it is notable that one of the 12 most-cited papers in the Stickler and Shi article focuses on the use of corpora for language learning in an L2 writing context (Gaskell & Cobb, 2004). Ever since the early pioneers of corpus linguistics noted that linguistic knowledge can be construed as knowledge of patterns (e.g. Sinclair's 1991 *idiom principle*) gained through our encounters with these patterns in use (e.g. Hoey's 2005 *lexical priming*), the use of corpora to extract these patterns – and to use corpus data to *teach* them – has been a major research area in applied linguistics over the past 25 years. Studies have focused on the use of corpus data presented to language students by their teachers or – increasingly – situations where the learners themselves develop the autonomy to discover the complexities of language through their own corpus consultation. These approaches, coined *data-driven learning* (DDL, Johns, 1990), have now been featured in over 200 empirical studies between 1989 and 2014 across a range of languages (Boulton & Cobb, 2017), and given the upwards trajectory in DDL studies since Gaskell and Cobb (2004), many more studies have recently been published or are in progress.

DDL is a pedagogical approach where direct learner engagement with corpus data in the form of either printed materials or learner-led hands-on corpus consultation using corpus tools allows for students to learn and internalise statistical and contextual information about language in use. Under a DDL approach, learners consult corpus data as "language detectives", with "every student a Sherlock Holmes" (Johns, 1997:101) as he or she queries, manipulates, and visualises a range of output data including concordances of query words with surrounding context, statistical information in the form of frequency or collocation lists, and increasingly visual or multimodal forms of data (see Hirata, this volume). DDL has often been described as an "inductive" approach to learning, where learners' active engagement with corpus data leads to increased focus-on-form (Long, 1991) and data-enhanced "noticing" of language features (Schmidt, 1990) that replaces the need to memorise abstract textbook "rules" while promoting a range of constructivist skills correlated with improved learning practices (e.g. Cobb, 1999).

The main reason for the sharp increase in DDL studies published over the last 25 years is that DDL *works*, and people are starting to take notice. Aside from the aforementioned cognitive benefits, DDL works because it represents the digital age we now find ourselves in, a world where information on any topic is available to learners at the touch of a button and where vast language resources are accessible and queryable in increasing numbers as corpus technology continues to improve. The more that language learners take charge of their own learning outside the use of contrived textbook examples – with this charge greatly facilitated by innovation corpus technologies – the more they are developing the skills for deductive reasoning, problem-solving, and autonomous learning so essential to the development of the modern twenty-first-century language learner. And the evidence is in – in an already much-cited meta-analysis of the effectiveness of DDL (as measured by DDL's ability to increase learners' skills or knowledge) across a range of learning goals and contexts, large positive effect sizes have been found (Boulton & Cobb, 2017). Lee, Warschauer, and Lee (2018)'s meta-analysis of the effectiveness of DDL for vocabulary learning shows similar positive results, with a range of other studies reporting positively on DDL's affordances for error correction (e.g. Crosthwaite, 2017), phraseology (e.g. Geluso and Yamaguchi, 2014), disciplinary-specific register and lexis (e.g. Crosthwaite, Wong, & Cheung, 2019), translation and interpreting (e.g. Sotelo, 2015), and many other of the "multiple affordances" (Leńko-Szymańska & Boulton, 2015) of language corpora for data-driven learning. Many of the contributors to this very volume have also experienced firsthand the effectiveness of DDL in their own contexts, disseminating empirical findings of data-driven learning in numerous publications while changing the learning habits of hundreds of students as they "spread the word" (Römer, 2009) as missionaries of data-driven learning.

So far, so good – so what's the problem? The problem is that if you ask anyone under the age of 18 or anyone responsible for teaching those under 18 what a corpus is, the chances are that you will get a blank look and a shrug of the shoulders. Put simply, while DDL is rapidly becoming established as a viable pedagogical approach in tertiary education, there is a real dearth of research into the affordances of DDL with pre-tertiary learners. Boulton and Cobb (2017) reported that only ten out of the 88 samples included in their meta-analysis of DDL studies involved secondary school students; six samples included between-subject designs, and four included within-subject designs. Pérez-Paredes (forthcoming) reported that only two out of the 32 studies exploring DDL or corpora in language education during the 2011–2015 period involved secondary school learners. Lee et al. (2018)'s meta-analysis did not include the age of the learners as a variable at all. Boulton and Cobb (2017) concluded that "unfortunately, there is little [DDL] research with high school learners" (p. 375), while the amount of DDL-focused research conducted with primary school learners can probably be counted on one hand (see Crosthwaite & Stell; Hirata, this volume).

Why have pre-tertiary learners been left in the cold when it comes to DDL thus far? We know of the "rational fears" (Boulton, 2009) affecting uptake of DDL generally, including the fears of learners regarding a switch to self-guided from teacher-led learning, the complexity of corpus consultation, and difficulties understanding corpus output; there are also fears of teachers, who feel their students would not be able to handle DDL or who may be distrustful of corpus resources (see also Schaeffer-Lacroix, this volume). Yet, despite ICT now being a core part of both primary and secondary school curricula as a twenty-first-century skill (Voogt, Knezek, Cox, Knezek, & ten Brummelhuis, 2013) and despite most international primary and secondary school assessments of digital literacy measuring skills such as "searching, retrieving, and evaluating digital information" (Siddiq, Hatlevik, Olsen, Throndsen, & Scherer, 2016, p. 58), the integration of corpus technology within the pre-tertiary classroom has not yet really begun in earnest. Eng (2005) describes three phases required for such integration, with the first (emerging) phase dealing with ICT infrastructure, a second (application) phase involving the application of technology within current teaching-learning processes, and a third (infusion) phase where teachers are able to use technology in different ways for innovative pedagogies. However, while many schools now have general ICT infrastructure in place (at least, for those with fairly privileged educational budgets), we are not yet at the point where infrastructure for corpora and DDL tailored specifically for younger learners is either available or appropriate for general use (Stenström, Andersen, & Hasund, 2002; Braun, 2007; Pérez-Paredes, this volume). In addition, we are still a considerable way off the aforementioned second "application" phase, primarily because of a lack of knowledge or training for pre- or in-service teachers in understanding and using corpora on their own, let alone having developed any interest or proficiency in DDL materials or lesson preparation. Given that a teacher's relative state of professional development in ICT is "the most significant variable in explaining classroom ICT use" (Gil-Flores, Rodríguez-Santero, & Torres-Gordillo, 2017, p. 447) and that failure to integrate ICT use into the classroom can be generally explained by a lack of "constructivist beliefs" by in-service teachers (*ibid*) who are not aware or even afraid of what corpora can bring to the classroom, it is obvious much more work needs to be done to persuade teachers that DDL can potentially bring enormous benefits for their students as well as contribute significantly to their own professional development. This situation obviously precludes that the third "infusion" stage for the normalisation of corpora into the pre-tertiary classroom may still be some way off. Add to this the various complexities of getting funding or ethical approval for school-based research, and it is not difficult to see why DDL has not gained a footing in mainstream pre-tertiary education.

This volume therefore presents a range of studies that finally seek to address how corpus-based data-driven learning with young learners is finally emerging, how it is being applied, and how it can be infused into classroom practice in innovative ways. The studies represent a broad range of international perspectives on the use of corpora for DDL, including contributions from Europe, Asia, and Australia. These contributions have been produced by both experienced DDL experts and early-career scholars who have each attempted to document the successes as well as the challenges involved in applying DDL to pre-tertiary teaching and learning. The volume is divided into three distinct sections, each of which is described in the following.

Part 1: overcoming emerging challenges for DDL with younger learners

Fanny Meunier's chapter discusses the need for *constructive alignment* for DDL involving younger learners in the L2 classroom. This requires that the curriculum and its intended outcomes, the teaching methods used, and the assessment tasks be consistently and coherently aligned – a coherence that so far is lacking in pre-tertiary DDL research. Corpora and DDL, Meunier argues, can greatly facilitate such alignment in terms of data-driven improvements to teachers' content knowledge, pedagogical knowledge, and technological knowledge. This can be achieved by expanding on the types of tools and tasks currently used in DDL activities to include software other than traditional concordancers or corpus platforms in favour of applications more likely to be appealing to younger learners but which still allow for DDL to occur. In support, Meunier presents useful examples of such tools (e.g. PlayPhrase.me, LyricsTraining) and how they can be used for DDL, and the chapter ends with a call for more researchers and teachers to build on the affordances of new digital tools to DDL-ise them, leveraging tools "from the wild" into the classroom.

Oliver Wicher's chapter presents a critical evaluation of DDL for younger learners from the perspective of foreign language didactics, which are theories of teaching and learning in classroom instruction. Wicher calls for pedagogic processing of corpora when teaching younger learners, simplifying the type of corpus data to be processed by the learners, as well as the processes by which young learners are expected to engage with such data. Wicher outlines two phase models currently in use for L2 lesson planning in secondary schools (PPP and TBLT) before outlining how DDL can be incorporated into each model, with useful accompanying sample activities. Wicher then calls for increased scaffolding to overcome individual differentiation in corpus abilities, with this scaffolding in the form of input enhancement (e.g. colour coding or highlighting/underlining concordance results), DDL assessments that vary according to learners' proficiency, and teacher manipulation of concordance results to avoid weaker learners becoming overwhelmed. Wicher also notes for DDL to truly succeed, the communicative dimension must not be ignored. Specifically, learners must be able to *use* the target structures in their own output afterwards.

Eva Schaeffer-Lacroix's chapter focuses on the training of pre-service teachers in corpus use and DDL lesson planning in a secondary L2 German context in France, dealing specifically with the barriers to trainees' appreciation and use of corpora for language learning. Her chapter outlines both technical and conceptual barriers to corpus innovations as evidenced in trainees' attempts to create an L2 learning activity involving the use of corpora for DDL, with evidence from observations and interviews. Technical barriers encountered by the trainees included limited knowledge of corpus query syntax and corpus functions, leaving their lesson plans lacking in innovation and variety, while conceptual barriers including teacher beliefs about younger learners' DDL capabilities and preferences for other teaching tools were raised in the interview data. To overcome these barriers, Schaeffer-Lacroix recommends the creation and use of more user- or child-friendly corpus tools and corpora, better samples of DDL activities, and greater alignment between the format of DDL tasks and other language learning tasks already commonly employed in the secondary L2 classroom.

Part 2: applying new DDL methods for younger learners

Pascual Pérez-Paredes' chapter explores the pedagogic advantage of teenage corpora for secondary school learners, noting that one of the biggest reasons for a lack of DDL uptake with younger learners is the lack of appropriate corpus resources. Such pedagogical corpora are advantageous over corpora collected for research purposes as they are specially designed with teaching in mind. Describing the SACODEYL-English multimedia pedagogic corpus of L1 teenage speakers of English, Pérez-Paredes outlines how a corpus of teenage talk can be used to teach English grammar to secondary L2 English students who might ordinarily have little access to authentic oral production from people their own age and who might typically have little interest in traditional textbook grammar exercises.

Eri Hirata's contribution explores the development of a multimodal corpus tool for primary learners of English as a foreign language before presenting a case study on its integration in a Japanese teacher education programme. Hirata argues that multimodal corpora are essential for the primary classroom as younger learners use a variety of textual and non-textual cues to comprehend meaning while reading. Presenting her multimodal corpus platform comprises children's texts with accompanying images, video, and subtitles, Hirata tests trainee primary school teachers' perceptions of this resource for L2 learning following a DDL training session, using a text-only corpus platform as a point of comparison. The findings suggest the trainees were significantly more positive about the use of the multimodal corpus platform over the text-only counterpart for DDL, with Hirata calling for greater integration of DDL training into pre-service teacher education generally if DDL is to find its way into mainstream practice.

Maristella Gatto's chapter explores the use of Google Web searches from a corpus perspective, looking at how younger learners can develop query complexity and query refinement skills for data-driven learning. Gatto emphasises that while there is a perception that younger learners (as "digital natives") already know all there is to know about technology, the reality is that such learners lack key skills in information retrieval and query refinement. While most young learners are familiar with Google's basic search functions, Gatto's chapter explores how to incorporate Google-as-a-corpus into DDL practice, reporting the findings of a series of training sessions with 15- to 17-year-old learners of L2 English in Italy as they learned about collocation, translation candidates, and query refinement. Gatto claims that advanced Web searches may be reinterpreted from a corpus linguistics perspective, an approach that cultivates in learners key skills for progressive query refinement. This can, in the long term, trigger an interest in other forms of DDL.

Part 3: infusing DDL into practice – new empirical findings from younger learners

Paweł Szudarski's chapter explores the effects of DDL on enhancing L2 English learners' knowledge of phraseology with L1 Polish secondary school learners. Szudarski's empirical study tracked learners' acquisition of target phrases (e.g. "by far" or "straight away") with a group using dictionaries and another group using printed handouts of selected concordances. Acquisition was measured by means of a test of meaning recognition and an L1–L2 translation test of meaning recall, as well as a questionnaire that explored students' perceptions of the treatments. Results revealed that DDL was more effective in enhancing learners' phraseological knowledge, while the questionnaire data confirmed that corpus-based exercises were perceived as beneficial. Szudarski ends his chapter by discussing the benefits and challenges of introducing DDL to lower-level L2 students and the implications of the study for secondary school language education more generally.

Peter Crosthwaite and Annita Stell's contribution explores the initial reactions to corpora of two Year 5 L1 primary school students in Australia as they write argumentative essays in a private tutoring setting. These young students revised lexical errors in their writing using Sketch Engine for Language Learning (SkELL) and the British Academic Corpus of Written English (BAWE) over a one-month period, with the tutor providing scaffolded help while taking observational notes and screenshots of the students' queries and search results alongside post-session interviews. Continued use of the corpus was shown to help improve students' self-efficacy as they used DDL to aid their revisions, although there was also significant individual variation in their initial reaction to and usage of the corpora across the revision sessions. Encouragingly, both students were positive about using corpora by the end of their training, suggesting that primary school students can be quite receptive to direct use of corpora for DDL despite their young age, at least when sufficient scaffolding is provided by a tutor proficient in corpus consultation. This study is one of the very few empirical studies of DDL with primary age learners, although there are many more to come.

Sonia Di Vito's chapter details a DDL experiment with L1 Italian middle school students who were studying elements of L2 French grammar through the use of concordances. Di Vito charts how DDL can aid younger learners to meet CEFR proficiency requirements in an increasingly multilingual L2 environment in secondary education, before outlining previous DDL findings for L2 French. Di Vito then describes in detail her experiences getting students to engage with DDL to learn a variety of French grammatical constructions, including many useful examples of DDL activities for the learning of possessive adjectives, pronouns, and verbs. Students reported positively about this "new method of learning" and the ease of the learning process, while teachers observed gains in learning.

Vasiliki Papaioannou, Marina Mattheoudakis, and Eleni Agathopoulou's chapter investigates the effects of a blended DDL approach in the acquisition of English modal verbs by high school students in Greece. Modal verbs are considered difficult for L2 English learners to acquire, particularly for speakers of L1 Greek because of potential for L1 transfer. However, as DDL can facilitate the analysis of relevant, authentic examples of modals (unlike traditional textbook treatments), Papaioannou and colleagues conducted an experiment with secondary school L2 English students in Greece using a pedagogic corpus of selected reading materials rich in modals and the general corpus COCA. Papaioannou and colleagues outline in detail a series of DDL training activities, before describing DDL activities focusing specifically on modals, with useful examples provided for the reader. Qualitative observations of students' corpus engagement and teacher-student discussions show positive results, with students often going beyond the provisions of the training materials when making corpus queries.

Finally, **Trisevgeni Liontou's** contribution reports on an empirical study with young EFL learners (12–15 years old) investigating the processing and comprehension of idioms through DDL activities. While idioms are notoriously difficult for L2 learners, Liontou explores whether exposing younger learners to authentic examples from a corpus and getting them to query corpus data could result in significant improvement in participants' overall ability to deduce idiomatic meaning and produce idiomatic expressions in their written scripts, with positive results. Liontou's chapter contains a series of accessible DDL activities that get students to look beyond the sentence level to the patterns found in extended discourse and explore the connection between different forms and senses of a word, which can be modified to suit a range of other DDL purposes.

Afterword

Following these contributions, I present an afterword that addresses future directions in DDL for younger learners in the hope of inspiring others to take up the mantle and work towards the adoption of DDL into mainstream primary and secondary education. Whether this is a goal worth working towards will depend very much on your evaluation as to the success of the contributions contained within this volume, yet we are confident that the research collected in this volume is a major step in that direction.

References

Bax, S. (2003). CALL – past, present and future. *System, 31*(1), 13–28.
Boulton, A. (2009). Data-driven learning: Reasonable fears and rational reassurance. *Indian Journal of Applied Linguistics, 35*(1), 81–106.
Boulton, A., & Cobb, T. (2017). Corpus use in language learning: A meta-analysis. *Language Learning, 67*(2), 348–393.
Braun, S. (2007). Integrating corpus work into secondary education: From data-driven learning to needs-driven corpora. *ReCALL, 19*(3), 307–328. doi: 10.1017/S0958344007000535.
Cobb, T. (1999). Applying constructivism: A test for the learner-as-scientist. *Educational Technology Research & Development, 47*, 15–33. doi: 10.1007/BF02299631.
Crosthwaite, P. (2017). Retesting the limits of data-driven learning: Feedback and error correction. *Computer Assisted Language Learning, 30*(6), 447–473.
Crosthwaite, P., Wong, L. L. C., & Cheung, J. (2019). Characterising postgraduate students' corpus query and usage patterns for disciplinary data-driven learning. *ReCALL*, accepted, in press.
Eng, T. S. (2005). The impact of ICT on learning: A review of research. *International Education Journal, 6*(5), 635–650.
Gaskell, D., & Cobb, T. (2004). Can learners use concordance feedback for writing errors?. *System, 32*(3), 301–319.
Geluso, J., & Yamaguchi, A. (2014). Discovering formulaic language through data-driven learning: Student attitudes and efficacy. *ReCALL, 26*(2), 225–242.
Gil-Flores, J., Rodríguez-Santero, J., & Torres-Gordillo, J. J. (2017). Factors that explain the use of ICT in secondary-education classrooms: The role of teacher characteristics and school infrastructure. *Computers in Human Behavior, 68*, 441–449.
Hoey, M. (2005). *Lexical priming: A new theory of words and language.* Abingdon, UK: Routledge.
Johansson, S. (1995). Mens sana in corpore sano: On the role of corpora in linguistic research. *The European English Messenger, 4*(2), 19–25.
Johns, T. (1990). From printout to handout: Grammar and vocabulary teaching in the context of data-driven learning. *CALL Austria, 10*, 14–34.

Johns, T. (1997). Contexts: The background, development and trialling of a concordance-based CALL program. In A. Wichmann, S. Fligelstone, T. McEnery, & G. Knowles (Eds.), *Teaching and language corpora* (pp. 100–115). Harlow: Longman.

Lee, H., Warschauer, M., & Lee, J. H. (2018). The effects of corpus use on second language vocabulary learning: A multilevel meta-analysis. *Applied Linguistics*, online ahead of print.

Leńko-Szymańska, A., & Boulton, A. (2015). Introduction: Data-driven learning in language pedagogy. In A. Leńko-Szymańska & A. Boulton (eds.), *Multiple affordances of language corpora for data-driven learning* (pp. 1–14). Amsterdam: John Benjamins.

Long, M. (1991). Focus on form: A design feature in language teaching methodology. In K. de Bot, R. Ginsberg, & C. Kramsch (Eds.), *Foreign language research in cross-cultural perspective* (pp. 39–52). Amsterdam: John Benjamins.

Pérez-Paredes, P. (forthcoming). *The uses and the spread of corpora and data-driven learning in language education in CALL research: An analysis of the 2011–2015 period.*

Prensky, M. (2001). Digital natives, digital immigrants. *On the Horizon, 9*(5), 1–6.

Romer, U. (2009). Corpus research and practice: What help do teachers need and what can we offer? In K. Aijmer (Ed.), *Corpora and language teaching* (pp. 83–98). Amsterdam: John Benjamins.

Schmidt, R. (1990). The role of consciousness in second language learning. *Applied Linguistics, 11*, 129–158. doi: 10.1093/applin/11.2.129.

Siddiq, F., Hatlevik, O. E., Olsen, R. V., Throndsen, I., & Scherer, R. (2016). Taking a future perspective by learning from the past – A systematic review of assessment instruments that aim to measure primary and secondary school students' ICT literacy. *Educational Research Review, 19*, 58–84.

Sinclair, J. (1991). *Corpus, concordance, collocation.* Oxford, UK: Oxford University Press.

Sotelo, P. (2015). Using a multimedia corpus of subtitles in translation training. In A. Leńko-Szymańska & A. Boulton (Eds.), *Multiple affordances of language corpora for data-driven learning* (pp. 245–266). Amsterdam: John Benjamins.

Stenström, A. B., Andersen, G., & Hasund, I. K. (2002). *Trends in teenage talk: Corpus compilation, analysis and findings.* Amsterdam: John Benjamins.

Stickler, U., & Shi, L. (2016). TELL us about CALL: An introduction to the Virtual Special Issue (VSI) on the development of technology enhanced and computer assisted language learning published in the System Journal. *System, 56*, 119–126.

Voogt, J., Knezek, G., Cox, M., Knezek, D., & Ten Brummelhuis, A. (2013). Under which conditions does ICT have a positive effect on teaching and learning? A call to action. *Journal of Computer Assisted Learning, 29*, 4–14. doi: 10.1111/j.1365-2729.2011.00453.x.

PART I
Overcoming emerging challenges for DDL with younger learners

2

A CASE FOR CONSTRUCTIVE ALIGNMENT IN DDL

Rethinking outcomes, practices, and assessment in (data-driven) language learning

Fanny Meunier

Introduction

Whilst recent meta-analyses (Mizumoto & Chujo, 2015; Boulton & Cobb, 2017) point to the benefits of using DDL in second/foreign language learning, Forti (2018, p. ii) adds that these meta-analyses also "reveal that the effects of the approach vary considerably when taking into account a number of moderator variables, such as teaching context, proficiency level of the learners and type of study design investigating these effects". She also mentions the scarcity of empirical DDL evidence for younger learners or for learners with proficiency levels other than upper-intermediate or advanced – a gap that the present volume aims to fill (also see Tyne, 2012). I argue in this chapter that DDL literature generally suffers from a lack of constructive alignment, which is unfortunate given the importance of aligned teaching and learning practices in instructed settings (particularly so when younger learners are involved). I also suggest ways of going off the beaten path of DDL concordance lines and adopting new ways of DDL-izing teaching practices by including more multimodality (sound, video, pictures), another asset for work with younger learners.

What is constructive alignment?

Put simply, constructive alignment (CoAl[1]) is a pedagogical principle for quality learning which requires that 1) the curriculum and its intended outcomes, 2) the teaching methods used, and 3) the assessment tasks each be consistently and coherently aligned.

When Biggs (1996) first discussed constructive alignment, he explained that it was an outcome-based approach related to both constructivist learning theory and instructional design literature. The constructivist side of CoAl comes from the fact that constructivist learning theories argue that reality and knowledge are "constructed" by the "knower" through engaging in activities (see Jonassen, 1991). Biggs (1996, p. 347) thus stresses the need for active participation from the learners to "create meaning". To give a concrete example related to language learning, if a learner knows how to transcribe a word using the phonetic alphabet, there is no guarantee that he or she will be able to actually pronounce the word correctly. It is only through actively engaging in speaking activities that pronunciation will be gradually acquired. As for the instructional design aspect of CoAl, it is related to the need for coherence and consistency between the definition of learning outcomes, the activities used to help students achieve those outcomes, and the way these outcomes are assessed. To give another concrete example related to language learning, if one of the desired learning outcomes of a course is that students should be able to interact orally with peers, it would make little sense to focus exclusively on written vocabulary exercises and to assess the learning outcome by asking students to match written words/expressions with corresponding pictures. In such a configuration, the course would not be aligned.

It is worth noting that the first tenet of constructive alignment, namely the centrality of the learner's activities in creating meaning, also lies at the core of many second language acquisition theories, including cognitive (see Ellis, 2006), social-interactional (see Pekarek Doehler, 2013), socio-cultural (see Aimin, 2013), and usage-based (see Eskildsen, 2009) approaches. In all those theories, the learner is actively involved in acquiring the second/foreign/additional language and is not considered a passive recipient of knowledge. Learners, teachers, peers, and speakers of the target language are all involved in the various steps of acquisition, for example as input providers, facilitators of intake, interactive participants, or (co-)producers of output.

As for the second tenet, namely the alignment of the objectives of a learning activity to the assessment of the learner's performance, it is widely used by teachers and educational stakeholders to increase programme/curriculum/course coherence and efficiency. Alignment can be found at not only various levels[2] of instructional design including specific teaching activities but also

- strategy (e.g. how students are taught within a school-improvement plan),
- learning standards (e.g. for the learning of an additional language: alignment on the CECFR levels [Council of Europe, 2001]),
- assessment (e.g. alignment of standardized tests to address the specific concepts and skills listed in curricula at various grade levels), and
- professional development (e.g. pre- and in-service training sessions to promote new educational approaches or teaching techniques).

CoAl can be described as a backwards type of instructional design[3] (Wiggins & McTighe, 2005) that should be applied as follows (based on Biggs, 2003):

1 Define the intended learning outcomes (content to be learned and what needs to be "done" with that content).

2   Create a learning environment that is likely to engage the student in activities that will bring about the intended outcomes.
3   Use assessment tasks that directly address the intended outcomes and enable assessors/teachers to judge if and how well students' performances meet the criteria.

In the next section, the rationale for using CoAl in DDL is presented in more detail. Going through this framing stage helps conceptualize – and better situate – the concrete suggestions provided in later sections. CoAl is particularly important in secondary contexts where pedagogic mediation is central (see Wicher, this volume, for a lengthier discussion and for concrete illustrations of pedagogic mediation).

Rationale for using CoAl in DDL: using the TPACK model to frame the reflection

Whilst the three steps described (outcomes, activities, assessment) can easily be applied to instructed second/foreign language teaching in general, they are particularly relevant in the specific case of DDL. The rationale for using CoAl in DDL will be framed using the Technology Pedagogy Content Knowledge (TPACK) model, developed to explain how teachers articulate different types of knowledge to teach effectively (Mishra & Koehler, 2006; Koehler, Mishra, Kereluik, Shin, & Graham, 2014). The authors updated Shulman's (1986) work on pedagogical content knowledge (PCK) to include one of the biggest changes in education, i.e. the use of technology in the classroom. As DDL contains a strong digital[4] component, it should ideally be smoothly integrated in classroom activities, and all this has strong implications for teachers' and learners' digital literacies. DDL is mainly used as a Focus on Form methodology (see Wicher, this volume) used to help learners become aware of the patterned nature of language. DDL

- relies on findings in corpus linguistic which show that language is highly formulaic and contains a large proportion of fully/partly/semi-fixed multiword units (see, among others, Wray, 2002; Conklin & Schmitt, 2007; Meunier & Granger, 2008; Ellis & Simpson-Vlach, 2009) and
- is in line with Second Language Acquisition findings in that the technology behind DDL helps learners access frequency information and visualize the saliency of form-meaning patterns, two aspects of language learning that are difficult to access for non-native learners, particularly in "low input" foreign language contexts (see Meunier, 2012; Lui et al., 2014; Ellis, Römer, & Brook O'Donnell, 2016; Ellis, 2017).

To better visualize the integration of DDL in TPACK, let us first consider the three key components of TPACK:

1   content knowledge (CK), which can be defined as the teachers' knowledge about the subject matter to be learned or taught (an additional language here);

2   pedagogical knowledge (PK), which is the teachers' knowledge about the appropriate and up-to-date processes and practices or methods of teaching and learning additional languages; and
3   technological knowledge (TK), which consists of an in-depth understanding of information technology, enabling the teacher to apply technology productively to assess whether information technology can assist or impede the achievement of a learning goal.

Figure 2.1 presents how I conceptualize DDL and CoAl as framed in the TPACK model (see also Meunier, 2018a and 2018b). I started from Koehler and Mishra's (2009, p. 63) graphical representation of the three key components of TPACK[5] (CK, PK, and TK), each consisting in a circle. Those three circles intertwine in dyadic ways (for instance when TK and PK overlap, we have TPK). Where/when the three circles intertwine, we get complete TPACK integration.

To me, TCK – technological content knowledge – is represented by the field of corpus linguistics, as the corpus linguistic methodology and tools (technology) have been instrumental in highlighting the patterned/multiword nature of authentic language use (content) (see also O'Keeffe & McCarthy, 2010, Biber & Reppen, 2015, Granger, Gilquin, & Meunier, eds., 2015). I view TPK – technological pedagogical knowledge – as being represented by DDL. The use of corpus-based concordance lines as a pedagogical tool for awareness-raising activities is a concrete example of how technology and pedagogy can be integrated (see Leńko-Szymańska & Boulton, 2015, Boulton, 2017, and Boulton & Cobb, 2017 for more illustrations of the potential of data-driven learning in language learning). As for PCK – pedagogical content knowledge – I see it as the core business

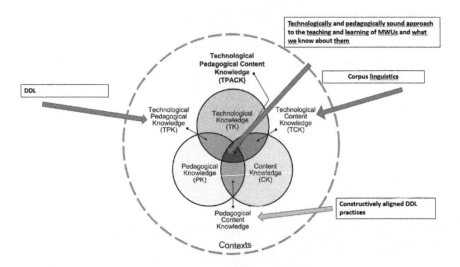

FIGURE 2.1   DDL and CoAl framed in the TPACK model

Source: (adapted from Koehler & Mishra, 2009, p. 63)[6]

of teaching, which notably includes the need for providing aligned courses. PCK here refers to the teachers' knowledge about the appropriate and up-to-date processes and practices or methods of teaching and learning the multiword/patterned nature of an additional language. This includes

1   the knowledge of overall educational purposes, values, and aims;
2   the mastery of general classroom management skills;
3   the understanding of how students learn/acquire language patterns/multiword units; and
4   the integration of what precedes in curriculum and lesson planning capacities, from preparation to assessment.

I argue that PCK is the "poor cousin" of numerous projects on DDL and deserves a lot more attention on the part of teachers and researchers. I also believe that working towards more aligned practices could be of tremendous help in promoting sustainable DDL practices, especially when working with younger learners in classroom contexts where pedagogical mediation, smooth integration of tasks in the curriculum, and scaffolded digital literacy practices are crucial. In the next sections I provide suggestions on how to better align outcomes, teaching/learning practices, and assessment in DDL.

Intended learning outcomes in DDL

Boulton (2010) tackles the issue of learning outcomes from corpus consultation. He found 27 empirical studies of DDL focusing explicitly on L2 learning outcomes. Some general observations on the bulk of studies analyzed are that the target language was mainly English (24/27), that over two-thirds of the studies involve learners in higher education, and that in most cases the learners accessed the data during the class or in special sessions in the computer room. Regarding the duration of the study, the average exposure to DDL is about 10 hours, but some studies have only a single contact with corpus data. In terms of learning outcomes, Boulton explains that a large variety of different tools were used for testing purposes but that most of them required learners to complete fairly closed tasks (e.g. cloze tests, matching, sentence completion, substitution, error-correction). Regarding learning outcomes specifically, the majority of the studies displayed rather encouraging results, but Boulton mentions some problems in design or quantitative analysis, and only six out of 27 studies provided unambiguously positive findings meeting the requirements of statistical significance. Whilst Boulton notes (2010, p. 18) that the results fall "short of conclusive proof of the effectiveness of DDL", he adds that they provide "grounds for optimism" and that the studies "show that DDL can be usefully employed for learners of many different language backgrounds and in different situations when appropriately adapted".

Several points of attention can be listed here. The first one is the linguistic scope of the outputs, which tends to remain fairly limited as the vast majority of tasks analyzed are closed tasks. The temporal scope is also rather limited in four ways: One, very few studies include delayed post-tests (I counted seven out of 27). Two, too many studies analyze the outcomes of DDL on the basis of limited encounters with the practice at hand (sometimes only one). The third limitation is the localization scope, as most studies are done in class or in computer rooms. The fourth one could be labelled as the competence scope, as most studies involve learners in higher education.

A widening of the various scopes listed is clearly in order. In terms of linguistic outputs it is essential to go beyond the typical closed tasks in writing activities. That would for instance entail a more frequent inclusion of DDL activities a) to train and practice more productive skills such as "open" writing tasks (story writing) or focus on orality (as is the case in studies using DDL for pronunciation, see Mairano & Romano, 2010 or Liakin, Cardoso, & Liakina, 2017), b) not necessarily carried out during in-class time, and c) with younger/less proficient learners; see concrete examples in the following section and in other chapters of the present volume. Another key issue that I would like to point out here (and which will be further expanded in Section 5) is the almost complete lack of DDL use in certification practices. Numerous written assessment tests do not for instance allow online corpus consultation, even in institutions/universities that overtly promote DDL. This is certainly a sign of a lack of constructive alignment and may, at least in part, be responsible for the lack of uptake of DDL practices often referred to in the literature (Leech, 1997; Chambers, 2007; Boulton, 2009; Wilson, 2013; Meunier, 2019).

Teaching and learning practices in DDL

Taking into account what has been said in the previous sections – and given the expected alignment between the learning outcomes, their assessment, and the practices required to help/train students reach the expected outcomes – I would like to stress the importance not only of an expansion of the types of tools and tasks currently used in DDL activities but also of a smoother integration of digital literacy tools inside and outside the classroom. As argued by, among others, Cobb and Boulton (2015) and Wicher (this volume), typical DDL may overwhelm weaker or less proficient learners who may expect/prefer more explicit guidance and for whom the "learner as a researcher" metaphor may not be appealing. In addition, teachers themselves may lack the necessary digital literacy to use existing corpus tools and may not always see the added value of integrating DDL in the prescribed curriculum they have to use.

If we consider that DDL is learning driven by the data (Johns, 1991a and 1991b), it seems to me that "the data" and the tools to access them have remained relatively similar over the years, despite the digital turn that has taken place in many educational areas. Whilst Boulton and Cobb (2017) note an evolution towards more computer-based (vs paper-based) practices in DDL over the years, it nonetheless seems to me that DDL has not (yet) taken a real digital turn. Boulton and Cobb (2017) list some of the reasons that might explain the reluctance of doing DDL in class. These include reluctance to work with computers and the lack of training that is often required to do so, the fact that the types of tasks may seem unfamiliar (vertical vs horizontal reading, learners as language analysts, etc.), and that the types of data contained in the available corpora and tools may not be appropriate for some learners' needs or levels. Forti (2018, p. 18) rightly mentions that some of the observed limitations can be overcome "with the many learner friendly corpus-search Web interfaces (justtheword, SkELL, BNC lab, etc.) that have become available in the past few years" and that "further possible developments in mobile-based versions of DDL can contribute in overcoming these perceived difficulties". This being said, there is also room for more creativity in the DDL tasks that could be proposed to younger learners, especially keeping in mind the affordances of current digital tools (multimodality, gaming options, easy access, intuitive use, etc.). Concordance lines are not the only possible triggers of frequency effects and form-meaning mappings in focus on form activities.

Expanding the scope of tools and tasks used in DDL activities

Due to space constraints, I present three concrete suggestions to expand the scope of tools and tasks in DDL activities. As will be shown, tools and tasks are often interdependent as the potential of the tool often guides the types of tasks that are feasible with the tool. I also aim to show that some tools – and the data they are working with – which while not initially created for DDL activities can easily be integrated in DDL focus-on-form types of activities, thereby doing what Ortega (2019) calls "domesticated CALL", i.e. leveraging tools "from the wild" into the classroom. This practice can be opposed to "dedicated CALL" which has been specifically created with language learning purposes in mind. I also try to present tools and tasks that can easily be used with younger learners but by no means exclusively so.

Tasks carried out on the basis of corpus-generated concordance lines are one of the most common approaches used in DDL. Such activities (and many others in DDL) are almost exclusively based on written texts (even if some of the texts are actually transcribed speech). Activities that include sound and videos are much less commonly used, which is a great pity given the multimodal nature of today's communicative interactions and the advantages of using various input types (see for instance Cho & Reinders's [2013] and Fatemipour & Moharamzadeh's [2015] studies on the effects of aural input enhancement on L2 acquisition).

One tool that could for instance be used for oral input-based/enhanced DDL activities is the PlayPhrase.me app or Web interface (see www.playphrase.me). PlayPhrase.me allows users to search for an almost endless list of common phrases of the English language. By inserting a word, the user is presented with words that are often used in "phrases" linked to that word. To give a concrete example, by inserting the word "give" in the search line, you are presented with possible options for multiword units or longer chunks related to "give". You can for instance decide to select "me" and then "a".

Imagine you decide to stop after "give me a" (see Figure 2.2) and press play; you will be presented with very short excerpts (often a couple of seconds) of recent

FIGURE 2.2 Screenshot from PlayPhrase.me (taken 11 April 2019)

video clips from films or series where the characters use that phrase. In the case of "give me a" the user will get 137 occurrences of the phrase in videos. Among them, students will hear – and see – numerous examples of "give me a break", "give me a reason", "give me a minute", "give me a hand", "give me a chance", "give me a call", etc. in films or series like *Breaking Bad*, *Sherlock*, *Game of Thrones*, *House*, *Big Bang Theory*, and the like. Besides the funny and addictive nature of the app (please continue reading the rest of the chapter before trying it out, or you might never finish this chapter!), it has numerous pedagogical advantages: multimodality (sound and images coupled to the text); links with real life activities, namely watching films and series (which may also prompt the use of the tool outside the classroom); or opportunities for the teacher to propose game-like tasks (e.g. "Who will be the first to find four expressions containing 'give me a' "?). One additional advantage is that the potential for receptive and productive SLA is often found to be enhanced thanks to the addition of the characteristics previously listed.

Another tool that capitalizes on multimodality and that could also be used to aid the learning of multiword units is LyricsTraining (https://fr.lyricstraining.com). As young people often spend a lot of time listening to music, the potential of this application is rather impressive. Initially, LyricsTraining (which is available in 13 languages: English, Spanish, Portuguese, French, Italian, German, Dutch, Japanese, Turkish, Polish, Swedish, Finnish, and Catalan) provides users with subtitled video clips of songs. Users can choose a song (among a list of available songs) and use one of the two following modes: karaoke style (to watch, read, and/or sing along) or fill-in-the-blanks (with or without suggestions) – see Figure 2.3.

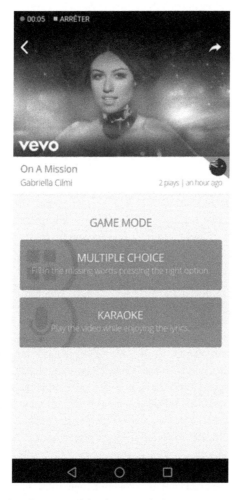

FIGURE 2.3 Screenshot from a mobile phone with the gaming options for the selected song

Whilst all this might look like a rather traditional fill-in-the-blank exercise based on songs in schools, it can be DDL-ized at various levels: The system allows users to choose their level, not in terms of the levels included in the Common European Framework of Reference for Languages (Council of Europe, 2001) but in terms of the number of words or expressions you have to pick up during the song. More importantly perhaps, teachers can also create their own gap-fill activities. This option makes it possible for teachers to tailor their activity to the needs/levels/aims of their own learners (e.g. by asking learners to find/hear/write language patterns that have previously been selected by the teacher as learning targets). To give just one concrete example, a song like "I Believe in You" by Michael Bublé (Sony Music, 2016) can be used to work on the [believe in + NP] or the [believe in + GERUND] patterns. Using such applications in (or outside) the classroom has several advantages. The first one is the motivational effect of working with songs in the classroom. Second, we have learning which is "driven by the data" in a format which varies from concordance lines, includes audio input in addition to the transcription, and is probably easier to handle for less advanced users. Third, the "frequency effect" in the data can be made salient by the task proposed by the teacher. Fourth, such apps are free and user-friendly and do not require specific training. Finally, the task is familiar both for learners and teachers. We also have additional features similar to those mentioned for PlayPhrase.me, namely multimodality, gaming options with the inclusion of scores, and increased likelihood of use outside the classroom. The DDL/focus on form activity presented here can also easily be integrated in meaning-focused activities (as the song can be used both for focus on form exercises and, say, discussions on topics like self-confidence, relationship with others, etc.). Here again, the use of oral input in one of its possible guises is a real plus (see Piske & Young-Scholten, 2008 regarding the various types of input and their related benefits in SLA), especially if it can then be recycled in additional form- and/or meaning-focused input, output, or interactional tasks.

LyricsTraining also has some drawbacks that should also be taken into account. Lewis (2017) in his review published on https://thedigitalteacher.com[7] mentions the fact that there is no filter for the videos or advertising and that teachers should be aware that the site content is unfiltered and hence be careful how they share it and when they demonstrate it. As the site's content is largely user generated, some errors might also appear in the lyrics. Despite those drawbacks, however, he comments that the app is easy to use (it takes 10 seconds to get started as a user), the site is generally problem free, it is an easy and fun way to learn, it improves foreign languages skills, it helps learners learn new vocabulary and expressions, and it reinforces grammar concepts through continuous exercise of writing the missing words and patterns.

The third example pertains to the need for more variation in tasks. Yoon and Jo (2014, p. 97) list various types of tasks implemented in writing classes and their related aims. A large body of studies report on tasks aiming at improving students' knowledge about common usage patterns of words, enhancing students' awareness of lexicogrammatical patterning and rhetorical functions, evaluating apprenticeship in corpus use and increasing vocabulary knowledge and use through concordance-based exercises (as alternatives to traditional gap-fill exercises). In contrast, fewer studies examine how students actually integrate corpus use for proofreading activities. Exceptions include Sun's (2007) study on using a Web-based scholarly writing template to enhance students' genre-specific language use or Gilmore's (2009) observations on learners' use of corpora to revise their writing to improve its naturalness. If one of the aims of DDL is to help students become independent corpus users (see Kennedy & Miceli, 2001; Sun, 2007; Yoon & Jo, 2014), it is of paramount importance to give them tasks that train their corpus use in meaningful and challenging contexts.

Such tools may, however, not easily be adapted for use by younger learners. With a view to progressively helping them to understand how digital tools can help them solve their language problems, they could be trained to use simple, free Web tools when working on writing tasks (or notes for speaking tasks). Such tools rely on language data analysis and natural language processing behind the scenes, but the output they offer to users is simplified. Learners do not need to perform a cognitively demanding task to access the information they need. One such example is using Google to search for "collocations for *x*". The first hit is very likely to refer learners to collocation examples, usage, and a definition of the word provided by an online dictionary. Even if the output may seem a bit abrupt at first sight, learners quickly understand that they can find useful words on the page. A test for "collocations for school" (see www.freecollocation.com/search1?word=school) returned the following suggestions – only a few examples are provided for illustration purposes:

> ADJ. elementary, high, middle, nursery, prep/preparatory, primary, secondary | special *She attends a special school for children with learning difficulties.* VERB + SCHOOL attend, go to | start | finish, leave | skip, (play) truant from | be/stay off, keep sb off *His mum kept him off school for two weeks when he was ill.* SCHOOL + NOUN curriculum | student | teacher (also schoolteacher) *She's a middle-school teacher.* PREP. after ~ *We're going to play football after school.* | at (a/the) ~ *She didn't do very well at school. Their son's at the school near the station.* | in (a/the)~ *Are the children still in school?*

We also see that the examples provided are accessible to younger learners, and even if the examples are simplified versions of what can be found in corpora of authentic texts, they are probably best suited for younger learners. In the present case, the data has been reorganized and simplified (e.g. easy example sentences that may not be exact copy-pasted authentic sentences from corpora). Whilst some may argue that the authenticity of the corpus is no longer guaranteed, it should be pointed out that pedagogic processing is beneficial for work with younger learners (see Wicher, this volume, for a discussion on the limits of "corpus fetishism" and on the advantages of pedagogic processing).

The second returned hit on Google for "collocations for school" referred me to https://prowritingaid.com/collocations-examples/294499/379418/Examples-collocations-of-education-and-school.aspx. I keyed in *school* in the "collocation search" box and got the following suggestions (only a few examples provided for common verb collocations of *school* for illustration purposes): *be, go, have, come, leave, attend, drop, can, should, do, complete, will, teach, enter, open, graduate, get, learn, must, belong, start, finish, begin.* As can be seen from only the first two hits returned after a very basic search on Google, such tools can provide students' first free, low-tech, and user-friendly approach to collocations. These websites can easily be used by learners independently in and outside school (e.g. for homework) but can also be used by teachers as prompts for further discussions or exercises involving the use of collocations.

As put forward by Trussart and Turgeon (2018) in their publication on student engagement strategies in the digital era, one of the key elements defining student engagement is the time and effort invested in the learning activities. In terms of strategies, it is also essential to make the learning activities significant for learners. In order to promote significance and engagement in DDL, I suggest providing students with tasks where the added value of corpus consultation/use of digital tools is made more salient (even if some of these tools offer simplified output). Examples include giving students the opportunity to access corpora/digital tools to edit their writing in exam conditions, not only for occasional in-class writing tasks or vocabulary exercises.

Towards a smoother integration of digital literacy tools inside and outside the classroom

Some of the suggestions provided in the previous section show that creativity is required in DDL activities and that more attention should be given to the integration of new tools for DDL, especially at lower proficiency levels or with younger learners with whom often-cited tools, such as BNCweb, COCA-BYU or Sketch Engine, might not be the ideal entrance to DDL. The use of various input sources, apparently funnier or game-like tasks, and tools usually helps trigger motivation in and outside the classroom. The ever-increasing options for mobile access to tools is also one of the keys to removing the walls of the classroom and to prompting students to use DDL for their everyday needs when they communicate in an additional language. Those needs may range from very basic communicative activities to more advanced academic challenges.

Here again, some learning apps used outside the classroom could easily be DDL-ized. One such example is Quizlet, an online tool or app that allows students to revise vocabulary and take tests online; it also contains some game-like options. As Quizlet allows teachers to create and use flashcards for vocabulary definition or review, teachers could easily integrate a few (input-enhanced) concordance lines in the flashcards to draw students' attention to the formulaic nature of some expressions. In addition to what teachers can implement, Quizlet already offers

A case for constructive alignment in DDL **25**

FIGURE 2.4 Some examples of collocations cards from Quizlet (including the collocation, an image for illustration and a translation – in Spanish here)

free material that has been shared by other teachers. For instance, if teachers of English go to https://quizlet.com/subject/collocations, they will find readymade cards that they can use with younger learners (only a few examples are copied in Figure 2.4 for illustration purposes):

The existing cards that I checked do not include concordance lines at the moment, but these can always be added by teachers later if they feel the need for it. What many of those cards do contain, however, is pictures. These pictures are a most-welcome help for younger learners. The cards also often contain translations, which may prove very useful as a scaffolding step towards more independent use of concordances and fewer guided exercises.

Assessing learning outcomes in DDL

As explained previously, CoAl recommends using assessment tasks that directly address the intended outcomes and enable assessors/teachers to judge if and how well students' performances meet the criteria. I have also argued that the expected learning outcomes of DDL activities tended to remain fairly limited to closed types of linguistic outcomes. To expand the nature of the learning outcomes, it thus seems essential to provide more open-ended tasks that require the use of DDL tools and strategies. In addition to the linguistic outcomes that can be expected, students should be tested on their ability to "DDLearn". Teachers might therefore consider including new items in their assessment grids. The typical "appropriate use of reference tools" that is sometimes found as one of the items in the assessment grids could be complemented/refined by the inclusion of "ability to revise a text using DDL tools" to improve accuracy, and/or fluency, and/or complexity. Some assessment tasks could also include rewriting or error-correction exercises where students could access any available online resources, among them corpora and DDL tools (see examples provided in the previous sections). This certainly requires a change in current assessment practices, but a digital turn is also required if one wants to contribute to Breiter and Jarke's (2016) notion of "datafying education" and embrace the potential of digital literacy and digital assessment practices. It is definitely time to go off the beaten path and accept the fact that students should be using online tools. It could be the case that teachers fear that cheating might take place or that students would stop studying their vocabulary. However, one way of overcoming such fears is to remember – and tell students – that if digital tools can be used to assess certain skills (e.g. written tasks), the tools will not be made available for other skills (e.g. spontaneous oral interactions).

Concluding remarks: a case for constructive alignment and innovation

The core of the TPACK model presented in the introductory section is a plea for a technologically and pedagogically sound approach to teaching content knowledge, i.e. the need for a smooth triadic integration of technology, pedagogy, and content. I have illustrated this plea by focusing on DDL in the teaching and learning of multiword units in additional languages. I have tried to demonstrate that corpus linguistics has largely fed the intersection of "content" and "technological" knowledge and that DDL studies have largely contributed to the intersection of "technological" and "pedagogical" knowledge. I also pointed to the fact that the intersection of "pedagogical" and "content" knowledge deserved more attention. More constructive alignment is needed in order to promote the TPACK, i.e. a clear definition of learning outcomes (in terms of the content to be learned and what needs to be "done" with that content), the creation of a learning environment that is likely to engage students in activities that will bring about the intended outcomes, and finally the use of assessment tasks that directly address the intended outcomes and that enable assessors/teachers to judge if and how well students' performances have met the criteria. I have presented concrete examples that strive towards increased alignment of outcomes, practices, and assessment and tried to focus on uses with younger learners. The examples presented are probably not appropriate in/for all contexts and can surely be criticized. There is, however, a pressing need to go off the current beaten DDL path and promote creativity in DDL. I hope that the few illustrations provided here will prompt more researchers and teachers to build on the affordances of new digital tools to DDL-ize them. The current scope of DDL should be expanded to integrate new tools, new input types, more multimodality, and inclusive DDL tasks that are integrated in meaning-focused curricular and extra-curricular activities. In sum, I plead for more efforts in domesticating CALL (see Ortega, 2019), i.e. leveraging tools "from the wild" into the classroom. In that respect, Sundqvist's (2019) paper on the use of commercial-off-the-shelf (COTS) games to enhance vocabulary learning offers is a much-welcome source of inspiration for future work and for the increased attention that should be paid to the impact of (what she calls) "extramural" language practice on the acquisition of an additional language.

The assessment of DDL outcomes should also be expanded and go beyond purely linguistic outcomes to include strategic ones too. This may require a shift in the vision that curriculum designers and/or teachers have about assessment. In that respect, it may be useful to keep Wiggins and McTighe's (2005, p. 146) suggestion in mind, i.e. before going on to the creation of any activity, teachers and curriculum designers must ask themselves questions like: "What would count as evidence of successful learning? Or what counts as evidence of the understanding sought?".

Notes

1 I have opted for the CoAl acronym to avoid confusion with the CA initialism, which is already used in my research domain for two different concepts, namely Contrastive Analysis and Conversational Analysis.
2 See www.edglossary.org/alignment for more concrete examples.
3 Backwards instructional designs are opposed to more traditional instructional designs in which the curriculum basically only lists the "contents" that need to be learned/taught.
4 It should be acknowledged that some DDL activities can be carried on paper, but even in such cases, the digital component (e.g. use of native and/or learner corpora and use of text retrieval and analysis tools) is often a prerequisite to the activity.
5 Their initial graph is included in the big (broken line) circle.
6 Reproduced by permission of the publisher, © 2012 by tpack.org.
7 See https://thedigitalteacher.com/reviews/lyricstraining.

References

Aimin, L. (2013). The study of second language acquisition under socio-cultural theory. *American Journal of Educational Research*, *1*(5), 162–167.
Biber, D., & Reppen, R. (Eds.). (2015). *The Cambridge handbook of English corpus linguistics* (Cambridge Handbooks in Language and Linguistics). Cambridge: Cambridge University Press. doi: 10.1017/CBO9781139764377.
Biggs, J. (1996). Enhancing teaching through constructive alignment. *Higher Education*, *32*(3), 347–364.
Biggs, J. (2003). *Teaching for quality learning at university* (2nd ed.). Buckingham: Open University Press/Society for Research into Higher Education.
Boulton, A. (2009). Data-driven learning: On paper, in practice. Corpus Linguistics in Language Teaching. In T. Harris & M. Moreno Jaén (Eds.), *Corpora in language teaching* (pp. 17–52). Bern: Peter Lang (Linguistic Insights).
Boulton, A. (2010). Learning outcomes from corpus consultation. In M. Moreno Jaén, F. Serrano Valverde, & M. Calzada Pérez (Eds.), *Exploring new paths in language pedagogy: Lexis and corpus-based language teaching* (pp. 129–144). London: Equinox. hal-00502629v2.
Boulton, A. (2017). Data-driven learning and language pedagogy. In S. Thorne & S. May (Eds.), *Language, education and technology: Encyclopedia of language and education*. New York: Springer. doi: 10.1007/978-3-319-02328-1_15–1.
Boulton, A., & Cobb, T. (2017). Corpus use in language learning: A meta-analysis. *Language Learning*, *67*(2), 348–393.
Breiter, A., & Jarke, J. (2016). *Datafying education: How digital assessment practices reconfigure the organisation of learning* (Communicative Figurations Working Papers. No. 11). Retrieved from https://www.kommunikative-figurationen.de/fileadmin/user_upload/Arbeitspapiere/CoFi_EWP_No-11_Breiter_Jarke.pdf. doi: 10.13140/RG.2.1.2565.9280.
Chambers, A. (2007). Popularising corpus consultation by language learners and teachers. In E. Hidalgo et al. (Eds.), *Corpora in the foreign language classroom* (pp. 3–16). Amsterdam: Rodopi.
Cho, M., & Reinders, R. (2013). The effects of aural input enhancement on L2 acquisition. In J. M. Bergsleithner, S. N. Frota, & J. K. Yoshioka (Eds.), *Noticing and second language*

acquisition: Studies in honor of Richard Schmidt.(pp. 133–148). Honolulu: University of Hawai'i, National Foreign Language Resource Center.

Cobb, T., & Boulton, A. (2015). Classroom applications of corpus analysis. In D. Biber & R. Reppen (Eds.), *The Cambridge handbook of English corpus linguistics* (pp. 478–497). Cambridge: Cambridge University Press.

Conklin, K., & Schmitt, N. (2007). Formulaic sequences: Are they processed more quickly than nonformulaic language by native and non- native speakers? *Applied Linguistics, 28*, 1–18.

Council of Europe. (2001). *Common European framework of reference for languages: Learning, teaching, assessment.* Cambridge: Cambridge University Press.

Ellis, N. C. (2006). Cognitive perspectives on SLA: The associative-cognitive CREED. *AILA Review, 19(1)*, 100–121. doi: 10.1075/aila.19.08ell.

Ellis, N. C. (2017). Cognition, corpora, and computing: Triangulating research in usage-based language learning. *Language Learning, 67*(S1), 40–65. doi: 10.1111/lang.12215.

Ellis, N. C., Römer, U., & Brook O'Donnell, M. (2016). *Usage-based approaches to language acquisition and processing: Cognitive and corpus investigations of construction grammar.* Hoboken, NJ: Wiley-Blackwell.

Ellis, N. C., & Simpson-Vlach, R. C. (2009). Formulaic language in native speakers: Triangulating psycholinguistics, corpus linguistics, and education. In G. Gilquin (Ed.), *Corpora and experimental methods.* Special issue of Corpus Linguistics and Linguistic Theory, 5(1), 61–78.

Eskildsen. (2009). Constructing another language – Usage-based linguistics in second language acquisition. *Applied Linguistics, 30*(3), 335–357. doi: 10.1093/applin/amn037.

Fatemipour, H., & Moharamzadeh, S. (2015). The impact of textual enhancement vs. oral enhancement on learning english language grammar. *Journal of Language Teaching and Research, 6*(2), 327–332.

Forti, L. (2018). *Developing phraseological competence in Italian L2: A study on the effects of Data-driven learning* (Unpublished PhD thesis). Perugia: University for Foreigners of Perugia.

Gilmore, A. (2009). Using on-line corpora to develop students' writing skills. English *Language Teaching Journal, 63*(4), 363–372. doi: 10.1093/elt/ccn056.

Granger, S., Gilquin, G., & Meunier, F. (Eds.). (2015). *The Cambridge handbook of learner corpus research.* Cambridge: Cambridge University Press.

Johns, T. (1991a). Should you be persuaded: Two examples of data-driven learning. In T. Johns & P. King (Eds.), *ELR Journal 4: Classroom Concordancing* (pp. 1–16). Birmingham: CELS, The University of Birmingham.

Johns, T. (1991b). From printout to handout: Grammar and vocabulary teaching in the context of data-driven learning In T. Johns & P. King (Eds.), *ELR Journal 4: Classroom Concordancing* (pp. 27–46). Birmingham: CELS, The University of Birmingham.

Jonassen, D. H. (1991). Objectivism vs. constructivism: Do we need a new philosophical paradigm? *Educational Technology: Research and Development, 39*(3), 5–14.

Kennedy, C., & Miceli, T. (2001). An evaluation of intermediate students' approaches to corpus investigation. *Language Learning & Technology, 5*(3), 77–90. doi: 10125/44567.

Koehler, M. J., & Mishra, P. (2009). What is technological pedagogical content knowledge? *Contemporary Issues in Technology and Teacher Education, 9*(1), 60–70.

Koehler, M. J., Mishra, P., Kereluik, K., Shin, T. S., & Graham, C. R. (2014). The technological pedagogical content knowledge framework. In *Handbook of research on educational communications and technology* (4th ed., pp. 101–111). New York: Springer. doi: 10.1007/978-1-4614-3185-5_9.

Leech, G. (1997). Introducing corpus annotation. In R. Garside, G. N. Leech, & T. McEnery (Eds.), *Corpus annotation: Linguistic information from computer text corpora* (pp. 1–18). London: Longman.

Leńko-Szymańska, A., & Boulton, A. (2015). Multiple affordances of language corpora for data-driven Learning. *International Journal of Corpus Linguistics, 20*(4), 560–569. doi: 10.1075/ijcl.20.4.07gar.

Lewis, R. (2017). *LyricsTraining: Brilliant adventure game for language learners*. Retrieved from https://thedigitalteacher.com/reviews/lyricstraining. Published on 13 July 2017.

Liakin, D., Cardoso, W., & Liakina, N. (2017). The pedagogical use of mobile speech synthesis (TTS): Focus on French liaison. *Computer Assisted Language Learning, 30*(3–4), 348–365.

Mairano, P., & Romano, A. (2010). Un confronto tra diverse metriche ritmiche usando Correlatore. In S. Schmid, M. Schwarzenbach, & D. Studer (Eds.), *La dimensione temporale del parlato* (Proceedings of the V National AISV Congress, University of Zurich, Collegiengebaude, 4–6 February 2009) (pp. 79–100). Torriana (RN): EDK.

Meunier, F. (2012). ARAL formulaic language and language teaching. *Annual Review of Applied Linguistics, 32*, 111–129.

Meunier, F. (2018a). Promoting TPACK and professional learning communities: Focus on teaching and learning multiword units. *EuroCALL*, Jyväskylä, Finland, 23 August 2018. doi: 10.13140/RG.2.2.26823.14244. Retrieved from www.researchgate.net/publication/ 327237628_Promoting_TPACK_and_professional_learning_communities_focus_on_ teaching_and_learning_multiword_units_EuroCALL_conference_paper_Jyvaskyla_ Finland_23_August_2018

Meunier, F. (2018b). *Data-driven learning: From classroom scaffolding to sustainable practices* (Plenary talk). Data-driven learning: A scaffolding methodology for foreign languages and CLIL classes conference, Torino, September 2018.

Meunier, F. (2019, in press). Resources for learning multi-word items. In S. A. Webb (Ed.), *The Routledge handbook of vocabulary studies*. London: Routledge.

Meunier, F., & Granger, S. (Eds.). (2008). *Phraseology in language learning and teaching*. Amsterdam: Benjamins.

Mishra, P., & Koehler, M. (2006). Technological pedagogical content knowledge: A framework for teacher knowledge. *Teachers College Record, 108*(6), 1017–1054.

Mizumoto, A., & Chujo, K. (2015). A meta-analysis of data-driven learning approach in the Japanese EFL classroom. *English Corpus Studies, 22*, 1–18.

O'Keeffe, A., & McCarthy, M. (2010). *The Routledge handbook of corpus linguistics*. Abingdon: Routledge.

Ortega, L. (2019). *Plenary address at mobile language learning experience* (MOBILE conference), Lycée Français de New York, New York City, 21–22 February 2019.

Pekarek Doehler, S. (2013). Social-interactional approaches to SLA: A state of the art and some future perspectives. *Language, Interaction and Acquisition, 4*(2), 134–160.

Piske, T., & Young-Scholten, M. (2008). *Input matters in SLA*. Bristol: Multilingual Matters.

Shulman, L. S. (1986). Those who understand: Knowledge growth in teaching. *Educational Researcher, 15*(2), 4–14.

Sun, Y-C. (2007). Learner perceptions of a concordancing tool for academic writing. *Computer Assisted Language Learning, 20*(4), 323–343.

Sundqvist, P. (2019). Commercial-off-the-shelf games in the digital wild and L2 learner vocabulary. *Language Learning & Technology, 23*(1), 87–113.

Trussart, J. L., & Turgeon, A. (2018). *Classroom management in the digital era (part 3): Student engagement strategies*. Retrieved fromwww.profweb.ca/en/publications/featured-reports/ classroom-management-in-the-digital-era-part-3-student-engagement-strategies.

Tyne, H. (2012). Corpus work with ordinary teachers: Data-driven Learning activities. In J. Thomas & A. Boulton (Eds.), *Input, process and product: Developments in teaching and language corpora* (pp. 136–151). Brno: Masaryk University Press.

Wiggins, G., & McTighe, J. (2005). *Understanding by design* (2nd ed.). Alexandria, VA: Association for Supervision and Curriculum Development ASCD.

Wilson, J. (2013). Technology, pedagogy and promotion. How can we make the most of corpora and data-driven learning (DDL) in language learning and teaching? *The Higher Education Academy*. Retrieved from www.heacademy.ac.uk/system/files/corpus_technology_pedagogy_promotion2.pdf

Wray, A. (2002). *Formulaic language and the lexicon*. Cambridge: Cambridge University Press.

Yoon, H, & Jo, J. W. (2014). Direct and indirect access to corpora: An exploratory case study comparing students' error correction and learning strategy use in l2 writing. *Language Learning and Technology, 18*, 96–117.

3
DATA-DRIVEN LEARNING IN THE SECONDARY CLASSROOM

A critical evaluation from the perspective of foreign language didactics

Oliver Wicher

Introduction

Data-driven learning (DDL) represents one of the most promising applications of corpus linguistics; the body of research is already impressive, regarding both its conceptual foundations and empirical case studies (cf. Cobb & Boulton, 2015 for an overview). Although the overall picture is filled with optimism, it must be noted that the use of DDL has been almost exclusively limited to tertiary learners with advanced foreign language (FL) proficiency. The secondary classroom, on the contrary, has been relatively uncharted territory. The reasons for this gap are well known by now: few child-friendly corpus resources, teachers' unawareness of existing corpus applications, and the paucity of empirical studies testing the actual effects of DDL, amongst others (Crosthwaite, this volume; Braun, 2007; Tyne, 2012).

Furthermore, there appears to be an emerging consensus that the use of corpora by younger learners must somehow be simplified, which is sometimes labeled *pedagogic processing* or *pedagogic mediation*. Following Flowerdew (2009, p. 43ff.), this includes two dimensions: *What* type of corpus data must be pedagogically processed, and *how* is it done? Whilst one may intuitively agree that this kind of processing is necessary, little is said about how exactly this may be accomplished (cf. also Pérez-Paredes, 2010, p. 56).[1] Early work on DDL in the classroom offers hands-on activities (Johns & King, 1991; Tribble & Jones, 1997) but does not provide information on the broader picture of decisions that teachers would have to make in planning an FL lesson: what competences to develop, what learning goals to set, and how to sequence exercises and tasks so that learners can reach these goals?

One cannot help thinking that the direct transfer of corpus linguistic methodology onto FL instruction is not really appropriate in a secondary school context without considering teaching and learning processes. In this regard, Gabrielatos (2005, p. 20) warns of "corpus worship", a metaphor that highlights the somewhat dogmatic assumption that corpus linguistic principles like frequency and authenticity are absolute and must be followed first and foremost in the FL classroom. I would also like to argue that such "corpus worship" is mistaken, in that if we want to pave the way for DDL to enter the secondary classroom, its use must be in keeping with theories of FL instruction, i.e. with didactics.

The notion of *didactics* can be said to mirror the terms *teaching methodology* or *pedagogy* popular in the Anglo-American research tradition, although it has a different conceptual background rooted in European educational research (Hamilton, 1999). In its former definition, didactics were concerned with the *what* and *why* of teaching as opposed to the *how*, which in turn was covered by the term *method* (Klafki, 1995). Over time, didactics have extended to methodological decisions of instruction, so that it has now become commonplace to speak of methodological-didactic decisions. A didactic theory takes a holistic stance to FL instruction, often visualized as the so-called didactic triangle, equally considering both the teacher and the learner as well as the content (cf. Pepin, 1999, p. 57ff.). This is the advantage over terms like *teaching methodology* or *instruction*, which tend to prioritize the teacher's perspective, neglecting learner-internal processes and the conditions under which learning takes place.

Didactic terminology is far from being used consistently across research communities. This chapter is written from a European, namely German, FL perspective with which not every reader may be familiar, and I now define some key concepts here for the sake of terminological clarity. By *secondary-level learner* (henceforth *learner*) I understand pupils aged from 10 to 18 who receive FL instruction at school. Their competence levels usually progress from A1 to B1 according to the Common European Framework of Reference for Languages (CEFR; Council of Europe, 2001). English is commonly introduced as the L2, followed by French or Spanish as the L3. Vocabulary and grammar are so-called *linguistic means* or *linguistic devices* (*sprachliche Mittel*) because they serve the development of functional-communicative competences: listening, reading, speaking, and writing, sometimes called *skills*.[2] The term *method* commonly refers to historical periods characterized by homogeneous didactic principles such as the Grammar-Translation-Method or the Audio-Lingual Method. In the context of everyday classroom practice, it describes the "planned way of doing things" (Klippel, 2013, p. 707). Methods may relate to class arrangement (pair-group work, *think-pair-share*, etc.) or to how content is presented (audio-visual aids, role-plays, etc.), and it is in this latter sense that I will use the term.

In order to illustrate what pedagogic – or rather didactic – processing of DDL can look like, I suggest discussing two interdependent questions:

1   Assuming modern FL instruction follows the principles of competence orientation and communicative language teaching and a typical lesson consists of several phases with respective functions, how can DDL activities be made compatible with these principles and be integrated into phase structure models?

2 What principles guide the design of DDL activities so that they can be tailored to the individual learning conditions of a group?

I now outline the main didactic tenets of competence orientation and of communicative language teaching, laying out the conceptual framework for the integration of DDL, before taking a closer look at phase structure models and discussing the place of DDL within them. I then investigate didactic decisions to make for "fine-tuning" DDL activities, before summarizing the lines of argument.

Setting the stage: competence orientation and communicative learning goals

The practice of FL teaching and learning is grounded in national curricula that specify learning goals, contents, progression, and the assessment of FL proficiency. The CEFR has arguably been the biggest influence on these curricula in European countries, and its introduction in 2001 marked the beginning of a new era in FL didactics. Learners' proficiency is objectively ranked according to six levels ranging from A1 to C2. Progress is no longer evaluated against the number of topics the learners have dealt with but against what communicative tasks they can actually perform with the target language, hence the term *output orientation* (Trim, 2013, p. 128f.). Most importantly, the central learning goal becomes the development of competences, "the sum of knowledge, skills and characteristics that allow a person to perform actions" (Council of Europe, 2001, p. 9).

Competences come in various shapes: The overall goal of FL instruction, as specified in most curricula, is the development of learners' intercultural communicative competence, i.e. the ability to cope with target language situations in a communicatively adequate way (Hymes, 1971; Byram, 1997). Apart from declarative knowledge (*savoir*), this includes the ability to interact appropriately with speakers from other cultures (*savoir-faire*); to reflect one's attitudes and motivations (*savoir-être*); and to improve one's learning process steadily (*savoir-apprendre*). To this end, FL lessons usually have the learners engage with communicative activities in the sense of the four skills previously listed. A meta-cognitive dimension is touched upon by the two transversal competences *language awareness* and *language learning awareness* (Müller-Hartmann & Schocker-von Ditfurth, 2011, p. 83; Trim, 2013, p. 129). Linguistic means are in a subordinate position to skills: Learning grammar or vocabulary is never a learning goal per se; it is considered a tool to overcome a communicative activity. For instance, learning past-tense morphology (Eng. *simple past*, Fr. *passé composé* and *imparfait*) serves to tell how one has spent the weekend. Being able to engage in such an activity constitutes a learning goal – not mastering the tense morphology itself. It is precisely in this regard that competence orientation differs from former historical methods alongside the balanced promotion of all four skills.

Competence orientation is reflected in the predominant FL methodology, the Communicative Method (Savignon, 2013) and its German variant, the Neo-Communicative Method (Reinfried, 2001), incorporating several popular, sometimes overlapping trends: *learner-* and *process orientation* emphasize that teachers should consider learners' interests, encourage their autonomy, and promote language (learning) awareness. If possible, their proficiency should be evaluated against the progress they have made, permitting a more individual assessment. A similar notion is *action orientation*, which makes a case for peer interaction and project work. *Task orientation* describes the commitment to complex, authentic situations with which learners are confronted (Willis, 1996; cf. Section 3). Finally, *content orientation* highlights the importance of developing both language and subject matter knowledge, which has been a key element of Content and Language Integrated Learning (Coyle, Hood, & Marsh, 2010). All these orientations express the cognitive-constructivist approach to FL didactics: Learners individually construct their own knowledge; teachers leave behind their traditional role as instructors and become moderators who accompany their learners in the learning process, providing the suitable environment for the (co-)construction of knowledge and competences (Pritchard, 2009, pp. 17–33).

How are these tenets put into practice? Take, for instance, the competence to "discuss what to do in the evening, at the weekend" (Council of Europe, 2001, p. 77), a component of the category "Informal Discussion" (A2). It is a basic element of dialogic speaking competence with considerable importance for younger learners. In planning the lesson, teachers have to make didactic decisions on how learners can attain this learning goal. Given that learner variables, teacher variables, and content variables all interact with one another, they must analyze the impact of these variables for the planned lesson in order to develop the most appropriate "package" of sub-learning goals, contents, and methods for the learners, suited to their needs and to the overall lesson structure. Such *didactic transformation* or *didactic reduction* (Niemeier, 2017) is crucial and concerns the question of *how* a teacher promotes competences to *what* kind of learning group by working with *what* type of content. Sticking to the learning goal previously mentioned, teachers may decide to have the learners present a role-play on weekend plans: One learner suggests an activity, e.g. going to the cinema, but the partner rejects it so that both learners have to come to a compromise. This particular situation implicates the selection of linguistic means: Learners are expected to use future tenses (Fr. *futur composé*), temporal and locative prepositional phrases (Fr. *à huit heures / au cinéma*), and conversational expressions for (dis-)agreeing or suggesting an activity (Fr. *ça j'aime pas trop / et si on allait au ciné / ça te dit*).

It is clear that learners do not produce such target language output immediately. They must have the opportunity to practice in a way that enables them to internalize the structures. Phase structure models serve as a template for this purpose.

A closer look at lesson structure: phase models in FL didactics

FL didactics distinguish at least two models of lesson structure, the traditional PPP approach and task cycles. In both cases, the lesson structure can be divided into several phases with respective functions.

PPP

PPP (Presentation – Practice – Production) has influenced decades of classroom instruction and follows a rather rigid procedure (Ellis, 2003, p. 29f.; Niemeier, 2017, p. 15f.). In the presentation phase, the teacher presents the new content to the learners, be it by means of auditory, visual, or textual material, e.g. a dialogue by two French students on their weekend plans. The material typically contains several instances of the target structure, e.g. the periphrastic future. The learners work through the dialogue, identify these new instances, and try to formulate a grammatical rule. The teacher may opt for an inductive or a deductive approach: In the former case, it is the learners who discover the rule by themselves; in the latter case, it is the teacher who provides the rule first and lets the learners apply it through examples. The subsequent practice phase is organized in a way that learners pass from form-focused to meaning-focused activities in order to attain a certain degree of automation in target language output (Doughty & Williams, 1998, p. 258). Depending on whether the form in question is phonological, morphological, or syntactic in nature, focus on form may include activities such as choral repetition, dictogloss, fill-in-the-gap, transformation exercises, or substitution drills. Meaning-focused activities like information or opinion gaps prepare target structure use with what Zimmermann (1988, p. 164) termed *communicative minimal situations*. Finally, the production phase expects learners to use the new structure freely, overcoming the communicative situation they faced at the beginning. If the overall learning goal is the development of speaking competence; then, learners typically simulate role-plays or give a presentation. Journal entries, postcards, or narrations may be products of lessons that focus on writing competence.

In sum, PPP tacitly assumes a weak interface: Declarative knowledge can be transformed into procedural knowledge by means of form- and meaning-focused instruction. In Germany, the approach has mainly been promoted by Zimmermann (1988), with his phase structure model still being taught to trainee teachers (cf. also Niemeier, 2017, p. 15). Its wide popularity notwithstanding, criticism has been equally severe. Most notably, learner autonomy is limited because it is the teacher who sets the assignments and controls the phase transitions. Furthermore, the body of research on second language acquisition has provided evidence that the restructuring of interlanguage systems simply does not correspond to the linear progression adopted in PPP (Ellis, 2003, p. 29). At least the first caveat, however, can be countered, as nothing prevents teachers from PPP in a more learner-centred inductive manner.

TBLT

The phase structure model of Task Based Language Teaching (TBLT; Willis, 1996; Ellis, 2003) is best seen in stark contrast to PPP. Fueled by the introduction of the CEFR and the increasing focus on the learner and his communicative needs, TBLT has steamrolled its way into what probably is the most popular learner-oriented methodology today. Although the definition of *task* is not uncontroversial, it is probably fair to consider a task a complex, authentic, and meaningful arrangement that confronts learners with a problem they must overcome by communicative means (Ellis, 2003, p. 2ff.). Tasks are therefore not to be confounded with *exercises*. On the contrary, they level out the sharp difference between formally practicing the FL and applying it in realistic communicative situations, thus representing a paradigm example of output orientation.

Following Willis (1996), TBLT posits three major phases, the *pre-task*, the *task*, and the *language focus*. Together, they constitute the *task cycle*. Before the learners work through the task itself, the pre-task essentially serves to motivate them by discussing the learning goals and the relevance of the task. Since learner-oriented teaching includes building upon prior knowledge, teachers should use this phase for the revision of important lexicogrammatical units. After the learners present their task results, the language focus allows them to pay attention to the errors they have made. Niemeier (2017, p. 35f.) criticizes that this phase, as originally conceived by Willis (1996), is little more than an "appendix" to the central task, as the form-focused activities in this phase are said to be incongruent with the communicative task tackled beforehand. Drawing on the role of the course book, which is still the pivot of everyday classroom teaching, Müller-Hartmann and Schocker-von Ditfurth (2011, p. 92) add a fourth preparation phase in which teachers analyze the course book and select tasks and material that can be used.

Where does DDL fit within these models?

Having outlined these two main phase models of FL didactics, the question arises of how to integrate DDL into them. Let us begin with PPP by reviewing its three phases and how a DDL activity can be placed. It comes as no surprise that the presentation phase of PPP is not suitable because learners are to be confronted with spoken or written texts as a whole, situated in their communicative context, not with corpus concordances. The latter bear a cotext (i.e. linguistic structure in front of and after the KWIC) but no context if no additional annotation is provided (cf. Kaltenböck & Mehlmauer-Larcher, 2005, p. 68). The production phase seems equally inappropriate: Learners are expected to produce FL output by speaking or writing, and it is clear that they do not do this during a DDL activity. Only the practice phase remains, and it is this phase that seems to be most appropriate to incorporate a DDL activity.

How can we characterize DDL in this practice phase? The starting point is the idea that DDL is essentially a *Focus on Form*–methodology (FonF; Doughty & Williams, 1998). Learners pay attention to structural properties of lexicogrammatical constructions; these are not presented in isolation but embedded in a context. Corpus concordances are a good example of such an FonF-approach because the target structure is flanked by its cotext and its usage patterns have to be analyzed against this environment. As for its degree of explicitness, DDL is implicit insofar as it heavily relies on input floods. The teacher may optionally increase the degree of explicitness via input enhancement, which is easily done by highlighting the KWIC or other usage-relevant items with colours or fonts (Doughty & Williams, 1998, p. 236f.).

That said, there is a difference to be aware of between the nature of DDL and the nature of the practice phase. Recall that the main function of the practice phase is to facilitate target language output by offering activities that enable learners to internalize the target structure. Noticing, i.e. becoming aware of the structure's form-meaning-correspondence, has already passed. This is opposed to DDL, which provides just such noticing opportunities. In other words, DDL serves for pattern recognition, but the practice phase does not, because the pattern is known at this moment. As a matter of fact, one can logically only practice what has already been grasped. It must therefore be asked how we can conceive a DDL activity so that it fits functionally to the practice phase.

Consider the two skills of speaking and writing. Proficient FL speaking is characterized by a balance between the components of fluency and accuracy alongside appropriacy and complexity, with fluency dropping out in the case of writing. One method to promote all these components equally is to adopt a phraseological, namely lexicogrammatical, approach to language (Pawley & Syder, 1983; Müller-Hartmann & Schocker-von Ditfurth, 2011, p. 210). This is where the multiple affordances of DDL (Leńko-Szymańska & Boulton, 2015) come into play. Concordances cater to these needs integratively, which is why they should best be conceived as proactive FonF-activities (Doughty & Williams, 1998, p. 205f.). The concordance in Figure 3.1 provides an example of this. Its data are extracted from a gigaword Web corpus of French, FRCOW16 (Schäfer, 2015; Schäfer & Bildhauer, 2012). Suppose the learning goal is the promotion of dialogic speaking and more precisely the competence to express emotions in informal conversations. Learners all too commonly get caught in the trap of literal translation, which leads to pragmatically inaccurate target language structures like *je ne peux pas le croire* (I can't believe i) or *je ne peux plus* (I'm fed up with) instead of their idiomatic equivalents *j'en reviens pas* and *j'en ai marre*. Concordances may serve as a model for exemplifying typical usage patterns that have been introduced in the presentation phase beforehand. In the case of *j'en reviens pas*, for instance, learners may discover that the construction is frequently flanked by emphatic expressions such as *flippant*, *hallucinant*, or *ça alors*.

```
D21 fr a tenu 50 minutes tu as vu ?    j' en reviens pas    . et je ne te crois pas . Pas de
hurler !!! Le pire après le huit ,     j' en reviens pas    , c' est flippant , on dirait une
rien que pour le soft ! Alors ça       j' en reviens pas    , c' est super cool ! Haut Qui est
ailleurs que chez nous ! ça alors ,    j' en reviens pas    ! je croyais que nous avions un
sans vergogne . C' est hallucinant et  j' en reviens pas    à quel point à chaque fois toute

n' empêche , je veux la victoire ...   j' en ai marre       de perdre des coupes ... Posté le
Je suis fatiguée de me battre ,        j' en ai marre       et en pleure . A l' assurance d
J' en ai marre des exams ,             j' en ai marre       de la fac . Jeudi j' arrête .
habituels , dans le cas d' haiti       j' en ai marre       de voir toujours les mêmes
venir tous les matins dire que         j' en ai marre       de me lever , d' aller bosser ...
```

FIGURE 3.1 Concordance of expressing disbelief with j'en reviens pas and frustration with j'en ai marre

Afterwards they use the practice phase to alter such concordance lines, producing their own minimal turn with a partner, which can look like the ones in examples 1 and 2. Feeding lexicogrammatical constructions of this kind into FL speech production improves both fluency and accuracy.

1   A: Écoute, j'ai passé l'examen avec 18 points!
        B: Ça alors, j'en reviens pas ! C'est vraiment hallucinant.
            Listen, I have passed the exam with 18 points!
            My goodness, I can't believe it. That's really cool.
2   A: Tu veux vraiment pas aller au cinéma avec moi?
        B: Écoute, j'en ai marre de tes questions.
            You really don't want to go with me to the cinema?
            Listen, I'm fed up with your questions.

It follows from this that activities such as those developed in Tribble and Jones (1997, pp. 40–58) are precious tools for raising consciousness, but they should be supplemented with assignments that have the learners engage in communicative activities and that are functional to the learning goal of speaking or writing. The 4xI-model developed by Flowerdew (2009, p. 407) already captures this shift of perspective well, providing a phase structure template for DDL lessons. It comprises the four phases "Illustration", "Interaction", "Intervention", and "Induction", differing from PPP in that the Interaction phase is dedicated for peer discussion. The Intervention phase allows the teacher to give further hints if learners do not immediately find the lexicogrammatical rule. A fifth phase "Integration", however, would be needed to make room for the communicative transfer of target language structures in complex situations.

Compared to PPP, TBTL offers a clearer link for the integration of DDL. The post-task phase explicitly encourages a focus on form, and DDL offers an excellent way to do that. But as this phase differs from the practice phase, so must the function of a DDL activity. Consider that learners have already produced target language output during the task. This is why a consciousness-raising activity aims at revising learner production, and it is preferable to use DDL in this phase for reactive error correction (cf. Ellis, 2003, p. 260f.). From a methodological point of view, this can be done efficiently via internal differentiation (cf. Section 4). Having corrected the learners' texts, the teacher may provide concordances with target language structures that are persistently erroneous in learner production or allow learners to consult the corpus themselves based on written feedback on their own work. However, this can come with its own problems, as summarized in Crosthwaite (2017, pp. 450–452) and the references therein.

Let us have a closer look at such an example of a DDL activity. Consider the competence of being able to present oneself in the FL (e.g. one's name, age, hobbies, what one (dis-)likes). The task – roughly sketched and simplified – is to design a poster including such information and a picture (*C'est moi* "That's me") presented to the other learners. Whatever pre-task the teacher opts for, the challenge for

```
et de l' île-themed party . S' ils     aiment jouer    au golf   , qui pourrait être un thème
sports vous aimez " ? Johnny : " J'    aime jouer      au football  . " Note : Hé ,
pur , nous sommes deux équipes qui     aiment jouer    au ballon . " Le match contre Milan
d' y aller , car c' est moi qui        aime jouer      au billard  , explique -t-elle .
Comme les indiens ! Vos enfants        aiment jouer    aux cowboys   et aux indiens ? Votre fille

jeune femme presque Parisienne . J'    aime la mode     , la photo , les nouvelles technologies ,
= / Bref ^^ il est gothique ,          adore le metal , c' est un geek , il a des cheveux
Merci pour ces réponses . J'           aime le froid  , la neige et la nuit et c' est pour cela
Ca tombe bien j'                       adore les abricots    . Cette recette a l' air très
Tu veux faire quoi ? Moi je            déteste les maths et   la physique ... Je kiffe la SVT et
```

FIGURE 3.2 Concordances of French "(dis-)like-constructions"
Source: Data from FRCOW16

beginner learners of French is the correct use of the definite article as in *j'aime jouer au foot* "I like playing football" (*le* contracted with the preposition *à*) and in *je déteste le fromage* "I hate cheese" (definite article despite generic reference). Suppose there are some learners who have problems with the first case and some with the latter. The two groups then receive concordances like the ones in Figure 3.2 that they can use as model texts to notice the correct lexicogrammatical pattern, enabling them to correct their own production afterwards.

It can be concluded that TBTL offers the most fertile terrain for DDL. Its post-task phase explicitly encourages the use of DDL for consciousness-raising activities like reactive error correction. Yet PPP is still a widespread practice in the secondary classroom. If teachers adhere to PPP, they are advised to place a DDL activity during the practice phase. In any case, they should understand that DDL activities will differ in their function depending on which phase model underlies the lesson structure.

Flexibly designing DDL activities

It follows from what has been said in the previous sections that didactic processing of DDL in the secondary classroom must recognize the complexity of FL teaching and learning processes. Taking account of this, the "possibility scenario" evoked by Pérez-Paredes (2010, p. 3f.) does not seem to be the right way for a stronger implementation of DDL in the secondary classroom. Therefore, the following section discusses major didactic decisions to be made for DDL activities and illustrates the arguments based on concrete examples. A flexible design is necessary, I like to argue, to account for the different teaching and learning conditions of a given group.

One of the most important didactic variables concerns the composition of a learning group. In one group of, say, 25 learners in their second year, individual proficiency can be extremely disparate, ranging from learners who have already developed some basic-intermediate proficiency to those who have not yet mastered even basic communicative situations. Furthermore, they come with individual predispositions: Apart from their general FL proficiency, learners may vary with respect to their sex, their L1, their learning styles, their learning speed, or even pathological conditions such as ADHD or dyslexia. Against such increasingly heterogeneous conditions, *internal differentiation* (also called *differentiated instruction*) in the classroom is crucial. The term describes the philosophy of tailoring FL instruction to the needs of the individual learner (Coffey, 2018). The most typical example of this is an FL teacher who provides different assignments, each targeting a different type of learner (*differentiation by task*). Assuming a PPP approach, the learners may choose between several learning products in the production phase, e.g. recording a podcast, drawing a graphic novel, writing a short piece of theatre, etc. Another example relates to pair work: After tackling a FonF-exercise, stronger learners are coupled with weaker ones; together they exchange their results and eliminate uncertainties. The stronger learner benefits because he or she assumes the role of a teacher-helper, taking responsibility for the weaker learner's progress. The weaker learner can discuss problems with his or her partner without fearing negative feedback from the teacher. In this regard, it is worth stressing that internal differentiation is explicitly recognized by the cognitive-constructivist approach to FL didactics.

How does internal differentiation concern DDL? It is a well-known fact that DDL is a methodology that can overwhelm weaker learners. These may prefer explicit guidance or simply have more difficulties in reading target language text (Cobb & Boulton, 2015, p. 481). Additionally, tertiary learners can have problems with the serendipitous nature of concordancing, and it is perfectly plausible to assume that secondary learners will encounter even more obstacles. Recall that tertiary learners studying a foreign language often already have a proficiency level around B2 and upwards, so that overall comprehension of concordance lines will not pose too much of a problem. In contrast, secondary learners normally reach B1 after five years of school instruction; up to this threshold they may get discouraged if too many items in the KWIC cotext are unknown.[3] Following the principle of didactic reduction, teachers must provide guidance to help them. How can they achieve this?

The key is to have a look at what determines the efficiency of a method. One central criterion is once again its "functional fit" to the learning and teaching conditions (cf. also Meunier, this volume). Let us examine some straightforward examples: A lesson with a priority on argumentative speaking in conversation would not have the learners prepare a monologic presentation. Likewise, unreflected use of cooperative methods may have a devastating effect if the overall atmosphere between the learners is marked by harassment and anxiety. In other words, a method must be functionally fitted to the attainment of the learning goal and suited to the learning conditions of the group. Translating this principle to DDL, I would like to offer three suggestions of how to fit a DDL activity to the individual classroom context: input enhancement, variable assignments, and the manipulation of concordance lines. Each of these examples may be representative of what didactic processing in the FL classroom can look like.

First, concordances can be processed via input enhancement. It has already been pointed out that input enhancement is a viable FonF-tool to draw learners'

```
encore plus vite que ça . Les balles se      perdaient      souvent dans le sable sans toucher
Août 2010 , 11:18 la horde sauvage je l'     ai vu          deux fois , la semaine dernière
devient grise et d' un vilain aspect J'      ai utilisé     une seule fois chez des amis une
Je prenais mes notes en Farsi ; je           faisais        souvent ça , et après , de retour,
qu' ils me foutent la paix ! - . On vous l'  a dit          mille fois , c' est qu' il doit y
rapides ( d'ailleurs parfois , elles         étaient        déjà là et je ne les voyais pas
le premier chapitre pour voir . Bon je l'    ai lu          trois fois ça doit aussi aider .
, les groupes de hard rock des 70 es         étaient        souvent dans un trip jam / longs
pas agréables , oui parfois les filles       étaient        chahutées ( pas plus que dans d'
y joue des rôles satyriques : deux fois il   a été          en France , deux fois lui et ses
```

FIGURE 3.3 Concordance of the French past tense alternation

Source: Data from FRCOW16

attention to specific structures, e.g. with coloured or underlined examples written on the blackboard. When teachers work with cotextually dependent target structures, they may decide to highlight these cotextual elements in the concordance. Figure 3.3 illustrates this issue. The goal of the activity is to raise consciousness of the usage difference between the French past tenses *passé composé* and *imparfait* with respect to adverbial co-occurrence. The former patterns with iteratives like *deux fois* "twice", while the latter triggers habitual aspect with frequentials such as *souvent* "often" or *parfois* "sometimes".

The adverbials are underlined in Figure 3.3. Without such a cue, learners would probably search for other potential elements than these temporal adverbials. However, input enhancement does not make the activity too easy. On the contrary, the main cognitive task to perform is preserved, i.e. abstracting the adverbial semantics and mapping them to past tense use.

Second, teachers can differentiate by modulating the degree of directionality in the assignment. This breaks down to the question of how explicitly the structure to be investigated is mentioned in the assignment. Weaker learners may need much more time if the assignment is relatively openly formulated, as they read the concordance lines horizontally. Let us take the same concordance from Figure 3.3, without the adverbials being underlined. Differentiation can be given by indicating the element to which attention shall be paid (cf. 4).

3   Have a look at these extracts of authentic French. Describe the difference between the usage of *passé composé* and *imparfait*. (openly formulated)
4   Have a look at these extracts of authentic French. Describe the difference between the usage of *passé composé* and *imparfait* by comparing the adverbials and what they express. (narrow)

The third option to discuss – and surely the most controversial one – is how to proceed if the concordance contains a number of unintelligible elements for the learners. Manipulating concordance lines seems to refute the basic DDL tenet of authenticity. The argument is that learners do not benefit from confected examples, deprived of any communicative reality. While this has some truth to it, it should be asked what the exact added value of authentic examples is and under what circumstances such added value is given. Pullum (2017, p. 285) alludes to this point by criticizing "corpus fetishism" in reference grammars. Additionally, there is no solid empirical evidence that learners do actually perform better if they have worked with authentic texts beforehand (Wulff & Gries, 2011, p. 82f.).

In fact, manipulating a concordance must not necessarily be seen as a crime against the "worship" position described by Gabrielatos (2005). Instead, it can be justified by considering it a procedure of internal differentiation: Stronger learners may plunge into unabridged concordances, as we can readily assume that their aptitude to derive meaning from cotext is more advanced. Weaker learners, however, lose motivation if a certain amount of cotextual elements is unintelligible for them. In any case, manipulating a concordance does not mean that its nature as a structured input flood is being stripped off. On the contrary, it is functionally fitted to the conditions of the learning group and to the learning goal. The following example may support this claim. I draw on a gap-fill exercise in Tribble & Jones (1997, p. 53), trying to show how it can be tweaked in terms of didactic processing. The learning goal is to "investigate the semantic network 'parts of the body' in French" with a selection of possible answers given in advance. Part of the concordance is displayed in Figure 3.4.

Several aspects must be mentioned with regards to the didactic processing of this DDL exercise. First, the straightforward extraction of a 60-character KWIC results in some words' endings being "snipped off". In a case such as line 9, it is evident that the adverb *sûrement* "surely" misses its final -*t*. In line 7, things get more confusing because the KWIC ends with an adjective phrase that lacks plural agreement on the noun (*de grands coup). Teachers must be prepared for questions if the concordance is presented in this way.

Second, some cotexts insufficiently disambiguate the correct answer. Help is provided insofar as the determinants (*le, la, son*, etc.) are already given, but some gaps simply permit several solutions (lines 5, 9, 10, and especially line 11 – the verb *se tordre* "twist" being able to collocate with *main* "hand", *cheville* "ankle", *cou* "neck", and *pied* "foot"). The authors are well aware of this fact and point out

```
 1 ous êtes debout, rincez-vous la        _____   à l'eau froide. (Profitez-en pour vous
 2 il se tirera une balle dans la         _____   et explosera parmi les célèbres lys de l
 3 e, enlevant ainsi le pain de la        _____   des nouvelles télévision privées. C'est
 4 t même qu'ils n'aient ouvert la        _____   . Le succès, c'est physique, c'est unreg

 5 latif. A l'ère victorienne, une        _____   entr'aperçue était troublante dans la
 6 ntre vous : vous vous foulez la        _____   au début du match, vous avez un point d
 7 tour de son cou et autour de sa        _____   Il aurait ensuite donné de grands coup
 8 s dans l'eau froide ; jusqu'aux        _____   . Faites cela même si vous avez pris un

 9 z-vous le bronze d'Amérique, le        _____   nu du Forez, le coureur indien ? Sûremen
10 xtrémité d'un fil autour de son        _____   et autour de sa cheville. Il aurait ens
11 r et entendre sans se tordre le        _____   dès qu'on est dans le fond d'une loge.
12 ier, le foulard rouge autour du        _____   , vous marchiez fièrement en tête de vot
```

FIGURE 3.4 Concordance of the lexical field of body parts

Source: Data from Tribble & Jones (1997, p. 53) with line numbers

that "cumulatively [the contexts] enable the astute learner to eliminate competing possibilities" (1997, p. 53). Yet it is difficult to see how less-astute learners are to cope with such ambiguities.

Third, at least some items are probably unknown to secondary learners and cannot be contextually inferred: *lys* (lily, line 2), *entr'aperçue* (catch a glimpse of, line 5, a low-frequent past participle), *n'aient ouvert* (subjunctive past of *ouvrir* "open", line 4), and *se fouler* ("twist", line 6).[4] Certain nouns form collocations (*se rincer la bouche* "wash one's mouth", *se fouler la cheville* "twist one's ankle", *se tordre le cou* "twist one's neck") or idioms (*se tirer une balle dans le pied* "shoot oneself in the foot", *enlever le pain de la bouche* "take away one's livelihood"). Both of these cases pose challenges. When acquiring collocations, it is the collocator, i.e. the semantically opaque verb, that must be learned explicitly, not the collocational base, i.e. the semantically transparent noun. This is contrary to what the gap-fill exercise expects learners to do. Idioms on the other hand should best be avoided until clear communicative contexts are given, as their usage conditions are often quite peculiar and pragmatically constrained.

What should teachers do given such caveats? The "worship" position would argue that concordance lines must not be modified. By contrast, a genuinely didactic perspective would see no problem in modification, since this methodological decision would functionally fit to the learning goal – to identify usage contexts of body parts. However, this leads to an even bigger issue. The activity has as its learning goal investigating the semantic network of the human body. But nothing is said about what learners do with the results, let alone what exactly is meant by "investigation". The communicative dimension is missing: Learners must use the target structures in their own output afterwards. Sticking to the example of body parts, one obvious communicative situation that comes into mind is the visit to the doctor. Learners may therefore present a role-play in which they use the vocabulary to indicate where they have pain. As a matter of fact, a communicative transfer of this kind is also in keeping with the proficiency scales of the CEFR, which mentions the competence to "describe symptoms to a doctor" (Council of Europe, 2001, pp. 34, 82) at the threshold level B1+. Consequently, the words related to the parts of the body should be presented in their typical lexicogrammatical pattern *avoir mal {au pied / à la cheville / aux yeux}* "have foot/ankle/eye pain". This is the type of pattern that should be prominent in a concordance and with which learners should work in DDL activities.

To summarize, examples have been given of how didactic processing may be put into practice in the FL classroom. When teachers work with corpus concordances, they are advised to check them for items unknown to the learning group. This should not pose much of a problem because course books often provide vocabulary lists that the teacher follows more or less closely. It goes without saying that only paradigmatically exchangeable items in the cotext should be replaced, not the KWIC itself. Depending on how difficult it is to infer the lexicogrammatical rule, teachers can provide additional differentiation by highlighting cotextual cues or formulating assignments in a narrower way. Finally, it is of utmost importance to link DDL to communicative tasks where learners use the target structures in their output.

Concluding remarks

This chapter argued that didactic processing of DDL is inevitable in the context of the secondary FL classroom. Starting from the assumption that a method(ology) must be compatible with a theory of FL learning and teaching, the argumentation focused on the tenets of competence orientation and (neo-)communicative language teaching and zoomed in on phase structure models of FL lessons. A DDL activity can be introduced to the classroom if it is functionally fitted to the learning goal and to the overall learning conditions of the group. To illustrate this, it has been shown how such activities may be placed with regards to the phase structure of a lesson (PPP versus TBTL); how they can contribute to the learning goal(s) (speaking and writing); and how to account for heterogeneous conditions in the learning group (internal differentiation). Among the latter, a case has been made for the manipulation of a concordance so that it is functionally fitted to the learning group.

The persistent gap between a corpus linguistic methodology for the FL classroom and its actual application seems to be symptomatic of a much larger issue at hand, the relationship between linguistics and FL instruction in general. Gabrielatos (2005) asks in the title of his article whether the relationship between corpus linguistics and language teaching is a "fling or wedding bells" – this chapter has shown, it is hoped, that it is time for DDL to listen to what its partner, didactics, has to say and to offer. We may abandon certain precepts in our "corpus worship", but the price to pay for such a change of perspective is small if it results in a stronger dissemination of DDL in the secondary classroom that is firmly grounded in a didactic theory of FL instruction.

Notes

1 As for the *what*, Flowerdew warns that some lexicogrammatical structures may be subject to register variation, constituting pragmatic pitfalls. As for the *how*, she emphasizes the usefulness of peer interaction during the analysis of concordances.
2 Mediation is increasingly being considered a fifth skill: Learners "act as an intermediary between interlocutors who are unable to understand each other directly" (Council of Europe, 2001, p. 87). It therefore is a competence that covers both receptive and productive components.
3 A similar situation may hold for tertiary university learners enrolled in FL courses of languages they do not study.
4 None of these items is attested among the 5,000 most frequent items in French (Lonsdale & Le Bras, 2009).

References

Braun, S. (2007). Integrating corpus work into secondary education: From data-driven learning to needs-driven corpora. *ReCALL, 19*(3), 307–328.

Byram, M. (1997). *Teaching and assessing intercultural communicative competence*. Clevedon: Multilingual Matters.

Cobb, T., & Boulton, A. (2015). Classroom applications of corpus analysis. In D. Biber & R. Reppen (Eds.), *The Cambridge handbook of English corpus linguistics* (pp. 478–497). Cambridge: Cambridge University Press.

Coffey, S. (2018). Differentiation in theory and practice. In M. Maguire, S. Gibbons, M. Glacking, D. Pepper, & K. Skilling (Eds.), *Becoming a teacher: Issues in secondary education* (5th ed., pp. 197–209). Milton Keynes: Open University Press.

Council of Europe. (2001). *Common European framework of reference for languages: Learning, teaching, assessment*. Cambridge: Cambridge University Press.

Coyle, D., Hood, P., & Marsh, D. (2010). *CLIL – Content and language integrated learning*. Cambridge: Cambridge University Press.

Crosthwaite, P. (2017). Retesting the limits of data-driven learning: Feedback and error correction. *Computer-Assisted Language Learning, 30*(6), 447–473.

Doughty, C., & Williams, J. (1998). Pedagogical choices in focus on form. In C. Doughty & J. Williams (Eds.), *Focus on form in classroom second language acquisition* (pp. 197–261). Cambridge: Cambridge University Press.

Ellis, R. (2003). *Task-based language learning and teaching*. Oxford: Oxford University Press.

Flowerdew, L. (2009). Applying corpus linguistics to pedagogy: A critical evaluation. *International Journal of Corpus Linguistics, 14*(3), 393–417.

Gabrielatos, C. (2005). Corpora and language teaching: Just a fling or wedding bells? *TESL-EJ, 8*(4), A1, 1–37.

Hamilton, D. (1999). The pedagogic paradox (or why no didactics in England?). *Pedagogy, Culture & Society, 7*(1), 135–152.

Hymes, D. (1971). *On communicative competence*. Philadelphia, PA: University of Pennsylvania Press.

Johns, T., & King, P. (1991). *Classroom concordancing*. Birmingham, UK: University of Birmingham, Centre of English Language Studies.

Kaltenböck, G., & Mehlmauer-Larcher, B. (2005). Computer corpora and the language classroom: On the potential and limitations of computer corpora in language teaching. *ReCALL, 17*(1), 65–84.

Kansanen, & H. Seel (Eds.), *TNTEE Publications, Vol. 2: Didaktik/Fachdidaktik as Science(-s) of the Teaching Profession?* (pp. 49–66). Umea: TNTEE.

Klafki, W. (1995). Didactic analysis as the core of preparation of instruction. *Journal of Curriculum Studies, 27*(1), 13–30.

Klippel, F. (2013). Teaching methods. In M. Byram & A. Hu (Eds.), *Routledge encyclopedia of language teaching and learning* (2nd ed., pp. 707–712). London: Routledge.

Leńko-Szymańska, A., & Boulton, A. (Eds.). (2015). *Multiple affordances of language corpora for data-driven learning*. Amsterdam: John Benjamins.

Lonsdale, D., & Le Bras, Y. (2009). *A frequency dictionary of French*. New York: Routledge.

Müller-Hartmann, A., & Schocker-von Ditfurth, M. (2011). *Teaching English: Task-supported language learning*. Paderborn: Schöningh.

Niemeier, S. (2017). *Task-based grammar teaching of English: Where cognitive grammar and task-based language teaching meet*. Tübingen: Narr Francke Attempto.

Pawley, A., & Syder, F. H. (1983). Two puzzles for linguistic theory: Nativelike selection and nativelike fluency. In J. J. Richards & R. R. Schmidt (Eds.), *Language and communication* (pp. 191–225). London: Longman.

Pepin, B. (1999). Existing models of knowledge in teaching: Developing an understanding of the Anglo/American, the French and the German scene. In B. Hudson, F. Buchberger,

Pérez-Paredes, P. (2010). Corpus linguistics and language education in perspective: Appropriation and the possibilities scenario. In T. Harris & M. Moreno Jaén (Eds.), *Corpus linguistics in language teaching* (pp. 53–73). Bern: Peter Lang.

Pritchard, A. (2009). *Ways of learning* (2nd ed.). London and New York: Routledge.

Pullum, G. (2017). Theory, data, and the epistemology of syntax. In A. Wöllstein & M. Konopka (Eds.), *Grammatische variation* (pp. 283–298). Berlin and Boston: De Gruyter.

Reinfried, M. (2001). Neokommunikativer Fremdsprachenunterrcht: ein neues methodisches Paradigma. In F. -J. Meißner & M. Reinfried (Eds.), *Bausteine für einen neokommunikativen Französischunterricht* (pp. 1–20). Tübingen: Gunter Narr.

Savignon, S. J. (2013). Communicative language teaching. In M. Byram & A. Hu (Eds.), *Routledge encyclopedia of language teaching and learning* (2nd ed., pp. 134–140). London: Routledge.

Schäfer, R. (2015). Processing and querying large web corpora with the COW14 architecture. In P. Banski et al. (Eds.), *Proceedings of the 3rd workshop on challenges in the management of large corpora (CMLC-3)* (pp. 28–34). Mannheim: Institut für Deutsche Sprache.

Schäfer, R., & Bildhauer, F. (2012). Building large corpora from the web using a new efficient tool chain. In N. Calzolari et al. (Eds.), *Proceedings of the Eight International conference on language resources and evaluation (LREC 12)* (pp. 486–493). Istanbul: ELRA.

Tribble, C., & Jones, G. (1997). *Concordances in the classroom: A resource guide for teachers*. Houston: Athelstan.

Trim, J. (2013). Common European framework of reference. In M. Byram & A. Hu (Eds.), *Routledge encyclopedia of language teaching and learning* (2nd ed., pp. 707–712). London: Routledge.

Tyne, H. (2012). Corpus work with ordinary teachers: Data-driven learning activities. In J. Thomas. & A. Boulton (Eds.), *Input, process and product: Developments in teaching and language corpora* (pp. 136–151). Brno: Masaryk University Press.

Willis, J. (1996). *A framework for task based learning*. Harlow: Longman.

Wulff, S., & Gries, S. Th. (2011). Corpus-driven methods for assessing accuracy in learner production. In P. Robinson (Ed.), *Second language task complexity*. Amsterdam: John Benjamins.

Zimmermann, G. (1988). Lehrphasenmodell für den fremdsprachlichen Grammatikunterricht. In J. Dahl & B. Weis (Eds.), *Grammatik im Unterricht* (pp. 160–175). München: Goethe-Institut.

4

BARRIERS TO TRAINEE TEACHERS' CORPUS USE

Eva Schaeffer-Lacroix

Introduction

Why is it that, after more than thirty years of history, corpus tools for language learning are nearly absent in French secondary schools? Are we experiencing a "tissue rejection" (Holliday, 1992), i.e. the failure of an innovation? Or is data-driven learning (DDL, Johns, 1991) finally going to make its breakthrough now that corpora are increasingly used in other educational sectors? There is some reason for hope: As direct corpus exploration by language learners has been proven effective within tertiary education contexts (see literature review in Chambers, 2005), research is now turning towards its affordances for younger learners, as showcased in this volume and in other studies. Such research has the potential to bring about significant changes to secondary language learning classrooms. However, despite an increasing number of useful studies on the use of corpora for language learning in secondary contexts (e.g. Rohrbach, 2003; Braun, 2007; Schaeffer-Lacroix, 2009; Frankenberg-Garcia, 2014), DDL has yet to truly make a breakthrough into the mainstream. There are a number of reasons for this delay cited in the literature, e.g. corpus functionality or interfaces being considered as too complicated by foreign language learners and teachers (Boulton, 2010, 2012; Vincent & Nesi, 2018), the overwhelming amount of corpus data novice DDL proponents inevitably encounter (Varley, 2009, p. 146), claims that corpus data that may be of "little interest or relevance to learners" (Hirata, this volume), the "the suspicion or doubt that some students have about the accuracy or reliability of corpus data" (Varley, 2009, p. 146), and the time-consuming nature of DDL materials preparation (Vyatkina & Boulton, 2017).

How then to convince secondary teachers of the usefulness and feasibility of corpus-based learning practices? As stated by Braun (2007, p. 326), one approach is to integrate training in corpora and DDL materials preparation into pre-service teacher training, leading to a "better understanding of the pedagogical (as opposed to the linguistic) needs of corpus analysis". Breyer (2009); Chambers, Farr, and O'Riordan (2011); Callies (2016); and Leńko-Szymańska (2017) have also reported about the importance of integrating DDL into teacher education programs. While this research has addressed difficulties in the development of corpus-based learning scenarios, user perceptions of DDL, or empirical learning results arising from DDL, there is still a need for further research into any potential barriers that may hinder trainee teachers from integrating direct corpus exploration into the secondary language classroom.

Barriers to learning?

In a literature review about teachers' adoption of learning design methods and tools, Dagnino, Dimitriadis, Pozzi, Asensio-Pérez, and Rubia-Avi (2018) note that determining potential barriers to such adoption is paramount when attempting to integrate new technology into the classroom. Referring to Ertmer (1999), they distinguish between *first-order barriers*, which are considered as extrinsic to teachers (e.g. tool features, time, and training), and *second-order barriers*, which are considered as intrinsic to teachers (e.g. previous use of ICT[1] motivation, teacher beliefs). First-order barriers to innovation in education date as far back as Rogers' (1962) innovation framework, involving four main factors likely to influence innovation processes (Rogers, 2003, p. 102):[2]

1 the characteristics of the innovation itself
2 the communication channels used to spread the innovation
3 the hosting social system
4 the elapsed time

To address the trainees' potential second-order barriers, Rogers' five-stage model (2003, p. 365) divides potential end-users into innovation adopters and innovation rejectors, proceeding through the different processes described in Figure 4.1. Each may change their minds at a more advanced stage according to the innovation's relative advantage, compatibility, complexity, trialability, and observability.

I used this model to search for clues regarding the extent to which the trainee teachers embraced either innovation "adopter" or "rejector" roles during group work sessions on corpus use and the design of DDL materials. The designer of the project may be considered as the "innovator", while the participants may adopt roles of early adopter, early or late majority, or laggard, according to their

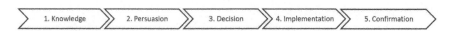

FIGURE 4.1   Rogers' model of stages in the innovation-decision process

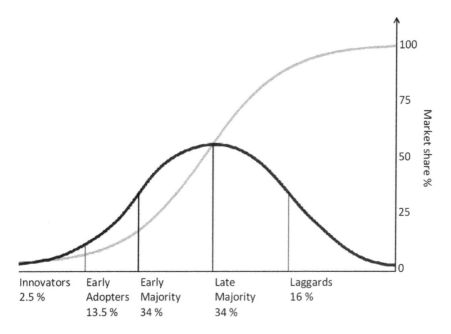

FIGURE 4.2 Innovation adopter categories

experiences (Rogers, 2003, p. 247) (Figure 4.2), or they could reject the technology entirely.

This study is therefore concerned with investigating which roles French trainees of secondary L2 German adopt when it comes to DDL innovation and the barriers (e.g. first-order, second-order) which may arise during DDL-focused language teacher training.

Method

This study details how trainee teachers of secondary L2 German in France created a "technology-enhanced" L2 German learning module, which required the design of a corpus-based learning activity integrated into a technology-assisted task-based language teaching and learning scenario (see also the section on TBLT in Wicher, this volume). This research project builds on a previous study conducted with future school librarians enrolled in a practical German course (level B1/B2 CEFR) who used the *Weissensee* corpus (see next section) as a support for metatalk and for L2 text revision (Schaeffer-Lacroix, 2016). In this chapter, the L2 German teachers were asked to design a learning scenario exploiting the same corpus, with a view to implementing the designed scenario the year after, during their secondary school in-service period. The rationale for this responds to the need for follow-up phases to be embedded within studies on the adoption of learning design methods and tools (Dagnino et al., 2018).

TABLE 4.1 Group composition (ICT abbreviations – communication tools = "ct"; online media = "om"; Internet search = "is"; gaming = "g")

Anonymised Forename	Gender (female = "f"; male = "m")	Age group (in years)	First Language	Previous extensive teaching experience	ICT use	Group number
Konstanze	f	30–40	German	no	ct, is	1
Laurie	f	20–30	French	no	ct, is, g	1
Valentine	f	40–50	French	yes	ct, is	1
Amandine	f	20–30	French	no	ct, is	2
Dora	f	20–30	Georgian	no	ct, is	2
Heike	f	20–30	German	no	ct, is, om	2
Henri	m	40–50	French	yes	ct, is	2
Anne	f	20–30	French	no	ct, is, g	3
Liliane	f	20–30	French	no	ct, is	3
Ninon	f	20–30	French	no	ct, is	3

The main research methods were those of recorded observations and screen captures of participants' experiences during training and descriptions of the corpus-based learning tasks the trainees created. Screencast-O-Matic (nd) was used to film the computer screen during the teachers' corpus explorations and make audio recordings of their verbal interactions. A set of final interviews was also conducted focusing on the future teachers' opinions and perceptions of DDL, which were videotaped and transcribed.

Table 4.1 describes the participants. None had previous experience of developing teaching materials using technology. According to an online questionnaire administered prior to the learning design module, their ICT competence was limited to personal use of communication tools, online media, Internet searches, and gaming.

Corpora and corpus tools used

The main corpus offered for DDL training contains the script of the first season of the television series *Weissensee* (Hess, 2010), a love story set in Eastern Germany during the Cold War. This corpus can be considered as pedagogically relevant for learners of German at level B1/B2 CEFR (Lee, 2011): It is "topic-driven", and it pursues "pedagogic rather than linguistic representativeness" (Pérez-Paredes, this volume) and was successfully tested with librarian students as previously reported (Schaeffer-Lacroix, 2016). I retrieved the PDF files of the six *Weissensee* episodes from the website *Stichwort Drehbuchautoren*,[3] storing them on a Sketch Engine account. The data (82,568 tokens) were processed with the RFTagger (Schmid &

Laws, 2008) offering fine-grained part of speech annotations, including gender, number, and case. The students were granted access to this corpus. In addition, I translated the first *Weissensee* episode into German and created a small parallel corpus (German – French; French – German), containing 23,553 German words and 15,830 French words.

Procedure

A regular first-year master's degree module dedicated to technology-enhanced learning design (15 hours, six sessions) was used to introduce basic corpus exploration methods to the trainees ($n = 10$), who were enrolled at the teacher training department of Sorbonne Université. Following an initial four-week classroom observation period in general classroom practice, the students then took their 15-hour course on technology-enhanced learning, which also involved training in DDL. During the first lesson of their learning design module, the students were offered a 15-minute introduction to the corpus query interface Sketch Engine (Kilgarriff et al., 2014). Afterwards, grouped in pairs, they were invited to explore the software themselves. During this period, *Screencast-O-Matic* (n.d.) was used to film the computer screens to record the conversations of the pairs during corpus exploration. The trainee teachers were asked to adopt a free exploration mode ("treasure hunting", Kennedy & Miceli, 2001) and to decide together which German corpus to explore, which question to start with, and which queries to do. The other five sessions of this module also involved training in corpus use for lesson planning. The participants carried out free or guided corpus explorations grouped in pairs, and they used the social learning platform *Edmodo* (2008) to develop, store, and share their lesson plans. As an assessment item, they were instructed to design a learning scenario containing at least one corpus-based learning activity involving the *Weissensee* corpus, shared with them via Sketch Engine. I framed the task as follows:

> *The concordancer does not have to be central to your scenario. But it must have its place in it, okay? You can even choose a paper version (. . .), with lines you have selected, or a combination of paper and (. . .) moments when you say (to the students): "Now, look for a little by yourself". It's your group that decides, depending on your affinity with this sort of things.*

Moments of collective feedback and group work activities were offered during each session, each of which was observed by the researcher. Following the final session and creation of the DDL task, a researcher from another university (called "investigator" in the following section), unknown to the participants, interviewed them as a collective.

Findings

Creating corpus-based learning activities

Group 1 (Konstanze, Laurie, Valentine): main task

The main learning task chosen by Group 1 was to have the young learners produce and orally present a scene extending the script of the first episode of the *Weissensee* series. The trainees designed a corpus-based activity for the learners based on the visualisation of short film excerpts displaying moments of intense emotion: a Stasi meeting, a family conflict, and a scene featuring leading actors Martin and Julia being spied on by Martin's brother Falk. The learners were expected to search the corpus to become acquainted with the use of words expressing *feelings*, for instance, "Spannung, enttäuscht, Wut, Freude, verliebt" [tension, disappointed, anger, joy, in love]. The young students would be instructed to write down two different expressions containing the search word. As a homework assignment, they would be asked to insert the retrieved elements into a short dialogue in which Martin discovers that Falk has been spying on him and Julia.

Group 1 integrated the concordancer into this task in a sensible way, and the corpus activity can be considered as an important step leading to the main writing task. However, I pointed out to the students that this activity could be improved by getting the young learners to access the full list of adjectives in the corpus rather than letting them explore the corpus without such scaffolding. Browsing the list obtained brings up several items linked to feelings, such as "verzweifelt" [desperate], "traurig" [sad] and, "besorgt" [worried].[4] A search for nouns in this corpus also leads to potentially useful results, e.g. "Angst" [fear], "Tränen" [tears], and "Herz" [heart] (Figure 4.3).

Further searches could help to identify word combinations like "Angst machen" [to scare, to frighten], "Keine Angst" [Don't be afraid"], or "Ich habe solche Angst gehabt . . ." [I was so scared . . ."], and the trainees were informed about these potential findings.

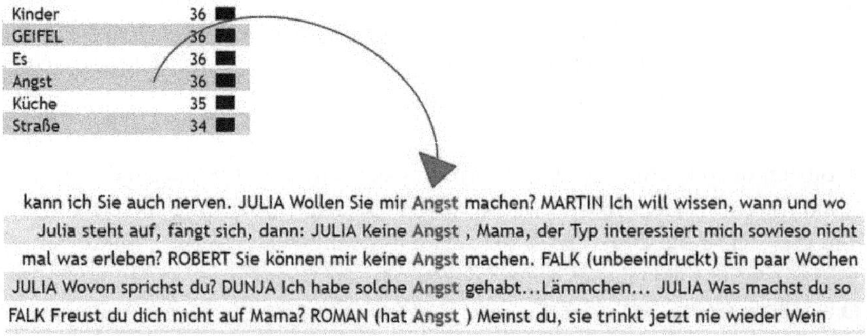

```
Kinder      36 ■
GEIFEL      36 ■
Es          36 ■
Angst       36 ■
Küche       35 ■
Straße      34 ■
```

kann ich Sie auch nerven. JULIA Wollen Sie mir Angst machen? MARTIN Ich will wissen, wann und wo Julia steht auf, fangt sich, dann: JULIA Keine Angst , Mama, der Typ interessiert mich sowieso nicht mal was erleben? ROBERT Sie können mir keine Angst machen. FALK (unbeeindruckt) Ein paar Wochen JULIA Wovon sprichst du? DUNJA Ich habe solche Angst gehabt...Lämmchen... JULIA Was machst du so FALK Freust du dich nicht auf Mama? ROMAN (hat Angst) Meinst du, sie trinkt jetzt nie wieder Wein

FIGURE 4.3 Search item "Angst" [fear]

Group 2 (Amandine, Dora, Heike, Henri): main task

Group 2's task asked students to create a multimedia poster (with the online tool Glogster) that reflects what the students have learned about the GDR (German Democratic Republic) from both a historical and a linguistic point of view. For the corpus-based activity, the group members provided a set of narrow queries which the learners were expected to enter into Sketch Engine: "Westen" [West] combined with "Staatsfeind" [state enemy] and "Republikflucht" [escape from the republic] combined with "Mauer" [wall]. The trainees even intended to tell the learners which concordance line out of several lines must be selected: *"Take only occurrence 1 (there are 6 in total)"*; *"Here are 3 occurrences, take the second"*, giving warnings such as *"Do not confuse this person with the other one having the same name"*.

The guidance provided by group 2 on the task is extremely limiting; its implementation is likely to prevent the discovery of other language features other than those selected by the teachers. In fact, the word "Staatsfeind" [state enemy] doesn't even exist in the corpus. In my comments on the designed activity (see Figure 4.4), I recommended the group tell the young learners to search the *Weissensee* corpus for nouns likely to help them understand that word meanings are shaped by specific cultural contexts. For example, in the *Weissensee* corpus, "Staat" [state] and "Republik" [republic] are both associated with Eastern Germany, and "Land" [country] and "Heimat" [native country, homeland] are forms referring to Western Germany.

[Translation of the comment:

> I didn't find "Staatsfeind" in the full corpus. "Staat" would be more interesting, or "Republik", & "unsere . . ." (& emotional connotation). See also "Land": & unser versus & dieses (& expression of a certain distance). See also "Heimat" and "drüben". What would also have been interesting: verbs from the lexical field "to observe, to look".]

⇨ Westen+Staatsfeind, 1 seule occurence.
Note sur Wolfgang Welsch né le 5.03.1944 (attention il y a un homonyme né le 17.10.1946)

⇨ Republikflucht+Mauer, prendre uniquement l'occurence 1 (il y en a 6 au total).

⇨ Westen+Volksarmee, ici 3 occurences, prendre la 2

anonym
Je n'ai pas trouvé "Staatsfeind" dans le corpus complet. Par contre, "Staat" serait intéressant, ou "Republik", & "unsere..." (donc & connotation affective). Voir aussi "Land" : & unser versus & dieses (& expression d'une certaine distance). Voir aussi Heimat et "drüben".

Ce qui aurait été également intéressant : verbes du champ lexical "observer, regarder".

FIGURE 4.4 Commented concordancing activity

Group 3 (Anne, Liliane, Ninon): main task

Group 3's task asked learners to choose one of the three topics covered in class (*committed speeches and dictatorship, restriction of freedom and imposition of power, authority and family conflicts*) and to invent a similar story focusing on the way people use language for reasoning. The corpus-based activity for this task was intended to focus on the use of logical connectors to support reasoning during a discussion. The trainees would ask students to read pre-selected concordance lines they obtained when searching for the logical connectors "da", "deshalb", "nämlich", "trotz", and "weil" [since, therefore, you know, despite, because] before being asked to think about the way the "words highlighted in red" (i.e. the search words, put in bold in the forthcoming sample) help to build arguments that can be used in a discussion. As a second step, students must insert these terms into a gap-fill worksheet: "Ich singe ohne Klavier, **da** mein Pianist sich geweigert hat, mich zu begleiten." [I am singing without the piano **as** the pianist refused to accompany me.]

Group 3 provided a list of logical connectors: "trotz" [despite], "nämlich" [you know,], and "da" [since] for query. However, the selected words are not very frequent in the Weissensee corpus; searches for all adverbs, conjunctions, and prepositions in the corpus offer other more frequent forms like "doch" [but, however], "aber" [but], "wegen" [because of], "allerdings" [however], and "(nicht. . .) sondern" [(not. . .) but]. It can be noticed that the learning activity designed by Group 3 focuses more on formal than on semantic features of logical connectors: by pre-selecting a number of concordance lines to be printed on handouts, the teachers unnecessarily restricted the context in which these items would appear, which may hinder the interpretation of their meaning. More training time would have been needed to explain to the teachers that direct access to corpus data on Sketch Engine offers the learners the possibility to play with the width of concordance lines and to click on a search word to further expand its context and so to go beyond the limits of printed concordance lines.

Summary

In summary, the three groups' corpus tasks showed first-order barriers linked to the limited knowledge of tool functions. For example, not all trainee teachers understood how to expand the size of concordance lines, and not all relevant functions (e.g. the creation of a word list restricted to adjectives) of Sketch Engine were used to design these tasks. A second-order barrier can also be realised from the trainees' task design: for each group, the trainees developed corpus tasks for students only in their last year of secondary school and did not envisage producing tasks for younger students in the first years of secondary school.

Exploring the barriers: trainee's observations and interviews

Having outlined the teachers' experiences developing the corpus-based tasks, I now turn to the teachers' qualitative discussions of the first- and second-order barriers to their corpus uptake during and after the training sessions.

First-order barriers: tool features and exploration methods

When using the corpus for the first time, the trainees explored several tool features and familiarized themselves with query syntax patterns. For instance, Heike and Laurie tried out several features of Sketch Engine apparently in a random-like manner, such as combining, for instance, the noun "Wolken" [clouds] with pronouns. This led to results like "zeigen **uns** die **Wolken** die Windrichtung an" [the **clouds** show **us** the wind direction] or "als **sich** die **Wolken** endlich lichteten" [when the **clouds** finally cleared]. This search is not methodologically sound: There is no morphological, syntactical, or semantic link between the noun "Wolken" [clouds] and the pronouns obtained. Konstanze and Valentine were observed to produce queries that were too narrow in scope: They combined the search word "Revolution" [revolution] with the adjective "französische" [French] appearing just to its left, while indicating the feminine adjective ending. They did not make use of the distance parameter setting or the lemma function that was presented to them during the training session.

In the follow-up discussion with the whole group, the trainer/researcher called Heike and Laurie's search method a "trial" and a "game":

Trainer: That is not a question, Laurie, that is, in fact, just a sort of trial, you can even say a game, to look at what will happen.

Anne and Ninon struggled with interpreting corpus output. For example, Ninon wanted to know which parts of the pattern "hohen Alters" [advanced in age] are fixed and which vary. The students discovered new adjective-noun combinations and seemed excited about other insights they gained when exploring the concordance lines. However, Ninon took "seit Alters" as a pattern; the whole pattern is, in fact, "seit Alters her" [since ancient times].

Ninon: Seit Alters, seit Alters – je le connaissais pas, moi, je le comprends quand je le lis (. . .). Si tu m'avais dit "depuis des siècles", j'aurais mis "seit Jahrhunderten".
[Ninon: Since ages, since ages – personally, I didn't know this one, I can understand it when I am reading it (. . .). If you had requested "depuis des siècles", I would have chosen "for centuries".]

Ninons' error shows the difficulties even very advanced learners of German may encounter in segmenting corpus data: They do not always understand which words form to produce a meaningful unit.

During the third session, the students had to use corpora to assist with tasks featured in the lesson plan they were currently developing. Group 2 had to look up the word "Mitarbeiter". This word means "colleague" but also "collaborator" (i.e. an informant in a totalitarian system). Henri started searching for the word in the parallel corpus without indicating a context, and then he tried to combine it with "Polizei" [police] with zero results. This could be explained by the fact that the activity of a collaborator is a secret one; the word "police" is not likely to appear within a context close to this word. Looking for verbs collocating with "Mitarbeiter" helped Henri identify relevant verbs like "to observe, to follow, to take photographs, to search a home, to inform about activities of a spy". During a follow-up discussion, the participants and I commented on Henri's results.

Trainer: *And the others who had to type "collaborator" for instance, did you get relevant results or not?*
Henri: *Yes, we found the verb "to observe" (. . .). This has to do with spying, in fact.*
Trainer: *Yes, okay. We can see that this is not neutral, this does not just mean "collaborator (. . .) at the university", in fact, but rather – What could you say instead of "collaborator", in fact?*
Konstanze: *Colleague.*
Trainer: *No, I mean, in this given context.*
Konstanze: *A shadow.*
Trainer: *A shadow, a spy, rather something like this, that's it. (. . .) You could tell the students (of your class): "You see, collaborator, we have already studied this word, its meaning seems rather neutral, but in this case, it (. . .) means something which is not neutral at all. You can do things (. . .) like that: observe what is written around this word, in which larger context it appears (. . .)".*

This verbal exchange helps us to understand that methodological and pedagogical competencies are intertwined: Searching a corpus for language learning purposes makes sense if you have a precise pedagogical goal which can be pursued by exploring an appropriate corpus. In the discussed case, the goal could be to help young German learners understand that the meaning of a word depends on, amongst other things, its use within a cultural context. Checking the verbs appearing with "Mitarbeiter" [collaborator] in a bigger corpus would have provided Henri with an even more prototypical meaning of this word, which can be applied to people who are cooperating within a professional context, e.g. employees of a company.

Trainees were also concerned about the reliability of the results obtained through concordancing. In the post-training interview, Laurie and Valentine (Group 1) say that corpus data are not reliable enough for less advanced learners who might not detect erroneous forms or labels in the corpus and could become confused by the way language is represented in concordance lines.

Laurie: *I think the use of Sketch Engine requires support. If you leave them [the students] alone, at some point there will remain mistakes, words that are misused, words that are not appearing in the right context.*
Investigator: *What do you mean by "mistakes"?*
Laurie: *In fact, a [highlighted] word that (. . .) belongs to another sentence and is combined with another word.*
Valentine: *The students don't see the difference.*

Konstanze, Laurie, and Valentine believed corpus exploration was suitable only for advanced students, as they felt this form of learning activity would require both enhanced linguistic and cultural background knowledge.

Konstanze: It's possible (...) with 12th graders (...).
Investigator: Not with other levels?
Konstanze: Oh, you have to admit that ... I think they have to understand the context, they need general knowledge. Vocabulary is not difficult, but you need to know (some) specific words. Maybe (it's possible) in the 11th form.
Laurie: The advantage of the 12th (graders) is that they also treat the same program in history, they also see the GDR in history, and as a result, they normally will already have some knowledge.

Second-order barriers: teacher's internal perceptions affecting adoption/rejection of corpora

In this section, I focus on the post-training interviews for evidence of embracing "adopter" or "rejector" roles in terms of corpus innovations (Rogers, 2003, p. 247), discussing firstly acceptance/adoption for L2 classroom use with younger learners (YL), followed by its rejection.

Acceptance/adoption of corpora for YL classroom

Ninon of Group 3 was a very enthusiastic corpus defender. She spoke more often than the other members of Group 3 about corpora and put forward strong pedagogical arguments to convince Liliane, who found, like Henri, that the use of corpus tools would require too much in the way of intensive preparation.

Liliane: Sketch Engine (depicts) a particularly grammatical + use and for vocabulary, it actually allows you to find + eh the exact use of words, for instance, knowing in which expressions (word) can really be used, in which form they can be used. (But) At the teacher's level, there's really a lot of clearing up things in German. We can't afford to let the students use Sketch Engine without facing the problems they may encounter.
Ninon: You have to know the subtlety of the language before you can use it by yourself, you have to be able to know it well, to differentiate + what is a verb, for example, what is a noun, and so on. But once they have grasped it, I think they can do very well.

After discussing with her group the possibility to understand the meaning of a word with the help of the context provided by concordance lines, Ninon made an enthusiastic plea for corpus use with young learners.

Ninon: Really, what I find good is that they learn the language without really ... well, themselves in fact, that's pretty easy learning. It's active in the sense that they still have to ask themselves questions, but that's quite easy because in the end, they

> acquire things they (normally) don't pay particular attention to, and finally, in the end, I think it will be very enriching for them.

By the end of the discussion, the members of Group 3 had linked corpus exploration with the linguistic concept of language in use, outlined a set of intellectual and pedagogical requirements for corpus use, and stated that DDL is compatible with action-oriented methods fostering language awareness and autonomous thinking. Ninon's view expressed in the final interview supports this idea.

> Ninon: I have found the use of Sketch Engine particularly interesting for all sort of students. From a very young age, you can do this with the students. That pushes them to try to find out (things) by themselves, and I think that they will memorize better this way. They will be able to reuse (an item) if they have discovered it themselves.

Aside from Ninon, Heike suggested that, while she was not keen on the use of corpora for L2 German, she was more favourable to its use with younger learners of Latin. During her interview, Heike reported that metalinguistic analysis activities of the type afforded by DDL are much more common in Latin courses than in other language courses.

Rejection of corpora for YL classroom

Contrary to the generally positive attitude of Group 3 towards DDL, all members of Group 1 and three out of the four members of Group 2 tended to reject the use of DDL for YL classroom purposes on the basis that corpus tools may require too much lesson preparation time, they may be too complex to handle for young learners, and the nature corpus output may be too unfamiliar for younger learners to process. The excerpt concerns the first two arguments put forward by members of Group 2.

> Investigator: What would you say in a few words about the advantages or disadvantages of using the Sketch Engine concordancer for teaching and learning German?
> Henri: I'm quite negative because (. . .) it is a tool for academics.
> Dora: For the students, it's really complicated.
> Amandine: As much as I was seduced by Glogster, basically, as much as Sketch Engine, well, if I project myself with students, (even) with the most advanced ones, it's true that I would not especially intend to use Sketch Engine.
> Heike: Our group has been working on vocabulary (. . .). If we are really working on grammar, if you wish to adopt a really authentic use of grammar, then (it's okay).
> Henri: Yes, but . . . again, it's for people at university.
> Amandine: Yes, that's right.
> Henri: But for middle schoolers and high school students fff I mean it's . . . I think it's too . . . too sophisticated.
> Investigator: Mrs. Lacroix did it with high school students.

Henri:	It requires a lot of preparation work
Investigator:	(which you find) too important.
Henri:	(Yes) too important, it's true that everything is relative, but it probably requires a lot of preparation work. You can't just (confront) the students like that with something like that. It's not possible.
Investigator:	And what about you?
Amandine:	Well, the same, as I said, I don't see myself using it. Sure, it was put into practice, but it is true that I personally am not very comfortable (with this tool), and I see more use for university students than for high school students.
Dora:	I don't think it's really suitable for to the level (of our students).

In the script documenting her first steps with the Sketch Engine, Valentine explains that she would never use corpus tools in the classroom and that she prefers lessons that use Internet searches. In their final interview, Valentine and Konstanze showed more interest in corpus tools than they had previously but confessed they were much more excited about other tools, such as online exercise generators (gap-filling activities; splitting spaceless text into words), which save the teachers time but are less likely to support student-centred discovery-based learning activities.

Valentine:	Regardless of Sketch Engine, I think that these exercises you can find (. . .) you enter a word, you say: I'm going to delete such a word, slap, you've done your exercise, I think it's miraculous, it's great.
Konstanze:	Even the snakes[5] there, you know, with markers where they must cut the words after, poof, I think it's great (. . .). That's amazing.
Valentine:	I think it gives you a lot of possibilities, actually.

The frankest rejection was pronounced by Henri: After having tried out Sketch Engine during the learning design sessions and at home, he told the whole group that he couldn't see any pedagogical goal for the use of this corpus analysis tool by younger learners. During the follow-up discussion at the beginning of the second course session, the teacher congratulated the group for the quick progress made with Sketch Engine during the treasure hunting period.

Trainer:	Some say that you can't use a concordancer at school; (. . .) you need kind of technical knowledge. However, during the last session, you proved that it is possible to understand nearly all of it within 15 minutes. I find that very positive.
Henri:	Personally, I find it still rather nebulous.
Trainer:	I think it is a matter (. . .) of acceptance. (. . .) Perhaps you were a bit reluctant and you were asking yourself: "Why this rubbish? Children are unable to manage it."
Henri:	Mhm.
Trainer:	In fact, I would like to know if this is true.

However, following this interaction, Henri suggested that corpus tools are too difficult to handle for children. In the final interview, several reasons for this belief are mentioned again, among them the idea (put forward by Anne) that direct access to unfiltered corpus data could be a possible source of error in concordance results, which may leak into student revisions.

Anne: The main disadvantage for me is that the provided context is actually quite broad. So, eh, the word is put in the middle of sometimes very long sentences and you may also find the end of the first one, and I think that for a student, it can be quite difficult to understand well how this word is used. That's why if I'm going to use the concordancer as a teacher with students, I would first make a pre-selection of relevant and really interesting sentences because I think that otherwise it is too complicated for the students. They don't keep enough distance and they won't realize that they're learning from a mistake, actually.

While two-thirds of the participants rejected the use of corpora for YL language teaching, one-third at least did accept their usefulness for other adult-focused academic tasks. Laurie said that she was already using Sketch Engine for translation exercises; Ninon planned to use corpora to create vocabulary lists helping her to pass her CAPES (certificate of aptitude for teaching at the secondary level), while Heike announced her intention to create a corpus for her own study of Latin, and Henri cited PhD students as the right target audience for corpus tools.

Discussion

This chapter aimed to identify potential barriers to trainee teachers' adoption of corpora for DDL in the secondary L2 German classroom. The data suggest that a range of extrinsic and intrinsic barriers appears to limit trainee's uptake of corpora for language teaching in this context. These barriers include issues with corpus tool complexity, trainees' limited capacity to generate suitable corpus queries for the corpus-based learning activities they had created, and their opinions about the suitability of DDL innovations as expressed in their final interviews. However, the results show that most of the participants accepted the idea that corpora were beneficial for other academic learning tasks, and three participants out of ten did consider using corpora with younger L2 learners in the future.

The model represented in Figure 4.2 (Rogers, 2003, p. 247) takes for granted that sooner or later, all participants will adopt the innovation. This was not the case for all members of our research project: Ninon clearly behaved as an "early adopter"; she was determined to try out corpus tools and to reflect on the possibilities they offer for German learning at secondary school. Her enthusiasm spread to Anne and Liliane, who then represented the "early majority" together with Heike from Group 2. However, the other participants remain very sceptical. At this stage of our research, it is impossible to predict if, with more observation and more training time, they would have become "late innovation adopters" or "laggards" or if they would have maintained their decision to reject the innovation.

Time, of course, is a major factor in the adoption of any innovation, and while modest technical first-order barriers do exist, e.g. knowing the main functions of the software and understanding how to do different types of corpus queries, it is likely these can be surmounted by offering corpus users more training and more exploration time. Amandine closed the interview of the reluctant Group 2 by saying, "Maybe we should . . . have a little more time".

In addition, both teachers and learners are willing to learn to use quite complex tools (e.g. Glogster) if they perceive that they offer exciting pedagogical features (cf. Dagnino et al., 2018). Heike suggested further development of the interface of Sketch Engine was needed to tailor it to a young audience: "Perhaps is it the interface. It is too complicated, in fact. Perhaps one should develop a concordancer for the young". Heike's claim for user-friendly corpus tools must be taken seriously (see also Hirata, this volume); encouragingly, the new Sketch Engine interface (designed in 2018) is evolving in this direction, and SkELL (Sketch Engine for Language Learning, Baisa & Suchomel, 2014) is finally available for German.[6] What is more, this corpus management system can now easily be accessed on tablets and smartphones, corresponding to the digital devices most often used by young people.

However, intrinsic second-order barriers are much harder to overcome (cf. Dagnino et al., 2018). This was evidenced in certain characteristics of the trainee-designed corpus-based activities of all three groups. Namely, the insistence on a narrow pre-selection of concordance lines or tasks based on printed query results reveals a tendency not to trust the tool as a means for knowledge creation in the language classroom. Even the members of Group 3, generally talking very positively about the use of corpus with young learners, produced corpus-based activity which did not really exploit the advantages offered by the tools.

As mentioned previously, an innovation must possess the following features to make its breakthrough in the secondary classroom: relative advantage (1), compatibility (2), level of complexity (3), trialability (4), and observability (5) (Rogers, 2003, p. 365). To what extent did the participants perceive that corpus tools possess or lack these characteristics? Ninon – and to a more limited extent, Anne, Liliane, and Heike – might have understood the relative advantages afforded by corpus tools. However, the other students did not find concordancing compatible with the maturity and the German level of younger learners (2), and they found the interface of Sketch Engine too complex for this kind of audience (and even for themselves) (3). Because of time restrictions, the various functions of the corpus tool could not be tried out extensively (4), and observability (understanding how others successfully used the tool before) was limited (5). Issues with first-order barriers in teacher training for DDL may then lead to the creation of perceptions acting as second-order barriers, as noted in Meunier (this volume), who explains that "teachers themselves may lack the necessary digital literacy to use existing corpus tools and may [then] not always see the added value of integrating DDL in the prescribed curriculum they have to use".

Based on these findings, I make the following recommendations to improve trainees' uptake of corpora for DDL in the secondary classroom:

- The choice of pedagogically relevant resources is crucial within DDL contexts.
- The students should be offered a user-friendly corpus analysis tool which they can access via their preferred devices.
- Sufficient training time is needed.
- Technical competencies can be enhanced with the help of sample queries that deal with questions corresponding to frequent errors made by young students.
- Trainees' motivation for using corpora might be increased by providing them with samples of corpus-based learning activities, which they can adapt to their own teaching projects and contexts (see the requirement of flexibility mentioned in Dagnino et al., 2018). Tim Johns's *Kibbitzers* exercises – accessible via the website WordSmith Tools (https://lexically.net/TimJohns/index.html) (Scott, nd) – show how corpus-based exercises (and even descriptions of their actual use) can be shared with others.
- Like Meunier (this volume), I would advise trainers to explain to corpus novices that corpus-based learning activities resemble, to some extent, the types of exercises and online tools they already like and that have proven their worth in the classroom. For instance, the "snake task" (mentioned earlier by Konstanze) trains learners to become competent in identifying words within a spaceless text, which can be generated with the help of an online tool. A comparable level of competence is needed when reading concordance lines, with the difference that working with concordancers or with other corpus functions (e.g. n-gram lists) offers a more flexible and integrated way to observe and to learn a foreign language.

By following these guidelines, the potential for first and second barriers to the adoption of DDL for trainee teachers is thus minimized, leaving future corpus classroom pioneers more likely to bring others into the fold.

Acknowledgements

My warmest thanks go to Annette Hess, who gave me the permission to use the scripts of the first season of the *Weissensee* series for teaching and research purposes.

Notes

1 Information and communication technology.
2 I am referring to the 5th edition (2003).
3 www.drehbuchautoren.de/stichwort-drehbuch
4 In the case of less advanced learners, it can be helpful to export the node form list and to have it translated by (*DeepL Translator*, 2017) or by another powerful translation tool.
5 Konstanze alludes to an online exercise generator focusing on word identification within a spaceless text accessed via LingoFox (2019). This tool is no longer available on the current version of this website.
6 deSkELL: https://deskell.sketchengine.co.uk/run.cgi/skell

References

Baisa, V., & Suchomel, V. (2014). SkELL: Web interface for english language learning. In A. Horák & P. Rychlý (Eds.), *Proceedings of recent advances in slavonic natural language processing* (pp. 63–74). Brno: Tribun EU.

Boulton, A. (2010). Data-driven learning: Taking the computer out of the equation. *Language Learning, 60*(3), 534–572. doi: 10.1111/j.1467-9922.2010.00566.x.

Boulton, A. (2012). *What data for data-driven learning?* Retrieved from https://eric.ed.gov/?id=ED544438

Braun, S. (2007). Integrating corpus work into secondary education: From data-driven learning to needs-driven corpora. *ReCALL, 19*(3), 307–328. doi: 10.1017/S0958344007000535.

Breyer, Y. (2009). Learning and teaching with corpora: Reflections by student teachers. *Computer Assisted Language Learning, 22*(2), 153–172. doi: 10.1080/09588220902778328.

Callies, M. (2016). Towards corpus literacy in foreign language teacher education: Using corpora to examine the variability of reporting verbs in English. In R. Kreyer, S. Schaub, & A. Güldenring (Eds.), *Angewandte Linguistik in Schule und Hochschule* (pp. 391–415). Frankfurt am Main, Berlin, Bern, Bruxelles, New York, Oxford, Wien: Peter Lang.

Chambers, A. (2005). Integrating corpus consultation in language studies. *Language Learning & Technology, 9*(2), 111–125.

Chambers, A., Farr, F., & O'Riordan, S. (2011). Language teachers with corpora in mind: From starting steps to walking tall. *The Language Learning Journal, 39*(1), 85–104. doi: 10.1080/09571736.2010.520728.

Dagnino, F. M., Dimitriadis, Y. A., Pozzi, F., Asensio-Pérez, J. I., & Rubia-Avi, B. (2018). Exploring teachers' needs and the existing barriers to the adoption of learning design methods and tools: A literature survey: Teachers' needs and barriers to adoption of LD. *British Journal of Educational Technology, 49*(6), 998–1013. doi: 10.1111/bjet.12695.

DeepL Translator. (2017). Retrieved from www.deepl.com/translator

Edmodo. (2008). Retrieved from www.edmodo.com/

Ertmer, P. A. (1999). Addressing first- and second-order barriers to change: Strategies for technology integration. *Educational Technology Research and Development, 47*(4), 47–61. doi: 10.1007/BF02299597.

Frankenberg-Garcia, A. (2014). The use of corpus examples for language comprehension and production. *ReCALL, 26*(2), 128–146. doi: 10.1017/S0958344014000093.

Hess, A. (2010). *Weissensee | Verband Deutscher Drehbuchautoren e.V. (VDD).* Retrieved from https://drehbuchautoren.de/podcast/2010-09-14/weissensee

Holliday, A. (1992). Tissue rejection and informal orders in ELT projects: Collecting the right information. *Applied Linguistics, 13*(4), 403–424. doi: 10.1093/applin/13.4.403.

Johns, T. (1991). Should you be persuaded – two samples of data-driven learning materials. In T. Johns & P. King (Eds.), *Classroom concordancing* (pp. 1–13). Birmingham: Birmingham University.

Kennedy, C., & Miceli, T. (2001). An evaluation of intermediate students' approaches to corpus investigation. *Language Learning & Technology, 5*(3), 77–90.

Kilgarriff, A., Baisa, V., Bušta, J., Jakubíček, M., Kovář, V., Michelfeit, J., . . . Suchomel, V. (2014). The sketch engine: Ten years on. *Lexicography, 1*(1), 7–36. doi: 10.1007/s40607-014-0009-9.

Lee, S. (2011). Challenges of using corpora in language teaching and learning: Implications for secondary education. *Linguistic Research, 28*(1), 159–178.

Leńko-Szymańska, A. (2017). Training teachers in data driven learning: Tackling the challenge. *Language Learning & Technology, 21*(3), 217–241.

LingoFox. (2019). Retrieved from www.lingofox.de/index.php?&page=start&lan=de

Rogers, E. M. (1962). *Diffusion of innovations*. New York: Free Press of Glencoe.
Rogers, E. M. (2003). *Diffusion of innovations* (5th Ed.). New York: Free Press of Glencoe.
Rohrbach, J. (2003). Don't miss out on Göttingen's nightlife: Genreproduktion im Englischunterricht der Jahrgangsstufe 9. *Praxis Des Neusprachlichen Unterrichts, 50*(4), 381–389.
Schaeffer-Lacroix, E. (2009). *Corpus numériques et production écrite en langue étrangère. Une recherche avec des apprenants d'allemand* (PhD thesis, Université de la Sorbonne nouvelle – Paris III). Retrieved from https://tel.archives-ouvertes.fr/tel-00439095/document
Schaeffer-Lacroix, E. (2016). Talking about German verb particles identified in concordance lines – from spontaneous to expert-like metatalk. *Language Awareness, 25*(1–2), 127–143. doi: 10.1080/09658416.2015.1122023.
Schmid, H., & Laws, F. (2008). Estimation of Conditional Probabilities with Decision Trees and an Application to Fine-grained POS Tagging. *Proceedings of the 22Nd International Conference on Computational Linguistics – Volume 1* (pp. 777–784). Retrieved from http://dl.acm.org/citation.cfm?id=1599081.1599179
Scott, M. (Ed.). (n.d.). *Tim Johns' Kibbitzers*. Retrieved from https://lexically.net/TimJohns/
Screencast-O-Matic. (n.d.). Retrieved from https://screencast-o-matic.com
Varley, S. (2009). I'll just look that up in the concordancer: Integrating corpus consultation into the language learning environment. *Computer Assisted Language Learning, 22*(2), 133–152. doi: 10.1080/09588220902778294.
Vincent, B., & Nesi, H. (2018). The BAWE quicklinks project: A new DDL resource for university students. *Lidil, 58*. doi: 10.4000/lidil.5306.
Vyatkina, N., & Boulton, A. (2017). Corpora in language learning and teaching. *Language Learning & Technology, 21*(3), 1–8. doi: 10125/44750.

PART II
Applying new DDL methods for younger learners

5

THE PEDAGOGIC ADVANTAGE OF TEENAGE CORPORA FOR SECONDARY SCHOOL LEARNERS

Pascual Pérez-Paredes

Introduction

Few young school learners use corpora to learn foreign languages during primary or secondary education. Braun's (2007, pp. 313–314) assertion about the use of corpora with young secondary school learners still resonates 12 years on: "To date very little is known about the use of corpus-based materials and learning activities in secondary education". It seems as if the corpus revolution predicted by Rundell and Stock (1992) has yet to reach these learners. The reasons are multiple. For example, young learners' lack of interaction with language corpora may be explained by their teachers' unfamiliarity with corpus resources. Mukherjee (2004) reported that 80% of the secondary school language teachers interviewed (*n* = 248) in Germany had not heard of language corpora, and Frankenberg-Garcia (2012) found that only a very small number of language teachers had actually used corpora. A recent European survey revealed that language teachers across different educational levels were not familiar with learner language corpora. In Spain and the UK (*n* = 230), according to this survey, language teachers' familiarity and use of L1 corpora was moderately low, and familiarity with part-of-speech taggers and corpus management tools (e.g. Sketch Engine) was extremely low (Pérez-Paredes, Ordoñana, & Aguado, 2018). This lack of familiarity and training echoes the sentiment of Braun (2007, p. 308), who stated that it would take a new generation of teachers "for corpora to find their way into the language classroom".

In addition, a lack of corpus use in instructed learning may stem from the limited amount of appropriate resources for pre-tertiary groups of learners. In fact, language learners in secondary education across the world seem to be invisible to designers of language corpora as a resource for language learning. Despite the widespread interest in language corpora in tertiary language education and the range of benefits for language learners found in the specialised literature

(Boulton & Cobb, 2017), very few learners in primary or secondary education have had the chance to explore such resources in instructed contexts (Braun, 2005, 2007; Pérez-Paredes, 2010; Boulton & Cobb, 2017). Indeed, the use of corpora in secondary schools is not high up on the agenda of researchers and teachers of teenage language learners. For example, Garton and Copland (2018) did not include a section devoted to corpora and young learners in their recent handbook on teaching English to young learners. Add to that the fact that teenage language has not attracted the attention of many linguists: "The dearth of investigations into teenage language is due in part to its under-representation in language corpora" (Stenström, Andersen & Hasund, 2002, p. x).

Paradoxically, *pedagogic corpora* (PC) have been around for quite some time (Lee, 2010; Chambers, 2010), which suggests that researchers in this field need to reassess how they bring these resources to the attention of language educators (Braun, 2007; Pérez-Paredes, 2010; Pérez-Paredes, Ordoñana & Aguado, 2018) and discuss what I describe in this chapter as their *pedagogic advantage*. As pointed out by Frankenberg-Garcia (2012, p. 486), we need to help language teachers to "take their first steps in using corpora autonomously [so as to] encourage them to want to find out more about using corpora in the classroom". The aim of this chapter is to contribute towards disseminating the huge potential of pedagogic corpora in secondary language education by discussing how SACODEYL can be used by language learners in instructed settings to promote language learning that is authentic to their learning contexts (Mishan, 2004). Focus is placed on some features of spoken language annotated by the language teachers who took part in the design of SACODEYL.

Designing corpora for teenage learners

Using L1 corpora with teenage learners

Some researchers have used L1 corpora resources with young learners of English. Soruç and Tekin (2017) adopted a control–experimental group research design ($n = 72$) to test whether the use of DDL was superior to traditional vocabulary learning. The teens studied English in Kampala and Uganda and were 12 to 15 years old. The DDL group was trained on how to use the British National Corpus and search for words. The learners were "asked to read and examine [. . .] concordances related to the words individually, and then to find and highlight key words around the target word in pairs" (p. 1,818). Soruç and Tekin (2017) appear to corroborate Chambers's (2005, p. 122) claim that "corpus consultation [. . .] favours learner autonomy and discovery learning" and Braun's (2007) positive evaluation of the use of a pedagogic corpus (Braun, 2006) with secondary school learners in Germany. Leray and Tyne (2016) used DDL in French primary schools to facilitate the learning of French spelling. The authors suggest that young learners and adults alike can equally benefit from corpus consultation. Crosthwaite and Stell (this volume) have also reported a positive impact of DDL with primary school learners.

Braun (2007) used one of the first PC ever developed: the English Language Interview Corpus as a Second-language Application (ELISA). This tool is a corpus made up of 25 video interviews featuring native speakers of English from different geographical backgrounds who talk about their careers, countries, cultures, and natural resources. These topics are interesting per se for secondary school learners, and their use is, therefore, potentially relevant to most school curricula. Braun (2007) used ELISA with 26 students of English ages 14 and 15 years during a one-month period. Braun selected interviews where Australian speakers discussed their professional lives as well as the country's culture. Students in the corpus group worked on activities that made use of wordlists, selected concordance lines, and hands-off concordancing, which allowed them to query the text version of the interviews. Students in the control group worked on more traditional, text-based activities. The corpus group yielded higher scores in perceived learning success for the second interview. Braun (2007, p. 322) argues that "the corpus-based activities were more effective and were perceived to be more useful than the more traditional computer-based activities". This significantly contributes to our understanding of the potential of pedagogic corpora in secondary schools.

Pedagogic corpora

Despite the huge potential of language corpora for language learning, the number of pedagogic corpora (Willis, 1998) is relatively limited. Frankenberg-Garcia (2012, p. 476) pointed out that the direct use of corpora in language teaching "has not caught on [because] the majority of corpus resources are neither pedagogically oriented nor user friendly". I would argue that the very concept of pedagogic corpora warrants further discussion in the specialised literature. In the context of this chapter, PC are corpora that follow design principles that differ from those present in corpora designed for research purposes: PC are topic-driven, they pursue pedagogic rather than linguistic representativeness, and they challenge traditional corpus-search behaviour. Walsh (2010) holds that PC can bring life to the language classroom and suggests that the use of invented dialogues and de-contextualised language in textbooks needs to be appraised. While Walsh (2010) describes PC as more relevant and appropriate than L1 corpora and highlights their superiority over language textbooks, pedagogic corpora are understood as "corpora of ELT textbooks" in Flowerdew (2012, p. 195). There is, however, a sense of recognition in the language education community that corpora have a potentially huge impact on the type of language that learners study in their schools (Braun, 2005, 2007; Chambers, 2005; Pérez-Paredes, 2010; Chambers, 2013). In the following paragraphs I will try to illustrate that, unfortunately, this argument has been *hijacked* by proponents of the use of "L1 corpora–only" in language education.

In Pérez-Paredes (2010), I discussed the existence of two main approaches or scenarios where language corpora may be used in language classrooms. Each scenario may be characterised by (a) the use of existing L1 non-pedagogic corpus resources or by (b) the use of specifically designed resources for language learning contexts. I call these two (a) the *possibilities* and (b) the *feasibility* scenarios, respectively. In the latter, language corpora are "specifically compiled, annotated and exploited with a pedagogic intention" (p. 10). Pedagogic corpora in the *feasibility* scenario become mediators (Braun, 2005) between language usage and the learners and are integrated with the methodology used in the classroom:

> The successful use of corpora for learning and teaching hinges to a great extent on a successful 'pedagogic mediation' between the corpus materials and the corpus users [. . .] to support learners and teachers in reconstructing the discourses which gave rise to the texts in the corpus.
>
> (Braun, 2005, p. 61)

In the *possibilities* scenario, however, corpora are adapted, not integrated. As a result, the corpus resources most likely to be used by language learners are *unmediated* L1 corpora. These corpora have been perceived by adult learners as challenging (Bernardini, 2004; Chambers, 2005) and messy (Braun, 2005). Santos and Frankenberg-Garcia (2007, p. 477) found that queries made by novice users of corpora reflect "serious misconceptions about the kind of information that can be retrieved from a corpus", and Pérez-Paredes, Sánchez-Tornel, & Calero (2012) report that, even after specific corpus training, university students tend to query the BNC as if it were Google, generally ignoring POS tags and regular expressions.

The notion that it is *possible* to use L1 corpora in classroom settings is at the heart of Römer's (2011) classification of corpus applications. While she distinguishes between indirect and direct applications, both types of uses draw on unmediated L1 corpora as the basis for introducing corpora into language education. If none of the existing L1 corpora are of interest, Reppen (2010, p. 54) suggests that the *ad hoc* compilation of a corpus for classroom use can be useful as long as "the teacher is interested in exploring types of language [. . .] not represented by existing corpora". The integration of representative L1 corpora seems to be successful in settings where the learning of the linguistic features of a variety is an educational aim. As noted by Flowerdew (2012), the uses of corpora in specialised contexts such as English for Academic Purposes (EAP) are approached from a genre perspective, although their integrations "have mainly remained at the institutional level and not filtered through to the language teaching community at large" (p. 203). Most research involving DDL has looked at either university students or EAP contexts (Boulton & Cobb, 2017; Pérez-Paredes, 2010, forthcoming), hence the tendency to embrace L1 corpora such as the BNC or corpora of academic texts as the basis for classroom interventions. The tendency to rely on existing L1 corpora in classrooms, together with the dearth of research designs using qualitative data to examine beginner and low-intermediate learners' use of DDL and corpora, may have contributed to the prevalence of the *possibilities* scenario. Rather than adapting corpus resources to the learners' world (Widdowson, 2003), researchers have reported repeated efforts to make L1 corpora such as the

BNC accessible to learners through training and guidance (Pérez-Paredes et al., 2012; Boulton & Cobb, 2017).

The SACODEYL approach: a pedagogic corpus for young learners of foreign languages

Corpora are powerful resources that, ontologically, try to represent how a community of speakers uses language or a language variety. In other words, corpora are used by corpus linguists as proxies of usage. The question is whether usage per se is of immediate use to every learner. Widdowson (2003, p. 126) maintains that the world to "replicate" in the learning experience is that of the learner; in other words, authentic language in the context of language learning differs from the range of attested uses recorded in representative L1 corpora.

The lack of appropriate corpus-based pedagogic resources in secondary school language education motivated the work developed first by the SACODEYL EU Minerva project from 2005 to 2008, and then by the BACKBONE EU Lifelong Learning project from 2009 to 2011. SACODEYL is a collection of seven topic-driven corpora (Braun, 2007) that seeks to incorporate corpus-based materials into secondary education language learning. The languages represented in SACODEYL are English, French, German, Italian, Lithuanian, Romanian, and Spanish. The design of the SACODEYL corpora follows the suggestions made by Braun (2005), who argues that mediation can be implemented through relevant content, a restricted corpus size, a multimedia format, and pedagogic annotation. For Thompson (2010, p. 4), *SACODEYL*

> exploits clips of commissioned video recordings of teenagers [. . .] speaking about their interests, experiences, friends and families [. . .] the video provides language learners with good listening practice, with orthographic transcripts provided so that the learner can check his or her understanding [and] the learner can search the data to locate certain features. The SACODEYL data have been annotated so that one can search by topic, grammatical point and part of speech [. . .] and one can also do concordance searches. When the concordance lines appear, it is then possible to select any one line, click 'Go to section', and open the relevant wider section of the transcript.

According to Timmis (2015), the only examples of teaching-oriented corpora available are ELISA, SACODEYL, and BACKBONE. Timmis draws on Leech's (1997) term "teaching-oriented", as these corpora focus not on research but on pedagogy. However, as Hoffstaedter and Kohn (2009, p. 293) point out, corpora are not intrinsically pedagogic: They assume their "pedagogic quality in a meaningful and relevant pedagogic discourse".

One of the features behind the *possibilities* scenario is that representative corpora of national varieties and registers are used in language classroom contexts where learners are trained to use software or interfaces whose primary aim is to derive linguistic knowledge about the textual nature (Braun, 2007) of the corpus. Bernardini (2004, p. 32), among many other authors, sees significant potential in DDL. However, she warns that

> learners require guidance and heightened awareness to learn from corpora and much of their potential [. . .] would be lost if learners did not have a chance to carry out relatively complex analyses, requiring them to observe phraseological regularities and restrictions and the functions associated with them.

Bernardini (2004) highlights the need for complex user searches to maximise the potential of corpora in the context of the *possibilities* scenario. Specifically, the affordances of corpora such as those described by Bernardini (2004) include noticing a set of phraseological regularities and their functions in discourse. This observation exercise may prove challenging for ELT learners in secondary schools and with a low proficiency level. Under these conditions a pedagogic corpus can mediate students' learning by providing some scaffolding in terms of facilitating the observation of communication and language phenomena. Besides pedagogic annotation, the design of the SACODEYL interviews sought to maximise the opportunities for learners to listen to, read, and engage with native speaker language, which presents fewer turns than one might expect in ordinary conversation, thus favouring language expression where clause construction and clause combining do not occur across turn boundaries (Carter & McCarthy, 2017).

SACODEYL-English (SACODEYL-EN) is a 53,090-word corpus of 20 video interviews with UK teenagers. Interviews followed a similar script: After allowing some time to introduce themselves, teenagers were asked to offer their comments on topics that had previously been identified by *SACODEYL* team members and EU teachers as relevant for their language learning and teaching in secondary education. Such topics included travelling, family, daily routines, plans for the future, the Internet, school, learning languages, and the EU. Figure 5.1 shows

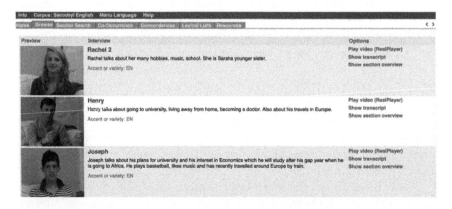

FIGURE 5.1 The "browse" interview interface of SACODEYL

the Interview browse interface of SACODEYL. As can be seen, the SACODEYL interface differs massively from most corpus interfaces that position the concordance search or, simply put, "search", as the main front end for the user. In SACODEYL, however, the teenagers themselves and the topics they talk about are presented first.

Pedagogic corpora such as SACODEYL and BACKBONE are designed following pedagogical usability criteria, including both horizontal and vertical reading that allow for an "easier construction of a discourse context in which the [. . .] results make sense" (Widmann Kohn, & Ziai, 2011, p. 322) to young learners. Similarly, different search modes (see Figure 5.1) help learners obtain a quick overview of the entire interviews and sections, zooming in on topic-specific sections, searching for several words simultaneously, and gaining an overview of the lexical content of the results, pattern search, use of wildcards, and the traditional KWIC display.

Interviews are divided into sections, that is, shorter pedagogic units of interest for learners and teachers viewed as pedagogically relevant (Braun, 2005) based on the segmentation carried out by language teachers. Every SACODEYL interview, therefore, is split into further pedagogic units, although the whole interview transcript or interview video can be accessed from the browser interface. Henry, a fictional name, is an 18-year-old boy living in Reading who plans to study medicine in Cardiff. His interview was divided into nine sections, all of potential interest to learners of English around the same age as Henry. Table 5.1 describes the section titles as well as the number of words and length of each section.

TABLE 5.1 Sections in one of the SACODEYL interviews.

Section titles	Words per section
Meet Henry	
Duration: 00:02:07	Word count: 426
Cardiff halls	
Duration: 00:02:09	Word count: 458
Living away from home	
Duration: 00:01:15	Word count: 256
Travels and hobbies	
Duration: 00:02:18	Word count: 401
Sports	
Duration: 00:00:59	Word count: 212
Interrailing	
Duration: 00:01:57	Word count: 374
Fear of flying	
Duration: 00:02:04	Word count: 496
Travelling in a group	
Duration: 00:00:38	Word count: 157
Future plans	
Duration: 00:00:52	Word count: 190

SACODEYL corpora (Pérez-Paredes & Alcaraz, 2009) were compiled, annotated, and distributed – not to be representative of teenage talk but to be pedagogically representative of the type of language required by teenage language learners across the EU. Despite its distribution in 2009, its spread and use has been somewhat modest. However, some researchers have used SACODEYL corpora to research teenage spoken language. Vandeweerd and Keijzer (2018, p. 92) used the French component of SACODEYL to "determine the extent to which FL in the dialogues of beginner French textbooks is representative of authentic language use". The authors looked at the average number of lexical bundles in SACODEYL and in the French L2 textbook dialogues and found that SACODEYL showed "more of the high frequency lexical bundles, indicating that the textbook dialogues were not representative of naturalistic speech in this regard" (p. 93). Buntinx and Van Goethem (2018) also used the French component of SACODEYL to explore the use of intensification in teenage L1 French. This interest in the oral dimension of language is shared by other researchers looking at the *possibilities* or potential of corpora in language education. For example, Surcouf and Ausoni (2018) developed a pedagogic spoken corpus for A2 learners of French as a foreign language (FLO-RALE) that uses TV shows. Although their target performance level is congruent with the curricula of most secondary schools, the type of discourse represented in the corpus may not be immediately related to young learners. Surcouf and Ausoni (2018, p. 87) note that it is essential for the spoken nature of the language to be mediated by the efforts of linguists and language educators in order to bring relevant pedagogic language into the language classroom: "Nul doute qu'un élément de réponse réside dans l'évolution des représentations de la langue que se font les didacticiens, les enseignants et les apprenants".

In the following section, I will show how L1 corpora such as SACODEYL can offer a pedagogic advantage over non-pedagogic L1 corpora in secondary school language learning.

Teenage corpora and spoken language

Using the rationale in Timmis (2005), McCarten and McCarthy (2010), and Carter & McCarthy (2017), I will demonstrate how pedagogic corpora of teenage talk may help teachers and learners discover and become aware of central features of spoken English as used by fellow UK students when using language to talk about topics of relevance in instructed L2 language learning. This is of huge importance, as cognitive and corpus linguists have shown that language usage is affected by, among other cognitive skills, the learners' strength of memory, the likelihood of recall, and fluency of production and comprehension (Ellis, 2017). Similarly, production and comprehension are affected by usage itself. As Ellis (2019, p. 39) put it: "Our understanding of language learning requires the detailed investigation of usage, its content, its participants, and its contexts – the micro level of human social action, interaction, and conversation, the meso level of sociocultural and educational institutions and communities, and the macro level of ideological structures". Timmis (2005, p. 123) encourages exposing learners to spoken grammar via real language to foster "awareness of spoken grammar, while accepting that learners may not necessarily always want or need to reproduce its forms". I will look at two types of pedagogic annotations implemented by language teachers who worked with the SACODEYL-EN corpus: the second conditional and the online edition of spoken language.

Contextualising the use of grammar in spoken English: conditionals

Enhancing the "description and pedagogy of languages" (Carter & McCarthy, 2017, p. 15) with data that emerge from conversational and spoken language can only contribute to improving learners' awareness and competence (Timmis, 2005; Aguado-Jiménez, Pérez-Paredes, & Sánchez, 2012), while multimedia corpora can be useful for both teachers and learners:

> We can no longer assume that the definition of a 'conversation' is anything as simple as a face-to-face or even an audio-visual encounter unfolding sequentially in real time; such explorations and re-thinking will need to take cognizance of multiple contextual dependencies of individual words and phrases. Multimodal corpora are a step in the direction of a fuller breaking down of boundaries between text and context [. . .] aiming ultimately at a more holistic grammar of speaking.
>
> (Carter & McCarthy, 2017, p. 14)

SACODEYL corpora were annotated by language teachers who selected sections of the interviews they considered particularly appropriate for language learning in secondary education. The annotators developed their own taxonomy of grammar based on the CEFR levels and their own experience as language teachers. The resulting taxonomy, which we call *grammatical characteristics*, includes a wide range of broad categories that represent the curriculum of language learning across the EU: tenses, passive voice, conditionals, modality, clauses, nouns, determiners and quantifiers, adjectives/adverbs, and other verbs. Each category was further expanded and annotated. Figure 5.2 shows the extended annotation tree of grammatical characteristics developed by the language teachers themselves.

In this section, I will illustrate how a pedagogic corpus can help teachers and learners use and acquire, respectively, grammar content that can be found in EFL secondary school curricula: the second conditional. Following suggestions made by McCarten and McCarthy (2010), I will observe how these annotated phenomena occur in context.

According to the English Grammar Profile (EGP), the use of conditional clauses spans all performance levels except for A1 of the CEFR. Uses by A2 learners include *if clauses* for future situations and if + simple present. B1 uses include *if clauses* for imagined situations, while B2 learners employ a wider range of

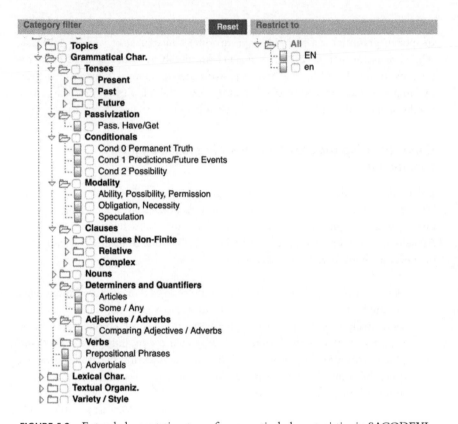

FIGURE 5.2 Extended annotation tree of grammatical characteristics in SACODEYL

conjunctions including *as long as* and *provided*. The EGP website[1] offers, among others, these examples from the Cambridge Learner Corpus (CLC):

> The next week I would have flown to Miami to meet George Clooney.
> (Italy; B1 THRESHOLD; 2008; Italian; Pass)

> If I were in your shoes I would have chosen the school which is in the centre of town.
> (Iran; B1 THRESHOLD; 2008; Farsi; Pass)

> I would suggest that you might bring a city map in case you lose your way.
> (Japan; B2 VANTAGE; 1993; Japanese; Pass)

Gabrielatos (2003) examined the representation of conditionals in an ELT corpus comprising 15 coursebooks and in a sample of <800 conditional clauses in the BNC. He proposed three assumptions behind the ELT approach to conditionals: (1) There are one-to-one form-meaning relations, (2) modality is expressed by modal verbs only, and (3) conditional sentences only express attitude to likelihood. Jones and Waller (2015) found the most common use of if-conditionals in the BNC to be the real non-past usage and that both *If I* and *If you* returned high MI scores in the corpus, which suggests a strong collocational profile. The authors suggest that an examination of concordance lines where both real and unreal uses are shown can make students aware of these patterns. A pedagogic collection of corpora such as SACODEYL, however, can help teachers and learners become aware of the situated uses of conditionals in L1 conversation in the context of topics that are relevant to EFL secondary school learners and thus complement the widespread exposure to de-contextualised uses (Walsh, 2010) including "If it rained, I'd get wet" or "If I went to bed early, I would not be so tired",[2] where the dynamic structure of conversational English (pre-clause dislocated topic + core clause + post-clause tail) (Carter & McCarthy, 1995; McCarthy & Carter, 1997) is rarely discussed or even presented to learners.

A search on SACODEYL-EN, the English SACODEYL corpus, returned seven sections that were annotated as suitable for learning the conditional type 2 (possibility). Figure 5.3 offers some extracts from these sections.

McCarten and McCarthy (2010) suggest that vocabulary is more functional in conversational English than in written communication, with references to the self and the listener. I would argue that conversational vocabulary is also more frequent and easier to understand. A subcorpus of the seven sections (words = 2,994) shows that 91.7 per cent of the words used by the teenagers belong to the family of the 1,000 most-frequent words in English, 4 per cent (hobby, exchange, improve, victim, decision) belong to the 2,000 most-frequent words, and only 1 per cent (complex, horror, audience) fall within the 3,000 most-frequent range. Figure 5.4 gives a breakdown of the vocabulary used by L1 teenage speakers in sections that were annotated by language teachers as pedagogically relevant for learning the second conditional in English.

The language used in conversational English is characterised by frequent hedging and stance expressions. Common chunks act as an invitation for the listener to explore the knowledge of a topic or their own experiences. These chunks are often found in textbooks; however, they are rarely presented in colligational contexts. Thus, the "cognizance of multiple contextual dependencies of individual words and phrases" (Carter & McCarthy, 2017, p. 14) is rarely explored in language instruction at lower levels. Some of the examples (Figure 5.3) involve different degrees of hedging before the conditional sentences are used, such as *I imagine* (section 1), *I don't know* (section 2) and *I think* (sections 3 and 4). In section 7 we find some conditional *would* uses and a use of the conditional type 2, where the learners can explore Sam's online edition of his reply to the original question. Teachers and learners can also explore the conspiracy of lexis and grammar behind the conditional type 2 in the context of natural L1 communication and how words, whether functional or content-based, are primed for their use in contexts that go beyond the strict formulation of grammatical rules so frequently taught to young learners in schools. However, the use of different types of conditionals is not uncommon, as shown in section 5.

Section	Interview	Topic	Example
1	Stuart	Films and filmmaking	– How could you improve it now? – Well **I imagine if I was to do it again I'd want to** make it a little more complex than just someone wandering upstairs and getting killed. Because it just seems that…
2	Hannah	Self-defence	– And have you ever been in a diff… in a dangerous situation? – No not yet thankfully. **I don't know if I'd actually remember what I was taught if I was in a dangerous situation.**
3	Viveca & Megan	Plans for the future	– I didn't really know I don't really know what to do with the animals so I don't really think it's that viable. – **I think if I was a vet there would be too much blood.**
4	Beatrice	Subjects at school	– Right and are you happy so far with your choice of subjects, or do you think if you had the opportunity again would you have chosen different subjects to do? – Well last year I did enjoy geography but as we started we started some of the A2 course this year as well and I've gone off the subject rather it's become much more in-depth and the topics have changed and have become less interesting in my opinion. So I think, I mean that's why I'm thinking of dropping it this year and, I think maybe last year if I, **if I did it again I'd do something like classics instead** cos I've started to think that would be maybe more interesting and something that I might do at university.
5	Ellen	Reading (UK)	– Ok so, when you go into town, do you enjoy Reading as a place? Can you tell me what you like about Reading or what you don't like about Reading? – I like it cos it's big and there's loads of places you can just go and hang out you don't have to do anything. **But it could probably be better if there was actually more stuff to do cos there's not**… if you're just going out with your friends you basically have the choice you can go to the cinema or hang around the shops for a couple of hours, but there's not actually that much to do.
6	Sean	On the Internet	– **If you became a teacher what would you teach?** – Oh I don't know. I love like teaching people things and you know some teachers you're like oh I could do such a better job than him. And I think yeah, I actually could because I like show people things sometimes when they get stuck on work and they're like you like teach it so much better than our actual teacher. To kind of take something really complicated and then explain it to someone really simply so you understand it is quite satisfying. So I was thinking of becoming a teacher but I don't know. It's kind of a clash between those two at the moment.
7	Sam	Plans for the future	– What do you plan to do after school? Are you planning to go to university? – Yeah I'd like to go to university. My grandparents live in Cambridge so I would quite like to go to that one because it's a really nice town and it's yeah, it's a very pretty town so it's nice to be there. I think my sister's gonna try to go there as well so **cos my it would make my granddad happy if we all went there cos he went there as well so it's it's like yeah.**

FIGURE 5.3 Sections annotated as suitable for learning the conditional type 2 (possibility)

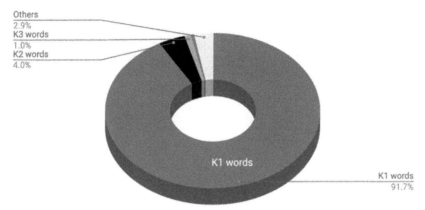

FIGURE 5.4 A breakdown of the vocabulary in the seven sections annotated as pedagogically relevant for teaching and learning the conditional type 2

This kind of wider context is rarely found in textbooks, where the focus is on decontextualised grammar practice and drilling (Cunningsworth, 1987). Furthermore, some uses of the conditional deviate from the prescribed (pedagogic) rule, as in section 5: "if you're just going out with your friends you basically have the choice you can go to the cinema or hang around the shops for a couple of hours". The examples given in Figure 5.3 not only challenge the speakers' adherence to the strict rules governing conditional clause use (Gabrielatos, 2003) but also bring to the forefront the role played by "small words" such as discourse markers, adverbs, and inserts that create the conditions for increased listenership as a conversation skill (McCarten & McCarthy, 2010). These are important findings that highlight the impact of corpora on younger learners across a variety of (multimedia) texts. As shown in Sealey and Thompson (2004, 2007) and Aguado-Jiménez et al. (2012), this exploration seems to facilitate the appreciation of how language patterns manifest themselves and shows the relevance of metacognition in understanding the statistical properties of language (Ellis, 2012). Sealey and Thompson (2007, p. 208) claim that the linguistic evidence found in corpora can contribute to "keeping teaching about language itself firmly anchored in genuine discourse". Pedagogic corpora thus facilitate the provision of genuine discourse against the backdrop of the topics and language that are needed by teenage secondary school learners.

Authenticating spoken grammar: foregrounding the online edition of language

Spoken pedagogic corpora showcase some of the language learning affordances most widely cited in the DDL literature (Pérez-Paredes, 2010), including the huge potential for language awareness raising (Aguado-Jiménez et al., 2012). However, corpora in the *possibilities* scenario fail to convey the communicative intent of the speakers:

> The corpus [. . .] cannot tell us why or how something was said, or how it was received. Indeed, the very act of transcribing real dialogue into writing distorts it, since this misleads us into regarding the spoken language as if it were identical with the written (ibid.).
>
> (Mishan, 2004, p. 220)

This is precisely where pedagogic corpora can be advantageous to young learners. Pedagogically annotated spoken corpora can offer learners a way into topic-relevant language usage that is rarely found in standard ELT materials, where we find restrictions in terms of, among other things, the unified, scripted lesson format in textbooks. In addition, PC such as SACODEYL can provide a multimedia experience of the L2, something which young learners would naturally expect as a normal affordance of L2 materials.

In particular, spoken discourse is misrepresented in ELT pedagogy. A study by Cunningsworth (1987, p. 46) highlighted a lack of spoken language representation in ELT materials and listed some of the resources available to language teachers interested in discursive competence:

a   partly-contextualized lists of form-function equivalences
b   an assumption that conversational skills are directly transferable from L1
c   a vaguely-defined expectation that learners will in some way "pick it up" through exposure to the language in contexts of use

While some of these "resources" challenge whether languages can be learned through explicit instruction – this being a most pertinent debate outside the scope of this paper – the use of pedagogic corpora can present opportunities for mediated language instruction that is appropriate to young learners. In the following paragraphs, I will explain how pedagogic corpora can be used by learners and teachers to situate the acquisition of spoken language by examining the emergence and use of extended lexical units in the context of topics of relevance to their own language learning experiences (hobbies, schools, travelling, friends, etc.). It is in this context that I intend to briefly discuss one of the features that characterise spoken English (Biber, Johansson, Leech, Conrad, & Finegan, 1999): the online edition of language.

Spoken language, and particularly conversation, is edited online; in other words, there is no time for planning, and the speaker has to maintain the flow of communication. The fact that turn-taking in SACODEYL interviews has been minimised favours (a) the interviewees' reevaluation of their thoughts and words and the emergence of self-restructuring and (b) the learners' focus on language produced by one speaker only. Figure 5.5 offers a selection of extracts from the

Section	Interview	Topic	Example
1	Rachel	A typical day	– Yeah, ok brilliant. So on a typical school day could you tell me what your routine is. – I get up about seven or quarter past seven and I go down and I have breakfast. Then I usually go up have a shower and brush my teeth **then get dressed and do my hair.** Then I go to school, and I meet Megan and we walk to school together. – And how about after school, what's your routine after school? – **Well usually, nearly every day I have an after school thing.** And when I get home I usually do my homework, or watch telly or do some piano practice **or, yeah.** – So you're playing the piano? – **Yep.** [. . .] – So why do you prefer piano now? – I dunno it just sounds, a bit better sometimes. – You like the sound of it? – **Yeah. It's really good.**
2	Helen	Education and gender	– Ok. I think you're also interested in education and how boys perform differently from girls in school and that that, that difference doesn't seem to be going away at all. [. . .] – **Well it's been a, you know, it's been a big issue for sociologists to study over the last, I dunno how long it's been, an issue for a long time that girls are constantly over, you know over-achieving and boys are under-achieving in schools.** I mean there is, I mean I dunno some of the theories are that girls they have better language skills than boys. **For example someone did a study into babies and talking to them and seeing their brainwaves and girls were able to distinguish between sounds more easily than boys were at a very young age and also because of the way boys and girls are socialised.** Boys tend to go outside more to play whereas girls stay inside and read more, which actually gives them a big head start in primary school.
3	Sean	A play in London	– Do you ever go to London or any other places near Reading? – I went to London a few weeks ago actually for a, with the, within the drama to see a performance. An' it was really cool. **I only found out like midway through the performance that it was actually the main character was actually a previous James Bond in the last film. Not James Bond, the bad guy against James Bond. And I think it's 'Tomorrow Never Dies'. I only remember the end scene really well, where they're in a plane and one side gets ripped off and obviously computers again I'll be able to do that if I get into that kind of job thing. But yeah the guy's got like an electric suit and he's fighting with Pierce Brosnan and it's so cool. And I only realised like part way through that that was the guy and I was like I have so much respect for that guy, so it was good to see that and. . .**

FIGURE 5.5 Some of the sections annotated as "typical examples of spoken language" in SACODEYL-EN

11 sections that were annotated by language teachers as pedagogically relevant for teaching and learning spoken English (typical examples of spoken language).

Most sections give examples of elliptical subjects (e.g. section 1) or delexicalised nouns (*thing*); restructuring and self-repair (section 1); and, among many others, uses of *yeah* to pass the turn to the interviewer for confirming or accomplishing acknowledgement functions. These and many similar features point to what Carter and McCarthy (2017, p. 6) have described as the "re-examining" of established features in previous face-to-face conversational language research. However, one of the most interesting areas where these sections can be used in L2 learning is to help students notice that everyday communication operates beyond the sentence level (Biber et al., 1999; Carter & McCarthy, 2017). In section 2, Helen is trying to put across the point that boys and girls behave differently according to different social roles. From a linguistic perspective, it is interesting to see how she struggles to find the words to say for how long this issue has been studied by sociologists:

> Well it's been a, you know, it's been a big issue for sociologists to study over the last, I dunno how long it's been, an issue for a long time that girls are constantly over, you know over-achieving and boys are under-achieving in schools. I mean there is, I mean I dunno some of the theories are that girls they have better language skills than boys.

However, the amount of repetition, hesitation, hedging, vague expressions, and self-repair observed in these few words is representative of what conversational English looks like (Carter & McCarthy, 2017). As is the case in everyday discourse, speakers often decide to introduce new "genres" as they speak or interact. In section 3, Sean is talking about a recent visit to London to see a performance there. However, Sean does not go into detail about the performance itself or about whether he enjoyed it. Instead, he gets carried away by other thoughts concerning the main character's name and then goes on to tell us about this film, in which the actor plays the bad guy:

> I only remember the end scene really well, where they're in a plane and one side gets ripped off and obviously computers again I'll be able to do that if I get into that kind of job thing. But yeah the guy's got like an electric suit and he's fighting with Pierce Brosnan and it's so cool.

He then reverts back to the performance:

> And I only realised like part way through that that was the guy and I was like I have so much respect for that guy, so it was good to see that and...

In just 90 words we have an example of authentic discourse (text + section + concordance + video), where a teenager tells other peers a story about going to the theatre and seeing a film, and it does so in a way which reflects how teenagers speak, that is, in a way that puts situational ellipsis at the centre of discourse. Interestingly, it forces listeners and interlocutors to take response into account, an area very rarely taught in L2 instructed learning.

Pedagogic corpora as opportunities for situated L2 learning

In this chapter, we have examined some of the advantages that pedagogic corpora can bring in to L2 secondary school classrooms. We have described what has been done in the last 15 years or so, but, most significantly, we have tried to argue that pedagogic corpora need to be conceptualized as resources that need to be designed following distinctive criteria.

Registering linguistic phenomena is a condition for language learners to acquire L2 language. From a usage-based perspective, what is not found in the input cannot be learned: "That language users are sensitive to the input frequencies of these patterns entails that they must have registered their occurrence in processing" (Ellis, O'Donnell, & Römer, 2015, p. 166). All of the input frequencies we find affect the relationship between practice and performance (Ellis, 2017), and it is precisely through performance that our knowledge becomes activated in real-life communication. Thus, our (implicit) knowledge of how language works is deeply affected by our perceptual systems, which, according to research in cognitive sciences, have become "attuned to expect constructions according to their probability of occurrence in the input" (Ellis, 2017, pp. 118–119). However, input in L2 and L1 contexts vary considerably. The idea that learners can pick up the frequency of L1 usage in EFL instructed settings will need to be further examined by researchers through a variety of research methods. Research such as (Szudarski, this volume) is essential to understand the role that DDL can play in attuning young learners' sensitivity to linguistic phenomena such as phraseology. What we know so far is that L2 learners exhibit distinct patterns from those observed by L1 speakers and that their phraseological competence is lower (Paquot & Granger, 2012).

Timmis (2005, p. 123) suggests that teachers and learners may exploit "a convenient harmony between a methodological emphasis on noticing, and [the] view that native speakers (and their cultures) should not be portrayed as models to imitate or aspire to". Pedagogic corpora can be beneficial when combining pedagogic foci (e.g. noticing, language awareness) and the provision of a more inclusive range on L2 speakers (e.g. age, race, gender, background, etc.). While the native speaker norms or uses are not necessarily the destination port for language learners, usage observed in L1 communication can be of tremendous use to explore the range of expressive form-function-meaning mappings that are at the disposal of learners of a foreign language. Pedagogic corpora can play a significant role as mediation tools in secondary school L2 instruction and can bring more authenticated (Mishan, 2004) and real usage (Walsh, 2010) into language classrooms. Further research in this area will enhance understanding of how pedagogic corpora can create better or different conditions for learning in L2 instructed settings and in multilingual contexts (Di Vito, this volume).

SACODEYL is a collection of corpora of teenage talk which was highly innovative back in the mid-2000s. However, its once-novel concept (Hoffstaedter & Kohn, 2009; Pérez-Paredes & Alcaraz, 2009; Widmann Kohn & Ziai, 2011) has not aged well in the era of mobile-assisted language learning (MALL) and Web-based services. While new online distributions of SACODEYL will become available in the coming years, the promise of developing pedagogic corpora should not live only within the community of corpus linguists. Schaeffer-Lacroix (this volume) believes that more friendly corpora will be necessary for both younger learners and language teachers. It will be down to the community of language teachers to decide whether pedagogic corpora are the right tools to successfully situate their students' learning needs and characteristics within an authenticated context (Mishan, 2004).

Notes

1 URL: www.englishprofile.org/component/grammar/content/631
2 These examples are taken from the English Grammar website of a major language teaching organisation.

References

Aguado-Jiménez, P., Pérez-Paredes, P., & Sánchez, P. (2012). Exploring the use of multi-dimensional analysis of learner language to promote register awareness. *System, 40*(1), 90–103.
Bernardini, S. (2004). In the classroom: Corpora in the classroom: An overview and some reflections on future developments. In J. M. Sinclair (Ed.), *How to use corpora in language teaching* (vol. 12, pp. 15–36). Amsterdam: John Benjamins.
Biber, D., Johansson, S., Leech, G., Conrad, S., & Finegan, E. (1999). *Longman grammar of spoken and written English*. London: Longman.
Boulton, A., & Cobb, T. (2017). Corpus use in language learning: A meta-analysis. *Language Learning, 67*(2), 348–393.
Braun, S. (2005). From pedagogically relevant corpora to authentic language learning contents. *ReCALL, 17*(1), 47–64.
Braun, S. (2006). ELISA – a pedagogically enriched corpus for language learning purposes. In S. Braun, K. Kohn, & J. Mukherjee (Eds.), *Corpus technology and language pedagogy: New resources, new tools, new methods* (pp. 25–47). Frankfurt: Peter Lang.
Braun, S. (2007). Integrating corpus work into secondary education: From data-driven learning to needs-driven corpora. *ReCALL, 19*(3), 307–328.
Buntinx, N., & Van Goethem, K. (2018). Cross-linguistic perspectives on intensification in speech: A comparison of L1 French and L2 English and Dutch. Poster presented at Louvain-la-Neuve, Université catholique de Louvain, Using Corpora in Contrastive and ranslation Studies.
Carter, R., & McCarthy, M. (1995). Grammar and the spoken language. *Applied Linguistics, 16*(2), 141–158.
Carter, R., & McCarthy, M. (2017). Spoken grammar: Where are we and where are we going? *Applied Linguistics, 38*(1), 1–20.
Chambers, A. (2005). Integrating corpus consultation in language studies. *Language Learning & Technology, 9*(2), 111–125.

Chambers, A. (2010). What is data-driven learning? In A. O'Keeffe & M. McCarthy (Eds.), *The Routledge handbook of corpus linguistics* (pp. 345–358). London: Routledge.

Chambers, A. (2013). Learning and teaching the subjunctive in French: The contribution of corpus data. *Bulletin VALS-ASLA, 97*, 41–58.

Cunningsworth, A. (1987). *Coursebooks and conversational skills.* ELT textbooks and materials: Problems in evaluation and development (ELT Documents 126). Oxford: Modern English Publications and The British Council.

Ellis, N. (2012). Formulaic language and second language acquisition: Zipf and the phrasal teddy bear. *Annual Review of Applied Linguistics, 32*, 17–44.

Ellis, N. (2017). Chunking in language usage, learning and change: I don't know. In M. Hundt, S. Mollin, & S. Pfenninger (Eds.), *The changing english language: Psycholinguistic perspectives* (Studies in English Language, pp. 113–147). Cambridge: Cambridge University Press.

Ellis, N. (2019). Essentials of a theory of language cognition. *The Modern Language Journal, 103*(S1), 39–60.

Ellis, N. C., O'Donnell, M. B., & Römer, U. (2015). Usage-based language learning. In B. MacWhinney & O. William (Eds.), *The handbook of language emergence* (pp. 163–180). Hoboken: John Wiley & Sons.

Flowerdew, L. (2012). *Corpora and language education.* Houndmills: Palgrave Macmillan.

Frankenberg-Garcia, A. (2012). Raising teachers' awareness of corpora. *Language Teaching, 45*(4), 475–489.

Gabrielatos, C. (2003, September). Conditional sentences: ELT typology and corpus evidence. In *BAAL 36th Annual Meeting.* Retrieved from www.academia.edu/2574542/Gabrielatos_C._2003_._Conditional_sentences_ELT_typology_and_corpus_evidence._36th_Annual_BAAL_Meeting_University_of_Leeds_UK_4-6_September_2003

Garton, S., & Copland, F. (Eds.). (2018). *The Routledge handbook of teaching English to young learners.* London: Routledge.

Hoffstaedter, P., & Kohn, K. (2009). Real language and relevant learning activities: Insights from the Sacodeyl project. In A. Kirchhofer & J. Schwarzkopf (Eds.), *The workings of the anglosphere: Contributions to the study of British and US-American cultures* (pp. 291–303). Trier: Wissenschaftlicher Verlag Trier.

Jones, C., & Waller, D. (2015). *Corpus linguistics for grammar: A guide for research.* London: Routledge.

Lee, D. Y. (2010). What corpora are available? In A. O'Keeffe & M. McCarthy (Eds.), *The Routledge handbook of corpus linguistics* (pp. 107–121). London: Routledge.

Leech, G. (1997). Introducing corpus annotation. In R. Garside, G. N. Leech, & T. McEnery (Eds.), *Corpus annotation: Linguistic information from computer text corpora* (pp. 1–18). Chicago: Taylor & Francis.

Leray, M., & Tyne, H. (2016). Homophonie et maitrise du francais ecrit: Apport de l'apprentissage sur corpus. *Linguistik Online, 78*(4), 131–148.

McCarten, J., & McCarthy, M. J. (2010). Bridging the gap between corpus and course book: The case of conversation strategies. In F. Mishan & A. Chambers (Eds.), *Perspectives on language learning materials development* (pp. 11–32). Oxford: Peter Lang.

McCarthy, M. J., & Carter, R. (1997). Grammar, tails and affect: Constructing expressive choices in discourse. *Text, 17*, 405–429.

Mishan, F. (2004). Authenticating corpora for language learning: A problem and its resolution. *ELT Journal, 58*(3), 219–227.

Mukherjee, J. (2004). Bridging the gap between applied corpus linguistics and the reality of English language teaching in Germany. In U. Connor & T. Upton (Eds.), *Applied corpus linguistics: A multidimensional perspective* (pp. 239–250). Amsterdam: Rodopi.

Paquot, M., & Granger, S. (2012). Formulaic language in learner corpora. *Annual Review of Applied Linguistics, 32,* 130–149.

Pérez-Paredes, P. (2010). Corpus linguistics and language education in perspective: Appropriation and the possibilities scenario. In T. Harris & M. Moreno Jaén (Eds.), *Corpus linguistics in language teaching* (pp. 53–73). Berlin: Peter Lang.

Pérez-Paredes, P. (forthcoming). The uses and the spread of corpora and data-driven learning in language education in CALL research: An analysis of the 2011–2015 period.

Pérez-Paredes, P., & Alcaraz, J. M. (2009). Developing annotation solutions for online data driven learning. *ReCALL, 21*(1), 55–75.

Pérez-Paredes, P., Ordoñana Guillamón, C., & Aguado Jiménez, P. (2018). Language teachers' perceptions on the use of OER language processing technologies in MALL. *Computer Assisted Language Learning, 31*(5–6), 522–545.

Pérez-Paredes, P., Sánchez-Tornel, M., & Calero, J. M. A. (2012). Learners' search patterns during corpus-based focus-on-form activities: A study on hands-on concordancing. *International Journal of Corpus Linguistics, 17*(4), 482–515.

Reppen, R. (2010). *Using corpora in the language classroom.* Cambridge: Cambridge University Press.

Römer, U. (2011). Corpus research applications in second language teaching. *Annual Review of Applied Linguistics, 31,* 205–225.

Rundell, M., & Stock, P. (1992). The corpus revolution. *English Today, 8*(4), 45–51.

SACODEYL. English corpus XML format. Retrieved from http://webapps.ael.uni-tuebingen.de/backbone-search/corpora/sacodeyl_english.xml Or www.perezparedes.es/sacodeyl_english-xml/

SACODEYL. System aided compilation and open distribution of European youth language. Retrieved from http://webapps.ael.uni-tuebingen.de/backbone-search/

Santos, D., & A. Frankenberg-Garcia (2007). The corpus, its users and their needs: A user-oriented evaluation of COMPARA. *International Journal of Corpus Linguistics, 12*(3), 335–374.

Sealey, A., & Thompson, P. (2004). What do you call the dull words? Primary school children using corpus-based approaches to learn about language. *English in Education, 38*(1), 80–91.

Sealey, A., & Thompson, P. (2007). Corpus, concordance, classification: Young learners in the L1 classroom. *Language Awareness, 16*(3), 208–223.

Soruç, A., & Tekin, B. (2017). Vocabulary learning through data-driven learning in an english as a second language setting. *Kuram Ve Uygulamada Egitim Bilimleri, 17*(6), 1811–1832.

Stenström, A. B., Andersen, G., & Hasund, I. K. (2002). *Trends in teenage talk: Corpus compilation, analysis and findings.* Amsterdam: John Benjamins.

Surcouf, C., & Ausoni, A. (2018). Création d'un corpus de français parlé à des fins pédagogiques en FLE: la genèse du projet FLORALE. *EDL (Études en didactique des langues), 31,* 71–91.

Thompson, P. (2010). Building a specialized audio-visual corpus. In A. O'Keeffe & M. McCarthy (Eds.), *The Routledge handbook of corpus linguistics* (pp. 93–104). London: Routledge.

Timmis, I. (2005). Towards a framework for teaching spoken grammar. *ELT Journal, 59*(2), 117–125.

Timmis, I. (2015). *Corpus linguistics for ELT: Research and practice.* London: Routledge.

Vandeweerd, N., & Keijzer, M. (2018). J'ai l'impression que: Lexical bundles in the dialogues of beginner French textbooks. *Canadian Journal of Applied Linguistics/Revue canadienne de linguistique appliquée, 21*(2), 80–101.

Walsh, S. (2010). What features of spoken and written corpora can be exploited in creating language teaching materials and syllabuses. In A. O'Keeffe & M. McCarthy (Eds.), *The Routledge handbook of corpus linguistics* (pp. 333–344). London: Routledge.

Widdowson, H. (2003). *Defining issues in English language teaching.* Oxford: Oxford University Press.

Widmann, J., Kohn, K., & Ziai, R. (2011). The SACODEYL search tool: Exploiting corpora for language learning purposes. In A. Frankenberg-Garcia, L. Flowerdew, & G. Aston (Eds.), *New trends in corpora and language learning* (pp. 167–178). London: Continuum.

Willis, J. (1998). Concordances in the classroom without a computer: Assembling and exploiting concordances of common words. In B. Tomlinson (Ed.), *Materials development in language teaching* (pp. 44–66). Cambridge: Cambridge University Press.

6

THE DEVELOPMENT OF A MULTIMODAL CORPUS TOOL FOR YOUNG EFL LEARNERS

A case study on the integration of DDL in teacher education

Eri Hirata

Introduction

Along with recent advances of corpus technology and concordance software development, analytical methods developed in corpus linguistics are now widespread in different areas of research, notably language teaching. Studies have reported on the direct application of corpora (i.e. DDL – data-driven learning, Johns, 1991) in language classrooms and its positive effects on vocabulary learning in both first (L1) and second languages (L2) (e.g. Lee, Warshauer, & Lee, 2018; Frankenberg-Garcia, 2012, 2014). With primary-age learners learning their L1, Sealey and Thompson (2004) conducted a study with English-speaking children using the CLLP (Corpus-based Learning about Language In the Primary-school) corpus, which consists of texts written for child readers extracted from British National Corpus (BNC). They report that colour-coded part of speech (PoS) information aided these L1 young learners to notice patterns and helped with "the grouping of items with similar properties" (ibid, p. 88) when analysing corpus output. However, DDL is still largely limited to adult learners, with relatively few attempts made to incorporate DDL in L2 pedagogy for young learners, especially at the primary school level. Reasons for this include difficulties for younger learners involved with the use of available concordance software tools, which were mostly created with adult learners in mind. In addition, classes with L2 young learners traditionally consist of teacher-directed activities, and interaction is emphasized in their learning. Though DDL provides inductive learning opportunities, it does not facilitate the kind of extended, direct, physical human interaction normally expected in TEYL contexts. Moreover, in the case of young learners who learn EFL, it may be too demanding to use traditional textual corpora for DDL, as the output can be very different from how young learners usually experience meaning-making, especially if they have not acquired sufficient reading skills in the L2. Another possible reason may be that corpus-based language learning and its possible application to TEYL are simply not recognised among practitioners. Clearly, there is little research conducted concerning DDL with primary YLs in EFL contexts, let alone the development of concordance software aimed at them.

Considering the challenges involved, it is necessary to develop appropriate tools for young EFL learners, taking into account how children learn to decode meaning. When very young children start to learn a language, they interact with many different modes to make sense of new words or expressions, utilise verbal information (sounds, tone of voice, etc.) and are particularly sensitive to non-verbal behaviours such as gestures, facial expressions, etc. For example, understanding the meaning of gesture is something children develop through "pragmatic scaffolding" in interaction with others (Thoermer & Sodian, 2001), and such a process also takes place when children learn their L2. In the case of children's literacy skills, early readers develop their skills through activities such as storytelling or reading picture books, experiencing meaning-making by weaving together both textual and non-textual features (Hassett & Curwood, 2009; Lewis, 2001). Through such experience, they also develop their understanding of each "visual, linguistic, spatial, and gestural" mode (Martens, Martens, Doyle, Loomis & Aghalarov, 2012, p. 287), with each contributing to the comprehension of meaning presented in the stories.

It is also important to consider young learners' increasing levels of experience with digital devices and the implications of this for teaching and learning. Recent research into children's literacy development points out that modern children's literacy experiences go beyond the traditional textual level and have become more "multi-stranded" (Parry & Taylor, 2018, p. 104) due to their increasing engagement with digital media in their everyday lives both at home and in educational settings (McPake, Plowman, & Stephen, 2013). Such exposure affects how they experience the process of discerning meaning and the development of early literacy (Burnett & Daniels, 2015; Levy, 2009; Yamada-Rice, 2011), since children are required to

> draw on their traditional literacy practices to decode not only print, but to negotiate diverse interactive and participatory modes of representation that frequently include images and videos and are authored by individuals from a broad range of backgrounds, locales and expertise.
> (Binder, Sorin, Nolan & Chu, 2015, p. 94)

It is also important for educators to realize how children comprehend the world around them, and to integrate children's social and cultural experiences into their educational contexts (Levy, 2011; Parry & Taylor, 2018). Since children's increasing engagement with multimodality is embedded in the "textual landscape" (Kress, 2003, p. 166) besides other experiences, it would be unrealistic to ignore its importance. Rather, it would be beneficial for children if educators were ready to incorporate children's multimodal daily experiences in their teaching and foster their learning by making use of the various "assets" they bring to the learning process (Parry & Taylor, 2018, p. 105).

Taking into account the various modes of interactions that children experience, corpora which only output textual information may appear overly decontextualised and far too challenging, especially for children who are learning English as a foreign language (EFL) and who may not yet have obtained enough literacy skills in their L2 or L1. It can be argued that having access to multimodal information would be worthwhile in assisting their comprehension of meaning. Reflecting the need to integrate multimodal information into the learning process, the *Multi-modal Corpus Tool 1.1* (henceforth *MmCT 1.1*) discussed in this study provides support for young learners' meaning-making through the simultaneous display of audio and visual information together with textual information. This may provide younger learners with the opportunity to learn in a manner closer to the way they process meaning in their everyday lives, making DDL more accessible for these younger learners.

The chapter firstly describes *MmCT 1.1*, providing its overall framework and features. I then report on a case study investigating the incorporation of DDL activities for EFL materials design in a younger learner teacher education programme, using *MmCT 1.1* alongside a general corpus, namely the Corpus of Contemporary American English through BYU (COCA, Davies, 2008). I present the results of a post-DDL survey conducted with pre-service teachers examining their experience of using DDL for lesson preparation, how their experience influenced their intention to use corpora themselves or with younger learners in the future, and their suggestions for appropriate corpus tools and functions. Remaining issues and challenges are discussed regarding the possible future integration of DDL in young EFL learners' classrooms.

The development of the *MmCT 1.1*

As previously mentioned, the *MmCT 1.1* (Hirata, 2017) is being developed for use in EFL education for YLs, with an aim of assisting their meaning-making by enabling them to interact with multimodal information through the use of application software. Figure 6.1 shows the overall framework and the search flow of the *MmCT 1.1*.

The search flow takes certain steps (i.e. 1–11 in Figure 6.1) in order to display appropriate information based on the search. Once the log-in and username are correctly entered, the system displays a search screen (Figure 6.2). The interface is intentionally kept simple. When the search word or words are entered by the user, the application accesses the database and extracts relevant files, i.e. SRT files, media files (MPEG), and the subtitle files (WebVTT) in which the search word or words appear. The locations of the search word(s) within each file are specified by making use of the time-codes within SRT files, and the extracted information is displayed together.

As previously mentioned, the primary aim of *MmCT 1.1* is to provide young learners opportunities to use corpora as a learning resource. To this effect,

An EFL-TEYL multimodal corpus tool **91**

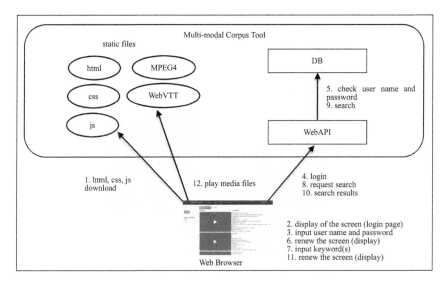

FIGURE 6.1 System framework of *MmCT 1.1* and search flow

FIGURE 6.2 Main "search" screen

MmCT 1.1 currently has the following main functions: 1) *MovieConc*, 2) *Wordlist*, and 3) *KWIC* display. *MovieConc* (Figure 6.3) is the main feature of *MmCT 1.1*; it enables the display of video, audio, and textual information together on the same screen in which the search word or words occur. The videos are displayed on the left side of the screen with the textual information on the right, showing a wider context than the textual concordances present (i.e. the search word displayed at the centre and five sentences at either side).[1] In addition, *MmCT 1.1* has a function which allows the user to set and adjust the playback speed. This function was considered essential as some EFL pupils may prefer the video and audio played at a slower speed in order to help their comprehension. Subtitles are also set to appear on each video, corresponding to each scene.

The *Wordlist* and *KWIC* (Key-Word-In-Context) are the same basic functions usually found in most concordance software. The *Wordlist* function allows the display of the words appearing in a corpus in order of their frequency or alphabetical order. *KWIC* allows the display of textual concordances alone at the top of the

FIGURE 6.3 Sample screen of *MovieConc*

display. It shows the search word(s) (i.e. "node[s]") in the middle, with surrounding text. It also has a "sort" function which enables the alphabetical sorting of the surrounding texts occurring at the specified position with respect to the search word(s) (e.g. 1L: one word to the left from the node). The *KWIC* display is useful in identifying the main patterns of search words. On the *KWIC* display (i.e. concordances), corresponding videos in which the search word or words appear are displayed so that it is possible for the user to check the usages in videos if necessary without having to go back to the *MovieConc* screen.

The *specialized multimodal corpus of YL teacher resources* provides the data used within *MmCT 1.1*, access to which is currently limited to non-commercial research and educational purposes requiring authenticated usernames and passwords in order to comply with data-protection regulation. The corpus includes media files (e.g. videos of songs and/or stories) with the corresponding text files of scripts created for young audiences for educational purposes or entertainment. The corpus is stored in simple text files saved in SRT format, including the time-codes, which allow the tool to identify the location of the search words within corresponding media files (Mpeg4) and the subtitle files (WebVTT) in order to display the information together on one screen.

Incorporation of DDL activities with a teacher training course: a case study

As previously pointed out, one of the main reasons for the lack of DDL within the TEYL context results from the lack of recognition among practitioners regarding corpus linguistics and its possible applications for language learning and teaching. Nevertheless, recent research has strongly recommended introducing corpus linguistics to ELT professionals, showing them how corpora can help with teachers' everyday problems (e.g. O'Keeffe & Farr, 2003). The direct use of corpora in language learning (i.e. DDL) encourages inductive learning by allowing learners to discover language rules through the exploration of concordances. This approach can be regarded as a "consciousness-raising" activity, promoting learners' language awareness with a particular focus on meanings and functions (Hunston, 1995). Since language awareness is one of the more important components to be included in teacher education (James & Garrett, 1992; Wright & Bolitho, 1993), DDL may significantly contribute to raising prospective teachers' language awareness. Generally, TEYL training tends to focus on the methodological aspects of teaching and provides fewer opportunities for in-depth consideration of language features, as the language presented to YLs is often simplified. However, recent research reports that the quality of input and teachers' language proficiency may affect YLs' learning outcomes (Muñoz, 2011), and it is clear that teachers of YLs should have a better understanding and command of the L2. It can be argued that incorporating DDL within teacher education not only serves to help develop language awareness among future practitioners but also may serve as an opportunity for introducing how corpora can help with materials preparation and improving the quality of language exposure provided to YLs. With this in mind, I now report on a case study incorporating DDL into a TEYL training course.

Context: participants and survey

Participants were pre-service teachers who are non-native speakers of English with Japanese as their L1 being trained to teach L2 English to young learners at the primary level at a four-year university in Western Japan. As a part of the training course, the participants were involved in tasks such as planning lessons, designing materials, and conducting lessons for pupils in Years 3–6. For this study, participants were invited to participate in DDL as a part of training in materials design during their teaching preparation. The DDL training incorporated in this study consists of three stages: pre-DDL activity, DDL activity, and post-DDL activity conducted under the following procedure:

Stage 1 – pre-DDL activity

Prior to DDL training, the participants were required to plan a lesson including the vocabulary and key expressions for certain teaching units in the designated textbooks published by the Japanese Ministry of Education, Culture, Sports, Science and Technology (MEXT) in 2018 (i.e. *Let's Try!1 & 2, We Can! 1 & 2*).

Stage 2 – DDL activity

Two types of corpora were used for DDL: a general corpus, i.e. the Corpus of Contemporary American English (COCA), and the specialized multimodal *MmCT 1.1* corpus described earlier. Though some participants (20 percent) had some experience in using corpora, most participants (80 per cent) were new to corpora. Participants were given brief introductory hands-on training by the researcher on how to use both COCA and the *MmCT 1.1* corpora. This training included how to access both corpora and to examine certain lexical items beyond the single-word level using concordances. The use of the "sort" function of *MmCT 1.1* was also presented in order to show how the function may help users discover patterns of lexical items. As for COCA, training in query syntax for BYU corpora (Davies, 2008) was also introduced.

Following the hands-on introduction, the participants were then invited to participate in DDL. They conducted analysis using the two corpora on the use of lexical items they had included in their pre-prepared lesson plans described in the pre-DDL stage and also items they found in designated textbooks. They were encouraged to compare how certain items were used in both corpora, finding any similarities or differences between the corpus examples and what they had included in their lesson plans. In particular, participants were encouraged to examine the phraseological features of the items together with the contexts in which the lexical items appeared in concordances. During the DDL session, participants were also encouraged to compare concordance output generated by the two corpora in order to see the differences between the output from COCA and that of the specialized multimodal corpus. Throughout the DDL session, each participant was asked to make a note of their findings, while considering the implications of these findings regarding the choice of lexical items, the design of teaching materials, and their teaching in general.

Stage 3 – post-DDL activity

After the hands-on DDL sessions, the participants had the opportunity to share their findings with other classmates and discuss the implications, e.g. whether it is necessary to reflect the findings in their material design in terms of lexical selections or whether any further consideration is needed in their teaching practice.

After the DDL sessions (Stages 1–3) described, a questionnaire was distributed to participants ($n = 47$) in order to learn about their DDL experiences, general impressions, and future intentions of using corpora for their own learning and teaching preparation. Out of the distributed 47 questionnaires, 45 responses were returned ($n = 45$, response rate of 95.7 per cent). The questionnaire included statements, and the participants were asked to choose the closest one to their answer to each statement from the four options (i.e. 1 = "I completely disagree", 2 = "I partly disagree", 3 = "I partly agree", 4 = "I fully agree"). A comment section was provided below each statement in which participants could provide more information about the reasons for their choice or state their opinions. The questionnaire also included topics such as the participants' general use of personal computers (PCs) and corpora, their prior experiences with any corpora, the participants' impressions of DDL in terms of both *MmCT 1.1* and the general corpus (i.e. COCA), participants' opinions about the appropriateness of corpus use with young learners, and their opinions about the useful features of the tool. Participants answered all questions, and almost all participants provided reasons for their choices as well as opinions on the useful features of corpora if they were to conduct DDL with young learners. The next section reports some of the key results of this survey and discusses their implications.

Results

Corpora vs. textbooks

As previously mentioned, participants were invited to participate in DDL training and asked to examine the lexical items they had prepared in their lesson planning by accessing both the specialized multimodal corpus and the general corpus. In relation to their experience of DDL for materials preparation, the participants were asked questions related to the following: 1) whether usages and expressions they had prepared in their lesson came from the corpus, 2) whether they found usages of lexical items which they had not expected or included in the lesson plan, and 3) whether the experience of DDL helped them to "notice" certain features of English.

Almost all participants, 97.7 per cent ($M = 1.33$, $SD = .52$), disagreed with the statement "I found the items or expressions used in the same way as I had prepared for the lesson". On the contrary, 97.8 per cent of the participants ($M = 3.76$, $SD = .48$) either partly or fully agreed with the statement "I found usages or expressions I had not expected or included in the lesson plan". Several participants commented that they noticed the contexts in which the lexical items or expressions were used were different from what they had thought "natural" or "normal". Some noted that the example expressions they had found in the textbook were much simpler compared with the examples they found in corpora, and some reported that they were "surprised" to find completely different usages in the concordances. Such results indicate that the presentation of lexical items in young learners' textbooks may be oversimplified and that the examples and contexts pre-service teachers include in their teaching may be restricted to those presented in designated textbooks. Moreover, the results also imply that the pre-service teachers' beliefs of what should be taught are influenced by or restricted to textbook usage.

Overall, most participants (93.3 per cent; $M = 3.47$, $SD = .62$) either partly or fully agreed with the statement "by consulting the corpora, I noticed some features of English that I was not aware of", indicating that the process of checking the items in corpora led them to notice different usages of the lexical items they included in their lesson plans. For instance, the following shows some of the comments referring to the expression "what do you want?":

- *"The expression (e.g. 'What do you want?') was used in different contexts from what we usually find (i.e. offering someone some food or drinks) in textbooks. In the corpus, when it was used, the people who used the expression always seemed disturbed or annoyed because they were busy doing something else."*
- *"The expression 'What do you want' was used either followed by to-infinitives (e.g. 'what do you want to do?'), or on its own (i.e. 'What do you want?'). When it was used alone, its use was different from what we normally see in textbooks. I had an impression that the person who was saying 'What do you want?' seemed irritated."*

Moreover, some also reported that "I noticed that the question form is not necessarily followed by an immediate answer", given they often observe such simplified interactional patterns in YLs' textbooks. Since the YL textbooks often tend to present dialogues with questions and their answers as "units" without any other alternatives, such noticing may encourage prospective teachers to be more flexible regarding the type of responses pupils may elicit rather than expecting the pupils to respond with "prescribed" model answers. In particular, this comparison made them aware that the usages appearing in textbooks may be introduced in somewhat "unsuitable" or "unrepresentative" contexts. Previous corpus studies of EFL or ESL textbooks often reveal contrived features or the tendency that "minor or less important features of usage are over-emphasized" (Römer, 2004, p. 197) in teaching materials. As the example indicates, it is important for pre-service teachers to be aware that "non-empirically based textbooks" (McEnery and Wilson, 2001, p. 20) may not always offer the best examples and that the materials may include oversimplified examples, where grammatical simplicity takes priority over the presentation of items in more common and suitable contexts. This is one of the areas where a DDL approach is useful for teacher education in providing opportunities for pre-service teachers to critically consider the presentation of language in textbooks as well as in their own lessons, through discovering language rules in an inductive manner by examining the concordances in corpora. Such activities aid increasing pre-service teachers' awareness towards the language they need to deal with in their future teaching.

In addition, while for most of the participants consulting the corpora led them to notice features in English which they were unaware of, others also commented that accessing corpora provided them opportunities to confirm their understanding about certain usages. Comments in this respect include:

- *"I realized how useful the corpus was in confirming our understanding."*
- *"It made me realize the importance of checking the examples in the textbook before we decide how to present them in our lessons."*

Participants thus realized the importance of accessing corpora before using the examples in the textbooks. Indeed, pre-service teachers will be able to evaluate such materials more objectively if they are equipped with the skills to access and use corpora. It can be said that such a process is useful in making them more than just "skilled material operators" (Gabrielatos, 2002/2003, p. 3) in their future teaching.

General vs. multimodal corpora

During the DDL activities, the participants were also asked to compare outputs generated in the multimodal corpus and the general English corpus (COCA) and their use of these two corpora. The survey addressed questions in terms of participants' impressions or opinions on 1) their accessibility and easiness of operation, 2) usefulness for checking usages and improving their English, 3) the intention to use them in future for their teaching preparation or their own study, and 4) appropriateness for TEYL if they were to use them for learning. Table 6.1 shows the overall results for the section.

In terms of the operational aspect of each corpus, most participants found the use of both *MmCT* and COCA easy. In addition, most participants agreed that both corpora were helpful to find examples of certain lexical items and their usages. All participants agreed with the usefulness of *MmCT*, with most of the comments mentioning the benefits of having the videos and scripts, which helped them to understand how certain lexical items were used in context. However, while the majority of participants generally agreed that the general corpus (COCA) was useful, 13.3 per cent partly disagreed and several commented that they found the amount of concordances somewhat overwhelming.

Regarding whether the participants intended to use a corpus in the future for checking usages or examples for their teaching preparation or for their own study, all the participants (97.7 per cent) agreed the multimodal corpus would be useful for their own study of English, and all participants showed an interest in making use of the multimodal corpus in the future. Qualitative comments also supported these findings, for instance:

- *"It would give us the confidence in using certain expressions for our lessons, if we have checked and found the usages and pronunciations in the corpus in advance."*
- *"We might have 'unintended' or 'accidental' findings by consulting corpora, provided with the contexts in concordances in MovieConc."*

The survey also looked at the participants' general ICT ability and their prior experience of using any corpora in order to see whether such experiences have had any influence on their attitude towards DDL. 35.5 per cent of participants answered they were not confident with using computers, while 64.5 per cent of participants showed their confidence with PCs by partly or fully agreeing with the statement "I regularly use PC and I am confident with its use" ($M = 2.76$, $SD = .76$). Regarding the participants' prior experience with corpora, 20 per cent had some experience of using corpora, while the majority (80 per cent) of participants were new to corpora.

TABLE 6.1 Descriptive statistics for items focusing on the DDL using the multimodal corpus and the general corpus

No.	Item	M	S.D.	Response (%) 1. completely disagree, 2. partly disagree. 3. partly agree, 4. fully agree			
				1	2	3	4
7.1	Using Multi-modal Corpus Tool (MmCT) was easy.	3.38	.68	0.0	11.1	40.0	48.9
7.2	It was useful to check the usages through MmCT	3.67	.47	0.0	0.0	33.3	66.7
7.3	I think using MmCT will help improve my English.	3.49	.54	0.0	2.2	46.7	51.1
7.4	I think Multi-modal Corpus is suitable for YLs' use.	3.00	.70	0.0	24.4	51.2	24.4
7.5	Multi-modal Corpus can he used (applied) in ELT.	3.49	.50	0.0	0.0	51.1	48.9
7.6	I would like to use Multi-modal Corpus for checking usages for my own study, teaching preparation etc. in future.	3.58	.49	0.0	0.0	42.2	57.8
8.1	Using the general corpus was easy.	3.02	.75	0.0	26.7	44.4	28.9
8.2	It was useful to check the usages through the general corpus.	3.07	.57	0.0	13.3	66.7	20.0
8.3	I think using the general corpus will help improve my English.	3.20	.58	0.0	8.9	62.2	28.9
8.4	I think the general corpus is suitable for YLs' use.	1.69	.66	40	53.3	4.4	2.2
8.5	The general corpus can be used (applied) in ELT.	2.76	.79	4.4	33.3	44.4	17.8
8.6	I would like to use the general corpus for checking usages for my own study, teaching preparation, etc. in future.	3.20	.62	0.0	11.1	57.8	31.1

In order to see the relationship between participants' ICT abilities or their experience of corpora and the participants' impressions or attitudes towards the use of corpora, Pearson product-moment correlation coefficients were calculated for each question shown in Table 6.2.

The data suggest there were no obvious relationships observed ($|r|<.15$, $p>.05$) between ICT ability and all the items concerning the use of *MmCT 1.1* (7.1–7.6). Similarly, there was no strong correlation between prior experience with corpora

TABLE 6.2 Pearson product-moment correlation of the Item 1 and Item 2 with the use of MmCT 1.1 and the general corpus

No.	Item	Ability	Experience
7.1	Using Multi-modal Corpus Tool (MmCT) nos easy.	-.08	-.05
7.2	It was useful to check the usages through MmCT	.14	.24
7.3	I think using MmCT will help improve mv English.	-.03	.25
7.4	I think Multi-modal Corpus is suitable for YLs' use.	-.08	.00
7.5	Multi-modal Corpus can he used (applied) in ELT.	.14	.16
7.6	I would like to use Multi-modal Corpus for cheeking usages for my own study, teaching preparation etc. in future.	.08	-.20
8.1	Using the general corpus was easy.	.09	-.06
8.2	It was useful to cheek the usages through the general corpus.	.09	-.04
8.3	I think using the general corpus will help improve mv English.	.46★	-.02
8.4	I think the general corpus is suitable for YLs' use.	.15	.27
8.5	The general corpus can be used (applied) in ELT.	.12	.06
8.6	I would like to use the general corpus for cheeking usages for my own study, teaching preparation, etc. in future.	.48★	-.20

$n = 45$
★$p < .01$

and their impressions of *MmCT 1.1* ($|r|<.30$, $p>.05$). In other words, most participants found operating *MmCT 1.1* easy, regardless of their level of confidence in using PCs in general or their previous experience with corpora. Judging from some of the qualitative comments (e.g. "Having the videos and scripts together helped me to understand the context more easily"; "It was helpful to have the videos"), participants seem to agree that having the multimodal features made it easier for them to deal with the corpus output in understanding the contexts in which their search words occur. Several participants also pointed out that *MmCT 1.1* was less challenging to use than COCA given the absence of complex search syntax on the former's platform. Since the initial motivation for creating *MmCT 1.1* was its direct use by young learners, the results imply their future teachers appear more willing to use *MmCT 1.1* with their own learners than would be found using a general corpus. While the majority of participants found DDL useful and seemed to have positive attitudes towards their future use of both corpora, participants who reported lacking confidence in using computers in general had a tendency to disagree with the usefulness of the general corpus for improving their English (Item 8.3, $r = .46$, $p = .0014$) and were less likely to use a general corpus in the future (Item 8.6, $r = .48$, $p = .00083$).

Several comments were observed indicating that these participants found it challenging to handle the general corpus. In particular, some reported that the number of concordances were somewhat overwhelming (e.g. "There were too many instances presented at the same time and I was confused"; "It was hard to interpret the data"). Given such results, it can be said that using general corpora may require extra training even with adult learners. This result also indicates that it is important for teacher trainers of younger learners to be aware that not everybody, even adults, can intuitively use such tools. Another possible reason may be that the language appearing in the general corpus might have been beyond some of the participants' level of English. Previous DDL research has shown the "importance of carefully selecting corpus data" (Lee et al., 2018, p. 5) for the direct use of corpora in L2 classrooms, adjusting the data to the level of the learners (Allen, 2009) rather than simply using readily available general corpora. This is particularly important when using corpora for YL teacher education with pre-service teachers who are non-native speakers of English.

The survey then addressed the participants' views regarding the use and appropriateness of DDL activities with younger learners. The majority of participants (93.3 per cent) either completely or partly disagreed with the use of the general corpus with younger learners. This is not surprising, as a number of the participants themselves commented that they found the interpretation of the output challenging in their DDL activities, even though they were convinced of the usefulness for checking English usages (cf. Table 6.1). As for the multimodal corpus, 75.6 per cent of the participants either fully or partly agreed with its usefulness for direct DDL with children. Those who agreed commented that having the audio and visual aids together with the textual data would help learners understand the contexts of what they were searching for. In addition, it was also noted that the multimodal features might support pupils who have not mastered reading skills in L1 or L2. As mentioned earlier, since the multimodal corpus includes media files which are created for a younger audience in mind, it is more likely to output samples which are relevant both in terms of levels and contexts to what the pre-service teachers may consider useful for young learners. Moreover, a multimodal approach led the participants themselves to consult the contextual clues, which is important for young learners when understanding the use and the meaning of certain lexical items. In addition, regarding the functions of the *MmCT 1.1*, some noted that the function of controlling the playback speed is helpful for young learners who may prefer to listen to the use in context at a slower speed.

Nevertheless, it is important to note that, while the majority of the participants were mostly positive about the use of the *MmCT 1.1* for YLs' DDL, 24.4 per cent selected "partly disagreed" with the direct use of the tool for this purpose. These participants mentioned:

- *"Letting young learners access and use the corpus by themselves might be difficult for them, and they might require some practice or support from teachers first."*
- *"DDL with young learners should be introduced and led by their teacher step by step as a part of in-class activity."*

- "*Young learners might have difficulties in using the tool by themselves, as the interface was displayed all in English.*"
- "*The icons should use accessible expression for children rather than using terminologies (e.g. KWIC)*"

These comments clearly indicate that some participants have reservations about the direct use of the tool with young learners as it stands. Some of them pointed out that young learners would need guidance with their DDL activity using the tool, and also indicated some ideas for future improvements of the *MmCT 1.1*, which are now discussed.

Summary and future work

Overall, the majority of participants found the positive benefits of corpora through DDL activities and were willing to incorporate corpus use into their lesson and materials preparation in the future. Participants were convinced that corpora could help them discover the main patterns of the target items and support them in clarifying their enquiries. The incorporation of DDL in teacher training also had a positive outcome on the attitude of prospective teachers, especially in terms of taking ownership of their teaching materials rather than blindly accepting the prescribed materials and teaching manuals. The survey results revealed that participants' DDL experience in comparing the use of lexical items in the official textbooks and the corpora made them realise the need to check the items and the associated contexts presented to young learners, as some expressions or usages presented in textbooks may be oversimplified and introduced in somewhat less-common or unnatural contexts. It can be argued that incorporating DDL during materials design has both served as a consciousness-raising activity – making these pre-service teachers more aware of the language they teach – and introduced the means to support their learning and teaching beyond textbooks or teaching manuals.

Generally, the participants agree that the use of a multimodal corpus is more suitable for young learners compared with that of a general corpus, which presents only textual information alone, and remarks were made in support of DDL activities with *MmCT 1.1*. Despite such positive reactions, some remaining challenges with *MmCT 1.1* were also identified. For instance, in terms of the design of the interface, it was pointed out that the functional display should be more child-friendly by using accessible icons or expressions suitable for young learners rather than using common terminologies in corpus linguistics. In addition, it was also mentioned that such functions should preferably be displayed in learners' mother tongue (i.e. Japanese) so that it is easier for the learners to work on their own after being introduced to the use of the tool.

Regarding the implementation of DDL with young learners, several participants commented that children might require training and/or assistance from the teachers. In relation to the issues of providing prior training with the use of DDL, Boulton (2009) reports that DDL with learners without any particular training can be equally as effective as when learners received training, and recent research also reports that beginning level learners also benefit from DDL (e.g. Vyatkina, 2016; Crosthwaite & Stell, this volume). However, although children are surprisingly intuitive users of digital tools in general, as suggested by the participants, extra attention may be necessary when it comes to DDL with YLs in EFL contexts. As Sinclair (2004, p. 7) suggests, "Corpus evidence is essentially indirect, which means that it cannot be taken at face value but must go through a process of interpretation". It can be easily assumed that such a process can be challenging for young EFL learners, and they may require additional support in their DDL. For this reason, as the comments show, it is important to make the interface more immediate for young learners, including its design and the language used with the tool. Moreover, as Lee et al. (2018, p. 28) point out, L2 proficiency level is one of the important factors for the effectiveness of DDL in vocabulary instruction; therefore, it is important to choose the appropriate corpus for a certain purpose. Since it is not realistic to expect young learners who are learning English as a foreign language to have the level of English proficiency to deal with DDL using existing general English corpora, the compilation of corpus data which are suitable for L2 young learners is necessary and clearly deserves more attention in future research (see Pérez-Paredes, this volume).

One of the main aims of this case study was to see whether the incorporation of DDL has a place in teacher education for TEYL. Such a suggestion is by no means new, and previous literature suggests the importance of promoting the integration of corpora within teacher education (O'Keeffe & Farr, 2003; Schaeffer-Lacroix, this volume). As reported, the overall results of the survey do bear out this view, confirming that DDL activities have contributed to raising prospective teachers' awareness towards language in use and the language presented in textbooks. Participants' willingness to use the corpora in the future was high, and the results clearly imply that participants were convinced of the general usefulness of corpora. As Kennedy (1992, p. 368) notes, "Many teachers need persuading that corpus linguistics can make a contribution to their professional activity". Judging from the results of the survey, it can be argued that the incorporation of DDL within teacher training is an effective way to introduce teachers to the value of corpora. Nevertheless, since most participants were new to corpora, it is important to continue to provide guidance and help throughout the teacher training course so that prospective teachers can be confident with its use when they become practising teachers. In addition, it is worth pointing out that being able to use corpora is different from being able to apply DDL when teaching YLs, which needs to be considered further (see Schaeffer-Lacroix, this volume, for practical examples) as it would require separate training, the compilation of appropriate corpora, and improving the quality of concordancing tools suitable for EFL young learners in order for young learners to fully appreciate the value of DDL.

Concluding remarks

This paper has attempted to highlight the need for developing multimodal concordance tools for EFL young learners given the children's increasing capacity to make sense of multimodal information in a progressively digitized world. It can be said that incorporating DDL in teacher training has proved to be useful not only in assisting prospective teachers' understanding of language features presented to young learners but also in contributing to the "popularization of corpus linguistics among teachers" (Mukherjee, 2004, p. 243). This, in effect, might lead to the increase of DDL in teaching YLs, which has yet to be appreciated widely either in the current Japanese TEYL context or elsewhere. However, the results of the case study with pre-service teachers also revealed challenges for the implementation of such an approach with YLs (e.g. child-friendly design, practical ways and methods to incorporate DDL in YLs' classrooms). It is no exaggeration to say that it would be impossible to realize the affordances of DDL for the teaching of YLs unless the YL practitioners themselves are aware and convinced of such an approach. It is therefore essential to incorporate the elements of DDL within teacher training, giving future practitioners the opportunities to appreciate the usefulness of corpora, as presented in this study. At the same time, it is important to bear in mind Bernardini's (2004, p. 32) suggestion that a "corpus-learner, and indeed corpus-teacher interaction are not replacements for learner-learner and teacher-learner interaction, but rather should be seen as an added value offered by corpus-aided discovery learning". Indeed, in order for such learning to take place for both young learners and their teachers in TEYL contexts, further development of suitable tools is a matter of great importance. Though several challenges remain, it is hoped that DDL for young EFL learners will become mainstream.

Note

1 Due to potential copyright issues, the concordances are blurred in this image.

References

Allen, R. (2009). Can a graded reader corpus provide "authentic" input?. *ELT Journal, 63*, 23–32.
Bernardini, S. (2004). Corpora in the classroom. In J. McH. Sinclair (Ed.), *How to use corpora in language teaching* (pp. 15–36). Amsterdam: John Benjamins.
Binder, M. J., Sorin, R., Nolan, J., & Chu, S. (2015). Multimodal meaning-making for young children: Partnerships through blogging. In S. Garvis & N. Lemon (Eds.), *Understanding digital technologies and young children* (pp. 92–111). Abingdon and New York: Routledge.
Boulton, A. (2009). Testing the limits of data-driven learning: Language proficiency and training, *ReCALL, 21*, 37–51.
Burnett, C., & Daniels, K. (2015). Technology and literacy in the early years: Framing young children's meaning-making with new technologies. In S. Garvis & N. Lemon (Eds.), *Understanding digital technologies and young children* (pp. 18–27). Abingdon and New York: Routledge.

Davies, M. (2008). *The Corpus of Contemporary American English (COCA): 560 million words, 1990-present.* Retrieved from https://corpus.byu.edu/coca/.

Frankenberg-Garcia, A. (2012). Learners' use of corpus examples. *International Journal of Lexicography, 25,* 273–296.

Frankenberg-Garcia, A. (2014). The use of corpus examples for language comprehension and production, *ReCALL, 26,* 128–146.

Gabrielatos, G. (2002/2003). Grammar, grammars and intuitions in ELT: A second opinion, *IATEFL Issues, 170,* 2–3.

Hassett, D. D., & Curwood, J. S. (2009). Theories and practices of multimodal education: The instructional dynamics of picture books and primary classrooms. *The Reading Teacher, 63*(4), 270–282.

Hirata, E. (2017, December). *Multimodal Corpus Tool for Young EFL learners.* Paper presented at Language Education Across Borders 2017, Graz, Austria.

Hunston, S. (1995). Grammar in teacher education: The role of a corpus, *Language Awareness, 4,* 15–31.

James, C., & Garrett, P. (Eds.). (1992). *Language awareness in the classroom.* Harlow: Longman.

Johns, T. (1991). Should you be persuaded: Two samples of data-driven learning materials, *ELR Journal, 4,* 1–16.

Kress, G. (2003). *Literacy in the new media age.* Abingdon and New York: Routledge.

Kennedy, G. (1992). Preferred ways of putting things with implications for language teaching. In J. Startvik (Ed.), *Directions in corpus linguistics: Proceedings (Nobel Symposium Proceedings)* (pp. 335–373). Berlin: Mouton de Cruyer.

Lee, H., Warschauer, M., & Lee, J. H. (2018). The effects of corpus use of second language vocabulary learning: A multilevel meta-analysis. *Applied Linguistics,* online ahead of print, March 2018.

Levy, R. (2009). "You have to understand words . . . but not to read them": Young children becoming readers in a digital age. *Journal of Research in Reading, 32*(1), 75–91.

Levy, R. (2011). *Young children reading: At home and at school.* London: Sage.

Lewis, D. (2001). *Reading contemporary picturebooks: Picturing texts.* New York: Routledge and Falmer.

Martens, P., Martens, R., Doyle, M., Loomis, J., & Aghalarov, S. (2012). Learning from picturebooks: Reading and writing multimodally in first grade. *The Reading Teacher, 66*(4), 285–294.

McEnery, T., & Wilson, A. (2001). *Corpus linguistics.* Edinburgh: Edinburgh University Press.

McPake, J., Plowman, L., & Stephen, C. (2013). Pre-school children creating and communicating with digital technologies in the home. *British Journal of Educational Technology, 44*(3), 421–431.

Mukherjee, J. (2004). Bridging the gap between applied corpus linguistics and the reality of English language teaching in Germany. In U. Connor & T. A. Upton (Eds.), *Applied corpus linguistics: A multi-dimensional perspective* (pp. 239–250). Amsterdam: Rodopi.

Muñoz, C. (2011). Is input more significant than starting age in foreign language acquisition? *International Review of Applied Linguistics, 49,* 113–133.

Parry, B., & Taylor, L. (2018). Readers in the round: Children's holistic engagements with texts. *Literacy, 52*(2), 103–110.

O'Keeffe, A., & Farr, F. (2003). Using language corpora in initial teacher education: Pedagogic issues and practical applications, *Tesol Quarterly, 37*(3), 389–418.

Römer, U. (2004). A corpus driven approach to modal auxiliaries and their didactics. In J. McH. Sinclair (Ed.), *How to use corpora in language teaching* (pp. 185–99). Amsterdam: John Benjamins.

Sealey, A., & Thompson, P. (2004). "What do you call the dull words?": Primary school children using corpus-based approaches to learn about language. *English in Education, 38*(1), 80–91.

Sinclair, J. McH. (Ed.). (2004). *How to use corpora in language teaching.* Amsterdam: John Benjamins.

Thoermer, C., & Sodian, B. (2001). Preverbal infants' understanding of referential gestures. *First Language, 21*(63), 245–264.

Vyatkina, N. (2016). Data-driven learning for beginners: The case of German verb-preposition collocations, *ReCALL, 28,* 207–226.

Wright, T., & Bolitho, R. (1993). Language awareness: A missing link in teacher education?. *ELT Journal, 47*(4), 292–304.

Yamada-Rice, D. (2011). New media, evolving multimodal literacy practices and the potential impact of increased use of the visual model in the urban environment of young children's learning. *Literacy, 45*(1): 32–43.

7

QUERY COMPLEXITY AND QUERY REFINEMENT

Using Web search from a corpus perspective with digital natives

Maristella Gatto

Introduction

Since the emergence of the notion of the "digital natives", derived from publications by Tapscott (1998) and Prensky (2001a, 2001b) and further supported by a range of other popular appropriations of the term, younger students have often been assumed to possess knowledge and skills that should allow them to handle ICT tools in a natural, fluent way. The very fact that younger people's lives appear to be saturated with digital media has led to the claim that "digital natives" (roughly identified as those born after 1980) might have developed different learning styles and behaviours in terms of abilities, preferences, attitudes, and even "productiveness" (i.e. focused attention, deep processing, and persistence) precisely as a consequence of their virtually total immersion in digital technology since early childhood and during adolescence (Thompson, 2013, p. 12). However, this assumption has not gone unchallenged. Indeed, ICT ownership and experiences and confidence with ICT devices do not necessarily imply competent use, and the overall conclusion of many recent studies is that digital natives are not necessarily ICT literates. On the contrary, it is advocated that information literacy should be explicitly enhanced with hands-on and minds-on courses (Šorgo, Bartol, Dolničar, & Boh Podgornik, 2016).

As far as Web search in particular is concerned, all models for information retrieval emphasize the dynamic nature of the search process, suggesting that users learn from their searches and that their information needs can be adjusted on the basis of retrieval results (Baeza-Yates & Ribeiro-Neto, 2011, p. 23). As suggested in Deschryver and Spiro (2009, p. 4), the ideal method of learning from the Web is an iterative search process where learners "create their own search phrases based on information they encounter on the Web". However, a tendency has been shown in digital natives towards "fast, expedient web search", which suggests that they mostly adopt a simplistic "get in, get the answer, get out" approach (Thompson, 2013, pp. 20–21). Such students may not be taking full advantage of the immense potential of Web search unless they learn to go beyond simple searches and exploit the full the affordances of search engines.

It is against this background that this chapter aims to contribute to the debate on the potential of Web searching for data-driven learning (DDL). In particular, building on existing literature on both the Web as corpus and on so-called Google-Assisted Language Learning (Chinnery, 2008; Gatto, 2009 and 2014; Eu, 2017), as well as on recent studies more specifically focused on uses of Web search in DDL (Boulton, 2015), I claim that using the Web as a corpus through ordinary search engines necessarily engages the learner in a process of progressive query refinement towards greater complexity, which can pave the way to a subsequent appreciation of dedicated corpus linguistics resources and tools. I discuss general issues concerning the learning styles of digital natives with a special focus on Web search as a pervasive paradigm in their everyday life before reconsidering key issues concerning the Web as corpus debate and the use of Web search from a corpus linguistics perspective. I then review existing literature on DDL using the Web for pedagogical purposes before reporting on a classroom experience based on the use of Web search from a DDL perspective with Italian secondary school EFL students. More specifically, the classroom experience is focused on language learning activities in which the students were asked to use the Web to gather evidence of language usage, explore phraseology, and test translation candidates. While using the Web for activities of this kind is increasingly seen as an appropriate DDL experience (Boulton, 2015), it is self-evident that the anarchy of the Web and the resulting problems in locating relevant and reliable results (Gatto, 2009) may impair the value of the experience as a whole. The study aims to show the pitfalls of a naïve use of Web search for linguistic purposes by so-called "digital natives", claiming that it is only when introduced to the principles of progressive query refinement, in which the Web is seen from the perspective of corpus linguistics, that the Web can really become the right place for a rewarding DDL experience. The basic assumption of the chapter as a whole is that, far from being naturally "fluent" users of technology, digital natives can benefit enormously by becoming familiar with basic notions of information retrieval for linguistic purposes and that using the Web as a corpus as part of DDL activities can contribute to the development of their general critical reasoning skills.

Deconstructing the myth: from digital native to digital wise?

Since Prensky's vision of younger generations as "digital natives" (2001a, 2001b), such students have been thought to have developed a distinctive set of characteristics including "preference for speed, nonlinear processing, multitasking, and social learning" (Thompson, 2013, p. 12) in a way which apparently marks a difference with that of previous generations. Indeed, as noted in Thomas (2011, p. 6), the discourse of digital natives is roughly based on three main assumptions in which younger generations are said to

1   constitute a largely homogenous generation and speak a different language vis-à-vis digital technologies, as opposed to their parents, the "Digital Immigrants";
2   learn differently from preceding generations of students; and
3   demand new ways of teaching and learning involving technology.

This characterization apparently assumes, especially in a teaching context, that younger people spontaneously know everything they need to know about technology rather than having to make the effort to learn about it. In fact, there is a correlation between confident use of digital technology and characteristics generally ascribed to digital native learners; ongoing research on such a correlation seems to suggest a less deterministic relationship between technology and learning. Recent research has shown that so-called digital natives are not necessarily information literate (Šorgo et al., 2016), while it has also been argued that parents and teachers often construct the image of their children/pupils as ICT experts (Buckingham, 2011, p. ix) without actually testing this supposed expertise. Indeed, when addressing the digital literacy skills of learners and the resulting necessary evolution of forms of pedagogy, teachers should rather be wary of adopting sharp dichotomies based on the binary logic of "natives" and "immigrants".

Prensky himself, in his contribution to the book *Deconstructing Digital Natives* (2011), considers how important it is to reflect on the way the metaphor of the "native" in the digital world has actually entered the popular imagination in ways he could "neither have imagined nor foreseen" (Prensky, 2011, p. 15). The metaphor of the native had been devised as an image for conceptualizing the differences that could be observed in the attitudes of younger and older people when faced with digital technology. While proving a useful, evocative metaphor, the image was eventually misunderstood as an "absurd claim [. . .] that if someone was born after a certain date, and was therefore included as a 'Digital Native', that person automatically knew everything there was to know about digital technology" (Prensky, 2011, p. 27). As Prensky himself maintains, "Having grown up with digital technology as toys, Digital Natives are much more at ease with its use than the generation that did not. But this surely doesn't mean they know everything, or even want to" (Prensky, 2011, p. 27). It is precisely this gap between supposed or assumed fluency and actual knowledge and competence that has made Prensky revise his concept of digital nativeness in terms of "digital wisdom" (Prensky, 2011, p. 30). Digital wisdom, according to Prensky, is a twofold concept which encompasses the "wisdom arising from the use of digital technology to access cognitive power beyond our innate capacity" and the "wisdom in the prudent use of technology to enhance our capabilities". Technology alone, he argues, "will not replace intuition, good judgment, problem-solving abilities, and a clear moral compass" (Prensky, 2011, p. 18).

It is against this complex background that views about the supposed technological fluency of digital natives are now challenged. While the use of digital technology for basic communication seems to be most common among digital natives, very few engage in more complex activities, and there seems to be evidence of a restricted range of technologies centred mostly on mobile phone features and basic Web use (e.g. sending an email or looking up information). Many so-called digital natives are no more intensive users of digital media than many adult digital immigrants, and young people's use of digital technology can be defined as "mundane rather than spectacular", i.e. characterized not by dramatic manifestations of innovation and creativity but by relatively routine forms of communication and information retrieval (Buckingham, 2011, p. x).

The Web as corpus: Web search from a corpus perspective

While it may be necessary to tone down enthusiastic claims about digital natives being *ipso facto* ICT experts, it cannot be denied that younger generations are very likely to be familiar with basic ICT activities such as Web search, which can be profitably used in language learning. Web search is ranked very high among the ICT skills which so-called digital natives are credited with (Thompson, 2013). Nonetheless, research on actual performance has shown that information-seeking behaviour by digital natives reflects "a culture of 'satisficing' decision-making that is in turn indicative of a surface approach to learning" (Kennedy & Judd, 2011, p. 240). Students often adopt a style of "fast, expedient web search, rather than a more iterative style of searching for information on the web" (Thompson, 2013, p. 21), a finding which is consistent with claims about digital natives being used to "twitch speed" (Prensky, 2001b, p. 442). This lends support to the widely held view that learners, whatever their age, might not yet be taking full advantage of the affordances of the Web for learning (Thompson, 2013). Indeed, online information seeking – performed through increasingly powerful and efficient search engines – has a great potential to support deeper learning, provided that students go beyond the simplistic "get in, get the answer, get out" approach previously mentioned.

The ideal method for learning from the Web has been described by Deschryver and Spiro (2009, p. 4) as an iterative search process, where learners

> create their own search phrases based on information they encounter on the Web, either by employing specific ideas from the current page as new search phrases, or by conceptualizing novel search phrases based on recent activity, past experience, and/or the related momentum web learning affords.

As argued in Thompson (2013), the distance between this ideal process and the "in and out" approach which seems to be common among younger learners suggests that the digital natives' supposedly innate confidence with technology needs to be complemented with explicit instruction in such skills as crafting and refining their query as well as evaluating the results in order to make effective use of the technology that surrounds their lives.

It is in this context that greater attention is being paid to the potential of Web search as a gateway to DDL and corpus linguistics. Despite obvious differences between proper corpus linguistics and using the Web as a ready-made corpus to be accessed via ordinary Web search engines (Gatto, 2009; Boulton, 2015), the Web is by now an accepted language resource with great potential as a source of evidence of attested authentic language use, and the Web can well be said to provide linguists (and learners) with "a fabulous linguists' playground" (Kilgarriff and Grefenstette, 2003, p. 345). Nonetheless, the way to treating the Web as a linguistic corpus is by no means straightforward. A comprehensive discussion of the differences between the Web as a spontaneous, self-generating collection of texts and a corpus defined as a finite-sized *body* of authentic text sampled so as to be representative of a language variety (McEnery & Wilson, 2001, p. 32) definitely falls beyond the scope of the present chapter. My own research (Gatto, 2009, 2011, 2014) has discussed a range of issues with the Web as corpus approach, including authenticity, size, representativeness, balance, and verifiability. Among them, authenticity and size have notable consequences for the potential of Web as corpus approaches and methods in the context of DDL. As the most prominent feature of the Web to have attracted linguists' attention, the Web's undisputable nature as a reservoir of authentic texts as produced in real human interactions is one of its most obvious strengths when considered as a corpus.

However, this is also one of its major flaws and the reason for being particularly cautious when using Web search for linguistic purposes. Owing to the Web's nature as an unplanned, unsupervised, unedited collection of texts, authenticity is often problematic. Everyday experience suggests that "authentic" in the Web often means "inaccurate" (misspelt words, grammar mistakes, improper usage by non-native speakers). As a consequence, it is of crucial importance that anyone purporting to look at the Web from a corpus linguistics perspective, especially for pedagogical purposes, needs to become familiar with some of its basic features so that he or she can profit from its potential without running the risk of being tangled in the Web itself.

Aside from authenticity, when frequency data obtained from the Web are to be used as evidence of attested usage, it is of fundamental importance for learners to be aware of the impact of size. In most cases, even a very large number of hits for a given query (especially for languages like English) does not necessarily imply uncontroversial validation of a hypothesis. A case in point in this respect is the example of the unusual collocation "suggestive landscapes" as discussed in Gatto (2009), where frequency data from the Web seems to provide abundant evidence of attested usage. The problem, then, concerns the correct interpretation of these results not only from a quantitative point of view (a task virtually impossible given the immeasurable nature of the Web) but also from a qualitative point of view. It requires a closer inspection into the results to probe their reliability, which – in this case – is called into question by the provenance of the results mostly from Italy or from sites referring to Italy (and possibly resulting, therefore, from a literal translation of the Italian "paesaggi suggestivi"). As a matter of fact, the number of hits for this query dramatically drops when resorting to the options "Pages in English" and "Pages from the UK", which retrieve only English pages coming from the United Kingdom.

Two more crucial issues among those discussed in the Web as corpus literature deserve special attention in this context, namely relevance and reliability (Lüdeling, Evert, & Baroni, 2007; Gatto, 2009), which relate to two aspects referred to in information retrieval as precision and recall. Any linguistic search carried out by means of specific software tools on a traditional corpus of finite size (such as the BNC) would report "only" results exactly matching the query (precision) and "all" the results matching the query (recall), while this is patently not so with the Web. This can be exemplified by a search aimed at evaluating "onset site" as a translation equivalent for "sede di insorgenza" to be used in a medical text about cancer, as discussed in Gatto (2011). By searching the exact phrase "onset site", the results returned by the search engine would provide a generic quantitative indication about its frequency of occurrence in the Web, which roughly gives an indication of appropriateness. In order to increase the relevance of the results to the domain of interest, one might include the word "cancer" in the query so as to retrieve only texts having the word "cancer" somewhere on the page and therefore more likely to be addressing this specific topic. The lower number of matches for the query *"onset site" cancer* when compared to *"site of onset" cancer* suggests that "onset site" may not be the preferred wording in this context. Moreover, it should be noted that most of the occurrences reported for the query *"onset site" cancer* feature the two nouns *onset* and *site* separated by punctuation marks (generally a comma), which suggests that these results cannot be considered as evidence of attested usage for the noun phrase "onset site" in this specific context. At this stage, further restriction of the query to a known domain such as a portal for the online distribution of scientific journals (e.g. Elsevier or Pubmed) or even Google Books can be attempted in order to boost the reliability of the results. This finally confirms the inappropriateness of "onset site" in this context, while the alternative search for *"site of onset" cancer* within the same restricted domains still produces a significant number of matches, all to be considered relevant and reliable. This example reveals that even the apparently trivial task of searching the Web for evidence of usage poses specific problems for the researcher which require that cautionary procedures are adopted both in the interpretation of the results and in submitting the query to the search engine.

More precisely, it can be argued that the query is the place where the practice of Web search meets a linguistically oriented approach to the Web as a corpus. Indeed, using the Web as a linguistic resource can be viewed as a specific case of information retrieval. The classic model, as reported in Baeza-Yates & Ribeiro-Neto (2011, p. 23ff), is formulated as a cycle consisting of four main activities:

- problem identification
- articulation of information need(s)
- query formulation
- results evaluation

Given the dynamic nature of the search process it is also stressed that users learn from their search and that their information needs can be adjusted as they see retrieval results (Baeza-Yates & Robeiro-Neto, 2011, p. 23). Using the Web as a corpus through ordinary search engines therefore engages the user in a process of progressive query refinement towards greater complexity which can only be supported by greater familiarity with the advanced search options provided by most search engines. As the examples provided have shown, each operator in advanced Web search can be interpreted from a corpus linguistics perspective. Thus, while a search for a single word can be compared to the creation of a sort of sub-corpus (made up of all the pages and only the pages containing that word), the search for phrases, possibly combined with the use of wildcards, can represent the search for collocates or patterns. Finally, language, URL, and domain restrictions, or searches in specific subsections of the Web, can each indirectly be read in terms of constraints at the level of geographical variation, register, and genre (Gatto, 2009, pp. 71–77). It is therefore only through a process of progressive query refinement towards greater complexity that the common practice of Web search and the linguist's approach to the Web as a corpus most fruitfully interact.

Using Web search in data-driven learning

Despite some *caveats*, the practice of using the Web as a corpus through ordinary search engines has received great attention in the context of Computer Aided Language Learning (Shei, 2008; Wu *et al.*, 2009; Sha, 2010; Geluso, 2011), sometimes even labelled as Google Assisted Language Learning (Chinnery, 2008). In all these studies, while the limitations of the Web as a source of language data are invariably acknowledged, its usefulness as a ready-made source of authentic language available at the click of a mouse button is undisputed, especially when one is to test personal intuitions about language use on the basis of existing data. Thanks to its nature as a low tech, low-cost, and ubiquitously available option, the Web often represents an immediate source of corpus-like linguistic information which makes it a perfect choice in teaching contexts at any level whenever there are limitations for the introduction of more traditional forms of DDL. Indeed, while attempts have been made over the past few years at making tools and resources more and more accessible – both in terms of availability for free and in terms of user-friendliness – barriers still exist that prevent a breakthrough of DDL in the classroom (Boulton, 2015, p. 267; Schaeffer-Lacroix, this volume). To say the least, corpus-based data-driven learning activities still require some comfort and confidence with the technology by teachers and students alike, which cannot always be taken for granted. By contrast, using the Web as a corpus surrogate (Baroni & Bernardini, 2006) with search engines as surrogate concordancers seems to provide a valuable opportunity to explore the undeniable de facto intersection between Web search as a common everyday practice and linguistically oriented Web search informed by the corpus linguistics approach (Gatto, 2009; Boulton, 2015). It cannot be denied in fact that the very act of searching the Web via an ordinary search engine and reading vertically through the results, as it typically happens even in the simplest Web search, is strikingly similar to what happens when searching a corpus through a concordancer. Furthermore, the results page resembles a concordance list, where the search item is highlighted within a small amount of cotext, even though this is by no means the same format as the Key Word in Context (KWIC) typical of linguistically oriented tools. It is as if reading "vertically" and "fragmented", looking for "repeated events", which Tognini Bonelli singles out as features that set apart the act of reading through a corpus from the common act of reading a text (2001, p. 3), is now everyday experience for people beyond the corpus linguistics community, including younger learners. Furthermore, as convincingly argued in Boulton (2015, p. 268), it should be borne in mind that DDL does not necessarily rely essentially on a corpus as it is generally understood in corpus linguistics: What is important is that the language should be pedagogically relevant (cf. Braun, 2005) and that the learner should engage directly with the data rather than relying on the teacher as intermediary (Boulton, 2015, p. 267).

As a matter of fact, many students acknowledge using the Web for linguistic purposes in many different ways. However, when it comes to using the Web as source of attested usage, they eventually display a limited awareness of the real workings of a search engine, which is fundamental knowledge if one is to avoid the common pitfalls and fully exploit the Web's potential. Certainly, search engines are designed neither for linguistic purposes nor for data-driven learning, as they aim, in fact, to meet a variety of other needs. Furthermore, it should be observed that the very strategies that enhance the effectiveness of search engines for general purposes, such as normalization of spelling and lemmatization or the inclusion of synonyms in the results, might fight against precision in a linguistically oriented Web search. And still, these limitations are only the tip of the iceberg. Today it should also be stressed that search engines are engaged in an unprecedented effort to shift the original query-based retrieval algorithm, in which the search engine's task was to find items exactly matching the query, into a context-driven information supply algorithm whose aim is to provide information that is supposed to be of interest to the user on the basis of elements not necessarily contained in the query itself (Broder, 2006; Gatto, 2014). It would be therefore an oversimplification to think that the problem posed by search engines for data-driven learning is that they are not designed for linguists and that they are geared "only" towards the retrieval of general information from the Web. The real problem is that the very needs which search engines address are constantly evolving, and next-generation search engines do not simply "passively" retrieve the information required but rather "actively" supply (unsolicited and often commercial) information in the form of banner ads or sponsored links and through algorithms aimed at behavioural and contextual targeting (Levene, 2010, p. 152 ff.). These new algorithms clearly tend towards strong customization of the results, creating a "filter bubble" (Parser, 2011) around each individual user, without the user even being aware of what is happening. This is the reason why most general-purpose Web search is now extremely effective and generally successful, even without particular effort on the searcher's part. In contrast, linguistically oriented Web search, which is quintessentially informational, needs to be grounded on greater awareness of both the nature of the Web as a surrogate corpus and of the real workings of search engines as surrogate corpus tools. Hence, a deeper knowledge of advanced Web search options has long been advocated as the only way to profitably use the Web as a corpus especially for DDL.

Among the various operators – such as inclusion/exclusion of context words to limit irrelevant hits for polysemous words; restriction by language, file type, and domain (e.g.. ac,. uk, or. edu for UK and American academic websites); and provenance of the results – the phrase search has been often singled out as a good starting point for entry into the Web as corpus, in particular by Maniez (2007), Shei (2008), Acar et al. (2011), and Geluso (2011). The next section focuses on the phrase search as a useful first strategy for younger learners negotiating the data-driven validation of collocates and for testing translation candidates through increasingly complex and refined queries.

Query complexity and query refinement: a classroom experience with digital natives

The approach to DDL used for this experience was mostly derived from research on the Web as corpus, with a special focus on the use of frequency data from the Web as evidence of attested usage for the validation of collocations and translation candidates. Before describing the methodology and discussing the results, it is indeed important to stress once again that one of the goals of the present study, as discussed especially in Section 1, was to show that ICT fluency is often more assumed than tested with specific reference, in this case, to Web search skills. The activities were accordingly designed so as to increase the students' awareness of the fact that a superficial, "satisficing" approach to Web search might lead to incorrect assumptions about the search results. On the contrary, by carefully refining their queries through inductive reasoning, the students could achieve the best results and – by doing so – have a rewarding experience in data-driven learning.

Participants

The school experience reported in this section involved a group of 15- to 17-year-old EFL students (12 male, ten female) from a scientific high school in Bari, in the South of Italy.[1] All students had been studying English as a foreign language at school for 5 to 7 years. This does not count English language learning in primary school, as this tends to be highly varied in Italy in terms of goals and standards and does not take into account any private language courses the students may have individually attended. Their L2 level was determined to be between A2 and B1 on average, as is typical in secondary schools in Italy. None of them had had previous experience with corpora or other forms of data-driven learning.

Procedure

Since it is not always easy to arrange a visit to pre-tertiary schools, even for research purposes, an English language teacher (Prof. Francesca Palumbo) acted as a "mediator" and "supervisor" as students were invited to perform specific tasks through a written assignment which I had designed for them (see Appendix). The set of activities proposed to the group of students was introduced with a note disclosing (very briefly and explained in simple terms) basic key concepts concerning quantitative evidence in empirical approaches to the study of languages. Using everyday examples (e.g. which is more common between "heavy rain" and "thick rain"), the students were invited to consider frequency of occurrence on the Web as a parameter to make an informed decision when in doubt about alternative wordings for similar concepts. Subsequently, the students filled in an online feedback questionnaire on the activities.

The methodology adopted was basically an inductive one. Rather than giving the students instructions about the potential of Web search for linguistic purposes according to the principles discussed in previous sections of this chapter, the students were faced with problems to be solved and were only later introduced to very basic Web search tips from a corpus linguistics perspective. The aim was indeed not so much to instruct them in the first place but to reveal shortcomings in their expedient approach to Web search and arouse interest in the potential of query refinement. Indeed, when asked whether they considered themselves well-equipped in terms of Web search strategy and whether they considered themselves capable of using Web search to find solutions to language questions, they all seemed to be very confident, as exemplified by the following sample for responses to Question 2 of the survey:

Would you be able to use web search to find a solution to problems concerning language use?
Yes, I would because I always use online dictionaries
Yes, I would because I often use the Internet to study.
Yes, I would because on the Internet there are a lot of examples
Yes, I would because it's so easy

Answers of this kind suggest not only that the group of students felt completely at ease with the task at hand and that introducing tasks based on Web search would not be problematic but also – significantly – that they were probably expecting nothing new from this experience. It is against this background that the classroom activities were designed, in the first place, as a way to "defamiliarize" Web search by showing how much is taken for granted – which, in fact, needs a more reflexive approach.

Warming up: calibrating the instrument

In its most basic form, using the Web as a source of evidence of attested usage can entail a simple search for a single word. A patently simplistic use of the Web for data-driven learning, searching for a single word is not devoid of interesting implications and provides a good starting point for exploring the potential

> 1) Warming up
>
> In this experience we are going to use the web as a tool for "measuring" language use. As is the case with many other tools for measuring things, we need first of all to 'calibrate' the measuring instrument, to see whether and to what extent it is accurate. More specifically, we are going to test the web for accuracy when providing quantitative evidence of attested usage.
>
> - Search the web for a number of commonly mis-spelt words (e.g. accomodation, beautifull, independant, unforseen...). How many hits have you found for each of them? How many hits for the correct spelling? What are the implications of this simple experience, as to the reliability of the web as a linguistic resource?
>
> Fill in a table with your results:
>
> | QUERY Wrong | # of hits | QUERY Correct | # of hits |
> | --- | --- | --- | --- |
> | accomodation | | accommodation | |
> | beautifull | | beautiful | |
> | independant | | independent | |
> | unforseen | | unforeseen | |

FIGURE 7.1 Section "Warming up" from the worksheet (See Appendix)

and limitations of the Web as a source of quantitative and qualitative data with students. It is in fact of crucial importance for anyone wishing to use the Web as a linguistic resource to be aware of the relative importance of quantitative data elicited from the Web. A case in point is spell-checking, which can be used as one of the most appropriate examples to show how misleading Web search can be. Considering that younger people tend to see the Web as a new *ipse dixit* whose reliability is not called into question, the warming-up phase in our virtual teaching unit was devoted to what has been termed "calibrating the instrument" (e.g. Figure 7.1).

When faced with the results of a Web search for misspelt words and their correct counterparts, which inevitably laid bare the extent to which the Web is also a repository for incorrect information (one needs only to consider the impact of such results as 86,100,000 versus 1,650,000,000 hits for *independant* vs *independent*), the students were shocked. How could the Web be used to find reliable answers to language questions when there was so much "noise" in it? This is what they were led to discover through the following activities.

Task 1 – evidence of attested usage for collocations

Being aware of "noise" in the Web is a good starting point for students to be engaged in DDL using the Web as corpus. This will give them a clue about the importance of devising a more refined and complex query to obtain the best results. Furthermore, it will make them more cautious in handling quantitative data as they become aware of how much that is patently "wrong" can be found online. Starting from these premises, the first activity was focused on collocation and was designed to introduce the students to the use of inverted commas to search for exact phrases. As discussed in literature on the Web as corpus (Gatto, 2009, pp. 59–65), using the Web to validate collocations can be a really rewarding experience, provided that the query is appropriate to the task. Now, again, rather than starting from explicit instructions, the students were invited to search the Web on the basis of their supposed skills as digital natives. The question concerned the evaluation of "big", "heavy", and "strong" as collocates for "smoker". The students were invited to answer this question on the basis of intuition and compare their hypothesis with information retrieved from the Web. Nine students out of 22 rightly indicated "heavy smoker" as the most appropriate collocation on the basis of their previous knowledge. However, when asked to support their answer on the basis of quantitative evidence form the Web, they were surprised, as the most frequent collocation seemed to be "big smoker". Indeed, none of the students were aware of the possibility of using inverted commas to search the Web for exact phrases, so they were faced with irrelevant results from the point of view of collocation, with "big smoker" and "strong smoker" finding more matches than the target collocation "heavy smoker".

As already argued, the methodology favoured an inductive approach. Not introducing advanced Web search tips before the task but only later was therefore functional to the goals of the study. Firstly, it demonstrated how naïve the approach to Web search is by so-called digital natives; secondly, it stimulated in

---

Which adjective among "big", "heavy", and "strong" would you consider most appropriate in the collocation with "smoker"?

☐ BIG SMOKER   ☐ HEAVY SMOKER   X ☐ STRONG SMOKER

Now use the web to support your answer:

QUERY	# of hits	
big smoker	132.000.000	
heavy smoker	38.200.000	
strong smoker	68.500.000	

TIP: use inverted commas to search for exact phrases

QUERY	# of hits	
"big smoker"	64.900	
"heavy smoker"	10.600.000	
"strong smoker"	15.400	

FIGURE 7.2 Section "Evidence of attested usage for collocation" from the worksheet (completed by one student).

the students an interest for advanced Web search tips through practice rather than on a purely theoretical basis. It goes without saying that experiences like this could be the gateway for a discussion of more complex issues concerning collocations, which younger learners would probably better understand after having had the possibility of appreciating it, so to speak, "hands-on".

Task 2 – testing translation candidates

Building on this task and taking "heavy rain" versus "thick rain" as translation candidates for the Italian "pioggia fitta" (literally "thick rain") as a new example, it was easy for our students to compare the frequency of occurrence of the two alternatives on the Web (see Exercise 3 in the Appendix). The students noticed that "thick rain" was fairly frequent on the Web, with 89,800 hits, though less frequent than "heavy rain". The problem was then how to interpret these results. Should the not negligible number of matches for "thick rain" be considered nonetheless as clear evidence of attested usage, or did it instead provide support to claims about the total unreliability of Web frequency data as a source of linguistic information (especially if the hits for "thick rain" are compared to the 34,100,000 hits for "heavy rain")? It was hard to provide an answer to a question like this since language itself constantly changes and what is untypical today might become the standard of tomorrow.

Furthermore, this example opened the door to more consideration concerning the potential unreliability of quantitative data elicited from the Web on a different level. In fact, one student observed that "Heavy Rain" is the name of a popular videogame, so the number of hits for this phrase was certainly inflated for this reason. This provided an opportunity to test the role of the minus sign to discard undesired results and to design a new query: *"heavy rain" -videogame*. Reference to the videogame also suggested that the results retrieved for a query like *"heavy rain"* could not necessarily contain only pages from the UK and in English, which paved the way for an introduction to advanced Web search parameters such as language and provenance of the query. Eventually, the more complex query submitted through the advanced search interface for the exact phrase "heavy rain" without the word "videogame", retrieving results only in English and from the UK, resulted in only 2,750,000 results, which still outnumbered the results for "thick rain".

This task was used as a gateway to proper data-driven learning using traditional corpora. Faced with uncertainties about the results obtained from the Web, the students appreciated the opportunity to query a more reliable resource for evidence of attested usage. Following a simple but detailed description on how to access the BNC through Mark Davies's Corpora (see Follow-up section in the Appendix), the students were asked to search the BNC for the two phrases to see which one was more frequent. The results provided by the BNC seemed to be indisputable: over 200 occurrences for "heavy rain" and only two for "thick rain", one of which was part of the phrase "thick rain forest". The difference between the Web as an anarchic though useful resource and a real corpus had been made clear.

Task 3 – query refinement in CLIL activities

Having introduced the students to some basic strategies for using the Web as a source of evidence of attested usage, thus improving their search skills, attention shifted to the importance of producing more complex queries so as to enhance the relevance and reliability of the results retrieved (as discussed in Gatto, 2014, pp. 69–70). This was done with reference to CLIL activities, where Italian students are asked to use English as a vehicular language for other subjects (e.g. physics). A case in point was the search for the most appropriate wording for the concept of *momentum* in physics, as reported in the following task.

In this case the students were already familiar with exact phrase match and all of them searched the Web accordingly. The results seemed to suggest that the most frequent phrases were "quantity of movement" and "quantity of motion". However, doubt was instilled in the students' minds as to the relevance of these results to the domain of physics, leading to the second part of this task:

Again, the results were daunting, and the students were enthusiastic about the impact that refining their query had had on the relevance and reliability of the results. In particular, a search restricted to Google Books forced them to consider other criteria besides frequency alone. Going back to the initial task, i.e. the validation on the phrase "motion quantity", the fact that it seemed to be attested and

---

In a paper by a schoolmate you read the following sentence:

Momentum, the motion quantity of a body, is given by the product of its mass and velocity.

Do you think that "motion quantity" is appropriate here? Can you use web search to support your opinion?

Consider alternative wordings. Can you use the web to find out which of the following, if any, is more appropriate in physics?

- motion quantity
- quantity of motion
- movement quantity
- quantity of movement

Take note of your queries and of the results you find (add lines if you need):

QUERY	N of hits	Notes

FIGURE 7.3 CLIC activity on alternative wordings for the same concept (see Exercise 4 in the Appendix)

> Was it easy to find an answer on the basis of the number of hits for your query? Are you satisfied with you results?
>
> If you haven't done so, repeat this exercise putting each phrase in inverted commas ("motion quantity", "quantity of motion", and so on) and adding the word *physics* to your search. This will increase the relevance of the results you get to the domain of physics, by including in the results only pages which also mention physics, which is what you are interested in:
>
> e.g. "motion quantity" physics
>
> Does the number of hits you get change?
>
> Finally you can restrict your query to "Google Scholar" or "Google Books", to increase the reliability of the results. Report your data in the following table and comment.
>
> | QUERY (Google Books) | N of hits | Notes |
> |---|---|---|
> | "motion quantity" physics | | |
> | "movement quantity" physics | | |
> | "quantity of motion" physics | | |
> | "quantity of movement" physics | | |
>
> Do these results validate or invalidate previous results? Comment.

FIGURE 7.4 Exercise on query refinement (see Exercise 4 in the Appendix)

validated in published books posed a new question: Could "motion quantity" still be considered a useful variant for the most frequent form, "quantity of motion"? At this stage, new qualitative criteria entered into play as the students realized that most of the results for the query "*motion quantity*" could not be considered as reliable evidence of attested usage, simply because they did not refer to the phrase "motion quantity" but were merely the result of spatial proximity of the words, often separated by a comma or some other punctuation mark, and not part of the same phrase (see Figure 7.4).

Conclusion

This chapter started with a reflection on the nature of younger learners as "digital natives" and eventually welcomed the revised version of this same concept by Prensky himself in terms of "digital wisdom" as a better way to address the relationship between younger learners and technology, which plays a key role in DDL. Digital wisdom is not just a matter of being clever in manipulating technology but rather entails "making wiser decisions because one is enhanced by technology". This means, in turn, one may rely on intuition, but let intuition be "informed, inspired, and supported by digital enhancements and by the additional

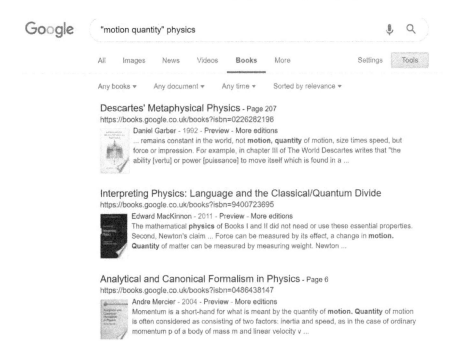

FIGURE 7.5 Search for "motion quantity" in Google Books

data digital tools provide" (Prensky, 2009, p. 26). The reported examples in this chapter suggest that using the Web as a corpus for DDL can positively contribute to this process. By learning how to use advanced Web search, students can query the Web in a more effective way in order to support intuition with data so as to find data-driven solutions to problems concerning language usage. Furthermore, using the Web as a corpus forces them into a process of progressive query refinement where each operator in an advanced Web search can be reinterpreted from a corpus linguistics perspective. This can, in the long term, trigger an interest in corpus linguistics and pave the way towards a competent use of proper corpus query tools, thus representing a potential gateway to all other forms of DDL.

Note

1 The school involved is Liceo Scientifico "G. Salvemini" (Bari, Italy). The author wishes to express her gratitude to Prof. Francesca Palumbo for her invaluable support and to all the students who took part in the project.

References

Baeza-Yates R., & Ribeiro-Neto, B. (2011). *Modern information retrieval*. Boston, MA: Addison-Wesley.

Baroni, M., & Bernardini, S. (2006). *Wacky! Working papers on the web as corpus.* Bologna: Gedit.
Boulton, A. (2015). Applying data-driven learning to the web. In A. Leńko-Szymańska & A. Boulton (Eds.), *Multiple affordances of language corpora for data-driven learning.* (pp. 267–329). Amsterdam: John Benjamins.
Braun, S. (2005). From pedagogically relevant corpora to authentic language learning contents. *ReCALL, 17*(1), 47–64.
Broder, A. (2006). *From query based Information Retrieval to context driven Information Supply.* Workshop on The Future of Web Search, Barcelona, 19–20 May 2006. Retrieved from http://videolectures.net/fws06_broder_qbirc/ (accessed 07 July 2019).
Buckingham, D. (2011). Technology, education, and the discourse of the digital native: Between evangelists and dissenters. In M. Thomas (Ed.), *Deconstructing digital natives* (pp. IX–XI). New York: Routledge.
Chinnery, M. G. (2008). 'You've got some GALL': Google-assisted language learning. *Language Learning & Technology, 12* (1), 3–11.
Deschryver, M., & Spiro, R. (2009). New forms of deep learning on the web. In Zheng (Ed.), *Cognitive effects of multimedia learning* (pp. 134–152). New York: IGI Global.
Eu, J. (2017). Patterns of google use in language reference and learning: A user survey. *Journal of Computers in Education, 4*(4), 419–439.
Gatto, M. (2009). *From body to web: An introduction to the web as corpus.* Roma – Bari: Editori Laterza University Press (available online).
Gatto, M. (2011). The body and the web: The web as corpus ten years on. *ICAME Journal, 35,* 35–58.
Gatto, M. (2014). *The web as corpus: Theory and practice.* London: Bloomsbury.
Geluso, J. (2011). Phraseology and frequency of occurrence on the web: Native speakers' perceptions of google-informed second language writing. *Computer Assisted Language Learning, 26*(2), 144–157.
Kennedy, G. E., & Judd, T. S. (2011). Beyond google and the "Satisficing" searching of digital natives. In M. Thomas (Ed.), *Deconstructing digital natives* (pp. 119–135). New York: Routledge.
Kilgarriff, A., & Grefenstette, G. (2003). Introduction to the special issue on the web as corpus. *Computational Linguistics, 29*(3), 333–347.
Levene, M. (2010). *An introduction to search engines and web navigation.* Hoboken, NJ: John Wiley & Sons.
Lüdeling, A., Evert, S., & Baroni, M. (2007). Using web data for linguistic purposes. In M. Hundt et al. (Eds.), *Corpus linguistics and the web* (pp. 7–24). Amsterdam: Rodopi.
Maniez, F. (2007). Using the web and computer corpora as language resources for the translation of complex noun phrases in medical research articles. *Panace@: Revista de Medicina, Lenguaje y Traducción, 9*(26), 162–167.
McEnery, T., & Wilson, A. (2001). *Corpus linguistics.* Edinburgh: Edinburgh University Press.
Parser, E. (2011). *The filter bubble: How the new personalized web is changing what we read and how we think.* New York: Penguin Group USA.
Prensky, M. (2001a). Digital natives, digital immigrants. *On the Horizon, 9*(5), 1–6.
Prensky, M. (2001b). Digital natives, digital immigrants, Part II: Do they really think differently? *On the Horizon, 9*(6), 1–6.
Prensky, M. (2009). Homo sapiens digital: From digital immigrants and digital natives to digital wisdom. *Innovate, 5*(3).
Prensky, M. (2011). Digital wisdom and homo sapiens digital. In M. Thomas (Ed.), *Deconstructing digital natives* (pp. 25–35). New York: Routledge.

Sha, G. (2010). Using google as a super corpus to drive written language learning: A comparison with the British national corpus. *Computer Assisted Language Learning, 23*(5), 377–393.

Shei, C. C. (2008). Discovering the hidden treasure on the internet: Using google to uncover the veil of phraseology. *Computer Assisted Language Learning, 21*(1), 67–85.

Šorgo, A., Bartol, T., Dolnicar, V., & Boh Podgornik, B. (2016). Attributes of digital natives as predictors of information literacy in higher education: Digital natives and information literacy. *British Journal of Educational Technology, 48*(3), 749–767.

Tapscott, D. (1998). *Grown up digital: The rise of the net generation.* New York: McGraw-Hill.

Thomas, M. (Ed.). (2011). *Deconstructing digital natives.* New York: Routledge.

Thompson, P. (2013). The digital natives as learners: Technology use patterns and approaches to learning. *Computers & Education, 65*, 12–33.

Tognini Bonelli, E. (2001). *Corpus linguistics at work.* Amsterdam: Benjamin.

Wu, S., Franken, M., & Witten, I. (2009). Refining the use of the web (and Web search) as a language teaching and learning resource. *International Journal of Computer Assisted Language Learning, 22*(3), 247–265.

APPENDIX

QUERY COMPLEXITY AND QUERY REFINEMENT: USING WEB SEARCH FROM A CORPUS PERSPECTIVE WITH DIGITAL NATIVES

1) *Warming up. Calibrating the instrument*

In this experience we are going to use the web as a tool for "measuring" language use. As is the case with many other tools for measuring things, we need first of all to 'calibrate' the measuring instrument, to see whether and to what extent it is accurate. More specifically, we are going to test the web for accuracy when providing quantitative evidence of attested usage.

- Search the web for a number of commonly mis-spelt words (e.g. accomodation, beautifull, independant, unforseen. . .). How many hits have you found for each of them? How many hits for the correct spelling? What are the implications of this simple experience, as to the reliability of the web as a linguistic resource?

  Fill in the table with your result:

QUERY Wrong	# of hits	QUERY Correct	# of hits
accomodation		accommodation	
beautifull		Beautiful	
independant		Independent	
unforseen		Unforeseen	

2) Evidence of attested usage for collocation

- Which adjective among "big", "heavy", and "strong" would you consider most appropriate in the collocation with "smoker"?

  ☐ BIG SMOKER   ☐ HEAVY SMOKER   ☐ STRONG SMOKER

  Now use the web to support your answer:

QUERY	# of hits
big smoker	
heavy smoker	
strong smoker	

  TIP: use inverted commas to search for exact phrases

QUERY	# of hits
"big smoker"	
"heavy smoker"	
"strong smoker"	

  Does anything change in the results? What? Comment.

3) Testing translation candidates

As seen in the warming up exercise, it is extremely important, when using web to search for evidence of language use, to be aware of the fact that web can retrieve an extremely high number of matches even for wrong spelling or unusual word pairs.

Nonetheless there are many situation in which web search can be profitably to find evidence of attested usage for phrases in both general and scientific English.

Consider the following situations:

- You are writing a text in English for your L2 class and you have doubts about using "thick rain" or "heavy rain" as an equivalent for the Italian "pioggia fitta". Which would you opt for on the basis of your intuition and/or previous knowledge? Is your bilingual/monolingual dictionary of any help?

  Intuition: ☐ THICK RAIN   ☐ HEAVY RAIN
  Dictionary: ☐ THICK RAIN   ☐ HEAVY RAIN

  Would you be able to use the Internet to support your decision?

Take note of your queries and of the results you find (add lines if you need):

QUERY	N of hits	Notes

If you haven't done so before, repeat your search putting the search string in inverted commas. In this way the search engine will return result for the exact phrase "heavy rain" or "thick rain". Has anything changed?

Click here to try a search for the exact phrase "thick rain"

Click here to try a search for the exact phrase "heavy rain"

If you want, comment on the results:

_____

_____

_____

_____

_____

- You are going to use the phrase *the key for success*, but you are not sure about it. Search the Internet or evidence of usage: what do the results suggest?

QUERY	# of hits
"the key for success"	

Now repeat your query using an asterisk instead of the preposition you are unsure about:

QUERY	# of hits
"the key * success"	

Do the results suggest any alternative? You will probably see many examples featuring "to *success*" instead of "*for success*". Now try the following and make your final decision:

QUERY	# of hits
"the key to success"	

4) Query refinement and CLIL activities

- Your Italian maths teacher has introduced you to the geometry of the so-called "anello di Moebius". You need to describe the experiment in English for your CLIL class.

  Which term is more frequent/correct among the following alternatives?

  Moebius ring

  Moebius strip

  Moebius band

  Take note of your queries and of the results you find (add lines if you need):

QUERY	N of hits	Notes

  Was it easy to find an answer? Are you satisfied with you results?

  In a paper by a schoolmate you read the following sentence:

  *Momentum, the **motion quantity** of a body, is given by the product of its mass and velocity.*

  Do you think that "motion quantity" is appropriate here? Can you use web search to support your opinion?

  Consider alternative wordings. Can you use the web to find out which of the following, if any, is more appropriate in physics?

  - motion quantity
  - quantity of motion
  - movement quantity
  - quantity of movement

  Take note of your queries and of the results you find (add lines if you need):

QUERY	N of hits	Notes

  Was it easy to find an answer on the basis of the number of hits for your query? Are you satisfied with you results?

If you haven't done so, repeat this exercise putting each phrase in inverted commas ("motion quantity", "quantity of motion", and so on) and adding the word *physics* to your search. This will increase the relevance of the results you get to the domain of physics, by including in the results only pages which also mention physics, which is what you are interested in:

e.g. "motion quantity" physics

Does the number of hits you get change?

Finally you can restrict your query to "Google Scholar" or "Google Books", to increase the reliability of the results. Report your data in the following table and comment.

QUERY (Google Books)	N of hits	Notes
"motion quantity" physics		
"movement quantity" physics		
"quantity of motion" physics		
"quantity of movement" physics		

Do these results validate or invalidate previous results? Comment.

FOLLOW UP

In contemporary linguistics, a corpus is a textual archive that can be queried to retrieve information about language use. For instance, the British National Corpus (BNC) contains texts of every type and genre, covering a moltitude of domains, amounting to 100.000.000 words. It can be queried to see how certain words are used in context. It is especially useful to investigate collocations. i.e. to explore word pairs, to see which wording is more common, as in the case of "thick rain" or "heavy rain".

In the following exercise will enter the BNC to check which of the two collocations, of "thick rain" or "heavy rain" is attested in this corpus:

Go to http://corpus.byu.edu/bnc/ and try the following exercises:

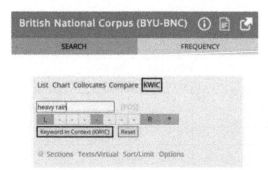

➢ HEAVY vs THICK RAIN
Under "SEARCH" click on "KWIC" and type *heavy rain* in the search box. Then click on "Keyword in Context (KWIC)". This search will retrieve results for the exact phrase *heavy rain*. How many hits have you found?

• Now type *thick rain* and consider the results you retrieve. What do they suggest? Do they confirm the results you got with your previous web search?

➢ KEY TO/FOR SUCCESS
Under "SEARCH" click on "KWIC" and type *key to success* in the search box. Then click on "Keyword in Context (KWIC)". How many hits have you found?

• Now type *key for success* and consider the results you retrieve. What do they suggest? Do they confirm the results you got with your previous web search?
• You can also try *key for the success*. Which word typically follows the pattern "the key to the success"? What do the results for this query suggest?

➢ Under "SEARCH" click on "KWIC" and type *Moebius* in the search box. Then click on "Keyword in Context (KWIC)". How many hits have you found? Which word typically follows Moebius – band, ring or strip?

PART III

Infusing DDL into practice – new empirical findings from younger learners

8
EFFECTS OF DATA-DRIVEN LEARNING ON ENHANCING THE PHRASEOLOGICAL KNOWLEDGE OF SECONDARY SCHOOL LEARNERS OF L2 ENGLISH

Paweł Szudarski

Introduction

Data-driven learning (DDL) is broadly defined as the use of corpus data in language teaching. It is an inductive approach based on the view that second language (L2) learners should be encouraged to use corpus data and immerse themselves in the analysis of naturally occurring language. Being an alternative to traditional teacher-led instruction, DDL gives learners direct access to corpus material either on computer screens or via printed handouts and emphasizes the role of self-discovery and more autonomous learning as a way of enhancing the process of second language acquisition (SLA).

While corpus-assisted language pedagogy is still a relatively new area of empirical work, the growing availability of open-access corpora and Web-based interfaces in recent years has resulted in the popularization of DDL. A good testament to this are two recent meta-analyses conducted by Lee, Warschauer, and Lee (2018) and Boulton and Cobb (2017), which offer convincing evidence in favour of using the techniques of corpus linguistics for L2 learning. The former reports an overall positive, medium-sized effect of corpus application on the short- and long-term learning of L2 vocabulary, while the latter, encompassing a variety of linguistic features and students from different learning contexts, shows that "DDL works pretty well in almost any context where it has been extensively tried" (Boulton & Cobb, 2017, p. 386). Importantly, Boulton and Cobb's analysis demonstrates that, while corpus-based treatments have been successfully employed to target a range of language points such as grammatical items (e.g. Moon & Oh, 2018) or writing skills (e.g. Charles, 2012), they are particularly effective in teaching L2 vocabulary, lexicogrammar, and phraseological patterning. However, most of this research has been conducted with older, university-level students who represent higher levels of L2 proficiency. With the use of DDL by younger, lower-level learners being the main focus of this chapter, what follows is a brief discussion of a selection of relevant studies from this area.

DDL and lower-level learners

As highlighted throughout this volume, the proponents of DDL emphasize a number of benefits associated with the integration of corpus work into formal language teaching. These include, among others, providing authentic examples, helping learners develop analytical and problem-solving skills, and promoting their autonomy (Vyatkina & Boulton, 2017). In practical terms, this means that in DDL learners are encouraged to adopt the role of language detectives (Johns, 1997), that is, engage in exploratory activities and discover language intricacies by themselves.

However, while potentially beneficial in many respects, the implementation of DDL may also present certain challenges, including issues such as explaining to learners the value of corpus analysis, familiarizing them with the format of data and corpus searches, and selecting which linguistic features to focus on (see Gilquin & Granger, 2010 for details). By way of example, research into perceptions of DDL has pointed to problems such as learners' difficulties in focusing on phraseological units when their understanding of individual words is limited (Granger & Meunier, 2008) or corpus consultation being seen as too time-consuming (Yoon & Hirvela, 2004). This is likely to be particularly true for younger, lower-proficiency learners, who often may feel unprepared to engage in pattern discovery or show reluctance to take on a more proactive role in the classroom. For these learners, "Hard [direct] DDL may be less helpful than softer [indirect] versions or traditional teaching methods" (Vyatkina and Boulton, 2017, p. 6).

It is fair to argue that success in implementing DDL in secondary education is largely dependent on fulfilling a number of pedagogical requirements. This is what Wicher (this volume) refers to as didactic processing or mediation of corpus data, with elements such as input enhancement or manipulation of concordance lines treated as additional scaffolding that supports the use of DDL. A similar definition of the pedagogical reality of DDL can be found in Smart (2014, p. 186), who promotes the use of carefully designed corpus-based activities as a way of assisting learners' work "with real language samples, whether on computer or not". In this view, DDL takes the form of guided induction in which instructors make pedagogically motivated choices, putting students in the centre of the teaching process. As Wicher asserts (this volume), in secondary school education, didactic processing of DDL is inevitable, with learners' linguistic development becoming paramount and the process of needs analysis driving the way in which corpus-based activities are successfully integrated into the broader language learning experience.

A good illustration of such teaching practice is Braun's (2007) study exploring the use of DDL in the context of secondary school language instruction in Germany. Using a four-week intervention based on a small corpus of video-based interviews with L1 users, the author investigated the conditions and challenges of introducing a corpus-assisted treatment to young (ages 14 to 15), non-expert language learners. Results revealed that, while the corpus-based work was perceived as a welcome addition, the corpus-based activities presented a number of logistical difficulties, such as learners' lack of analytical skills and autonomy in interpreting concordances. This led Braun to conclude that the integration of corpora into secondary education required a number of pedagogical modifications and a move away from classic concordancing towards needs-driven approaches and more individualized methodologies.

The role of methodological modifications within DDL has also been highlighted by Kennedy and Miceli (2010), who explored the perceptions of a semester-long corpus apprenticeship by intermediate-level learners of Italian. Through case studies with three individual students, the authors delved into the pedagogical mechanics of using corpora as a tool for enhancing the process of creative writing and found that the success of DDL was dependent not only on developing learners' corpus skills but also on raising their awareness of principles that underpin corpus-assisted work, including, for instance, understanding distinct functions of corpus searches or realizing that gaining corpus literacy is a long-term process.

Of particular importance for the current chapter is Boulton's (2010) study which examined the use of mediated DDL materials with intermediate-level L1-French speakers of English. Focusing on a range of difficult target items (e.g. irregular plural forms such as *person/people* or collocations such as *play / practice / do sports*), the author compared the effectiveness of corpus- (handouts with data from the BNC) and dictionary-based materials and also examined the attitudes of students towards corpus-assisted teaching. Results of a multiple-choice post-test revealed that, while both approaches led to significantly improved scores, it was only the corpus-assisted method that was significantly better than the control condition with respect to the knowledge of the target items. Crucially, qualitative insights into learners' perceptions not only pointed to considerable enthusiasm for the use of concordancing but also indicated how pedagogical decisions such as presenting concordances on paper rather than on a computer can contribute to more effective applications of DDL with lower-level learners.

DDL and formulaic language

Phraseology is the study of different types of word combinations or formulaic sequences (Wray, 2002), including idioms, collocations, phrasal verbs, and many more. Since the advent of corpora, there has been a significant increase in the number of studies devoted to the importance of such phrases, and formulaic language has become a key topic in applied linguistics (see Chapter 5 in Szudarski, 2018a).

The term "formulaic language" encompasses a wide range of sequences that recur in different types of discourse (e.g. *in particular, at once, at all*). Such units characterize fluent language use, afford processing benefits, and perform a number of pragmatic functions, making them a key element of naturally occurring language. Regrettably, the acquisition of formulaic sequences is known to pose a serious challenge for L2 learners, with factors such as L1 influence (Wolter & Gyllstad, 2011) or the quality of input (Northbrook and Conklin, 2018) being key determinants of this process. However, while the topic of formulaic language has received an impressive amount of attention in recent years, establishing the optimal classroom conditions for learning L2 phrases is still an open question that remains to be addressed (Szudarski, 2017). Considering that one of the tenets of DDL is that it increases learners' exposure to authentic language and context-specific variation, one can easily imagine how corpus-based interventions could serve to facilitate the acquisition of formulaic sequences.

Indeed, there is a growing body of work demonstrating the positive impact of DDL on learning different types of phrasal units, including pragmatic routines (Bardovi-Harlig, Mossman, & Vellenga, 2015), phrasal verbs (Boulton, 2008), and collocations (Vyatkina, 2016). Further evidence can be found in studies which have adopted a more holistic approach and examined the impact of DDL on developing general L2 phraseological competence. A case in point is Huang's (2014) study into the effects of paper-based DDL on L1-Chinese learners' writing as measured by phraseological patterns around abstract nouns such as "criticism", "situation", or "effect". In terms of treatment, an experimental group studied concordance lines (ten concordances per word), while a control group followed a dictionary-based approach. The quality of learners' post-treatment production was assessed by two L1 expert users, showing that essays from the DDL group contained a higher variety of phrases and fewer phraseological errors. Additionally, participant questionnaires and learning journals revealed that concordancing was perceived as a useful tool for noticing lexicogrammatical patterns.

In a similar design, Geluso and Yamaguchi (2014) investigated the effectiveness of DDL in relation to improving L2 phraseological competence and spoken fluency. Based in the context of teaching English to university-students in Japan, the study took the form of a corpus-based intervention built around the notion of "pattern hunting", that is, encouraging students to discover key words and their phraseological patterns (e.g. *hope for* or *look forward to*). Employing a range of tasks (e.g. speaking journals or student-led lessons), the intervention was aimed at improving learners' lexical knowledge by encouraging them to analyze examples of phraseological patterns in authentic corpus data. Expert-user ratings of L2 speech indicated positive effects of the treatment on learners' performance, as revealed by their improved skill to employ contextually appropriate phrases. However, the study also reported certain difficulties in learners' application of DDL, including issues such as learning how to use corpora effectively or sifting through the abundance of concordances.

In short, while there is a substantial body of findings pointing to DDL as a worthwhile pedagogical endeavour, most of this research has been conducted with college- or university-level students representing higher levels of L2 competence. As a result, little is known about the implementation of corpus-assisted teaching with younger and lower-proficiency learners. For instance, with a strong correlation between lexical knowledge and performance on the four main language skills (Milton, 2013), the acquisition of L2 phraseology is likely to look different for adults, whose vocabulary is large, versus younger learners, who may be yet to master even the most commonly used words. Following Cobb's (2019, p. 206) argumentation that "there is little evidence of a word-formula dichotomy", it is conceivable that, if properly supported, the learning of single-word and phrasal vocabulary can be complementary. With the attested benefits of DDL (Boulton & Cobb, 2017), it emerges as a natural candidate for introducing new phraseology to younger learners. However, until this hypothesis is tested empirically, such claims remain speculative. Consequently, to address this gap, the present chapter focuses on the use of DDL as a way of improving the phraseological competence of secondary school L2 learners.

Current study and research questions

The aim of the study was to examine the effects of two types of instruction on the learning of phraseology by lower-level EFL learners in Poland: corpus-inspired paper-based DDL versus more traditional dictionary-based teaching. More specifically, the study sought to address the following research questions:

1   Do lower-level EFL learners improve their knowledge of L2 phrases following paper-based DDL?
2   Is there a difference in the effectiveness of DDL and that of a dictionary-based approach?
3   What are L2 learners' attitudes toward the direct use of corpus data in language teaching?

Procedure

The study followed a quasi-experimental design and took the form of a pre-test–post-test experiment. It started with a pre-test (week 1) followed by a treatment phase (weeks 2–4) and ended with a delayed post-test (week 7). Both the pre-test and the delayed post-test consisted of two measures of phraseological knowledge (see Figure 8.1). During the treatment phase, three groups of learners were assigned to the following teaching conditions: paper-based DDL (DDL group), dictionary-based work (dictionary group), and a control condition. Since learners in the control group served as a benchmark, they participated in regular classes and completed only the pretest (week 1) and post-test (week 7). In terms of teaching, it was delivered by two experienced L1 Polish teachers of English. After agreeing to participate in the experiment, they were briefed about the use of corpora and the benefits of introducing authentic corpus examples. Further, when the experiment ended, a short questionnaire tapping into learners' perceptions of the treatments was also administered. It was based on a format used by Boulton

FIGURE 8.1 A sample of concordances for the phrase "take over"

(2010) and consisted of five Likert-scale questions translated into English. One open-ended question was also included with the aim of encouraging learners to comment on their learning experience.

As regards the teaching process itself, the DDL treatment was based on printed handouts, each of which contained a sample of 25 to 30 concordances per target phrase. Prepared in advance, the materials were handed to both teachers before the start of the experiment. All the corpus data were retrieved from the BYU-BNC interface (Davies, 2004) and, as Figure 8.1 demonstrates, the handouts followed the usual key-word-in-context format, with the search term presented in the centre of the screen. As can be seen, the interface uses color-coding to highlight words from specific word classes as well as examples of collocates or textual neighbours of the search items. Crucially, care was taken to include such concordances that were relatively simple to decode and provided a sufficient amount of context for the analysis of the target phrases.

Throughout the treatment, the selected concordances were treated as the main source of information regarding fifteen phrasal units (see "target items"). Considering that the main goal of the classes was to introduce the target phrases and focus on their meaning, the learners' attention was specifically drawn to the examples presented on the handouts. In light of their unfamiliarity with this format of teaching, pair work was used first followed by individual analysis, with the teachers monitoring the process and making a conscious effort to highlight frequent collocates or grammatical features co-occurring with the target phrases. The students also had a chance to create Mind Maps as a way of visualizing the meaning of the target items and presenting new insights into their use. Crucially, towards the end of each class, after the meaning of the phrases became clear, the students were also encouraged to use them productively by, for example, practicing dialogues or writing sentences. Finally, because of the focus on the analysis of authentic corpus data, throughout the entire experiment the teachers were asked to use mainly English and avoid translating into Polish.

The dictionary group, in contrast, followed a more traditional approach, with the target phraseology being presented in a more deductive way. Specifically, while the focus of the classes was the same, dictionary definitions and example sentences were treated as the main source of information. With respect to learners' interactions, they worked both individually and in pairs, and their main task was to focus on the target items and decode their meaning. Both mono- and bilingual dictionaries were allowed, with some participants also using online dictionaries to check the meaning of unknown vocabulary. Similarly to the DDL group, the learners were asked to create Mind Maps as a way of processing the new input and highlighting the importance of phrasal vocabulary. After becoming familiar with the meaning of the phrases, the students were also encouraged to apply them in dialogues or short sentences. In short, both treatments reflected contemporary teaching practice, ensuring the ecological validity of the study.

Participants

In total, twenty-two Polish secondary school students participated in the study. All of them were EFL learners who regularly attended standard English classes at school (three 45-minute classes a week, with some participants following an extended language program and attending up to six classes). All participants were 16 to 18 years old, and Polish was their first language. Given potential differences in their levels of proficiency, during the first week of the study all learners were administered Schmitt, Schmitt, and Clapham's (2001) Vocabulary Levels Test (VLT), a matching-format test of written receptive vocabulary. A compound score of the first 2,000 and 3,000 words was treated as a proxy for their vocabulary size. The average overall score across these two levels was 58 per cent (M raw score = 34.95/60, SD = 15.57), with the average raw score amounting to 19.77 (SD = 7.90) and 15.18 (SD = 8.03) at the 2K and 3K levels, respectively. These results showed a fairly low level of lexical competence, where even the most common English words from the 2K frequency band were yet to be fully mastered. Furthermore, high standard deviations suggested a large amount of variation in the analyzed sample.

Target items

Fifteen expressions from the PHRASE List (Martinez and Schmitt, 2012) were selected as target items. The list contains 505 non-transparent English phrases divided into five 1,000-word frequency bands representing the most common English vocabulary. Thus, by combining information on frequency and semantic opacity, the list serves as a practical guide for identifying phrases that are useful to know but difficult to decode by L2 learners. In order to include a wide variety of items in the study, three different phrases from each of the frequency bands were selected and spread across the three weeks of the experimental instruction. For instance, during week 2 the treatment included not only the phrase "at all" (first frequency band) but also "by far" (fifth frequency band). Thus, in terms of the teaching process, each week the learners were presented with five different phrases, grouped in the following way:

>Week 2: *at all, take over, other than, run out of, by far*
>Week 3: *is likely to, in particular, get rid of, take advantage, as of*
>Week 4: *deal with, carry out, at once, by no means, take for granted*

This meant that by the end of the three-week treatment the learners were exposed to fifteen phrases in total. While it could be argued that more target phraseology could have been introduced during this time, given the fact that the experiment constituted the first contact of participants with corpus-assisted teaching, this volume of new input was deemed appropriate, ensuring ample time to provide guidance for the analysis of concordances.

Testing instruments

In terms of measurement, the knowledge of the target phrases was tested by means of two tests: Martinez's (2011) Phrasal Vocabulary Test (Phrasal test henceforth) and a researcher-developed L2-L1 translation test. The former is a multiple-choice measure of English phraseology which tests the knowledge of 60 English expressions selected from the PHRASE List. Using Schmitt's (2010) categorization, the Phrasal test can be perceived as a receptive test of meaning recognition:

>**At all**: I don't like it at all.
>a.   all the time
>b.   in any way
>c.   at first
>d.   sometimes

The other test was a simple instrument through which learners translated phrases from English into Polish. The test consisted of 30 items in total: 15 target items and 15 filler phrases (also taken from the PHRASE List). Using such a format was deemed important as it provided a means to test the learners' ability to recall the meaning of the target phraseology. It should be added that including multiple measures of knowledge is commonplace in vocabulary research, enabling researchers to tap into learners' competence at multiple levels and produce richer insights into the multifaceted nature of L2 lexical competence (Schmitt, 2010).

Results

Table 8.1 presents descriptive statistics for both the pretest and the posttest sessions. As the average results of the pretest show, some of the phrases were known before the treatment, but crucially there were no significant differences between the results of the three groups.

To answer the first research question, a comparison was made between the pre-test the and post-test results. As far as the Phrasal test is concerned, a paired-samples t-test revealed a significant increase in the DDL group ($t(8) = -2.36$, $p = .046$, eta squared = .41), while this difference in the dictionary group only approached significance ($t(4) = -2.75$, $p = .052$, eta squared = .65). Somewhat surprisingly, the post-test results of the control group were significantly lower than their pre-test results ($t(7) = 3.64$, $p = .008$, eta squared = .65). All the effect sizes were small according to the benchmarks suggested by Plonsky and Oswald (2014).

A similar analysis was conducted for the translation test, using non-parametric tests (the data were not normally distributed). A series of Wilcoxon Signed Ranks tests indicated a significant increase in the DDL group ($z = -2.55$, $p = .01$, $r = .85$), but no significant effect was found in the dictionary group ($z = -1.34$, $p = .18$, $r = .60$). Similarly, the results of the Phrasal test showed a marginal decrease in the results of the control group ($z = -1.89$, $p = .058$, $r = .68$).

Given that the second research question concerned the effectiveness of the teaching process, the post-test results of the groups were compared with one another. On the Phrasal test, a one-way between-groups ANOVA revealed a significant difference between the groups ($F (2, 19) = 5.87$, $p = .01$, eta squared = .38). A *post hoc* analysis, a Tukey HSD test with a Bonferroni adjustment, indicated no differences in the performance of the experimental groups, but only the DDL group was significantly better than the control group ($p = .008$). With reference to the translation test, while the DDL group obtained a descriptively higher mean than the dictionary group, this difference was not significant on a Kruskal-Wallis test ($X (2, 22) = 4.71$, $p = .09$).

TABLE 8.1 Descriptive statistics for both tests of phraseological knowledge (max score = 15)

Condition	Session	Phrasal Test Mean (SD)	Translation Test Mean (SD)
Dictionary group (N=5)	pre-test	4.2 (1.8)	0.8 (1.3)
	post-test	5.6 (2.9)	1.6 (1.3)
DDL group (N=9)	pre-test	5.8 (3.0)	2.6 (3.8)
	post-test	8.0 (2.9)	5.0 (3.9)
Control group (N=8)	pre-test	8.3 (2.6)	3.6 (2.7)
	post-test	3.5 (2.4)	1.5 (1.1)

Further, it is noteworthy that the statistical analysis revealed a significant positive correlation between the learners' post-test scores on the Phrasal test and the translation test (Spearman *rho* = .60, p = .003), suggesting that the two measures tapped into related aspects of phraseological competence. However, when correlated with the results of the VLT, a test of general vocabulary size, only the translation test revealed a significant relationship (Spearman *rho* = .55, p = .008). This points to a complex relationship between L2 learners' knowledge of individual words and formulaic sequences, and aligns with the findings of Schmitt, Dornyei, Adolphs, and Durow (2004), who reported only moderate connections between L2 learners' vocabulary size and productive and receptive knowledge of formulaic units.

The third research question explored the attitudes and perceptions of learners from both experimental groups. When it comes to DDL (Figure 8.2), answers to questions 2 and 3 of the survey showed that concordancing was assessed favourably by the majority of students, who stated that the corpus-based exercises were useful and helped them avoid errors. However, none of the participants reported that the corpus consultation was easy. Additionally, while 44 per cent of the students confirmed they would like to do more corpus exercises in the future, there was also a high percentage of undecided students in both question 1 (89 per cent) and question 5 (56 per cent), which could be interpreted as some uncertainty or potential reservations about the use of corpora. Having said that, the experiment was the first contact of the participants with this form of teaching; therefore, it would have been unrealistic to expect an automatic appreciation of DDL, particularly in such linguistically homogenous groups, where learners were used to working with L1-L2 translations. This observation is supported by the results from the dictionary group (Figure 8.3), where 100 per cent of the students reported that the dictionary-based work was useful, and 60 per cent wanted to do similar

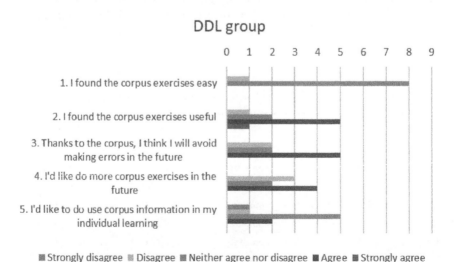

FIGURE 8.2 Questionnaire results in the DDL group (N = 9)

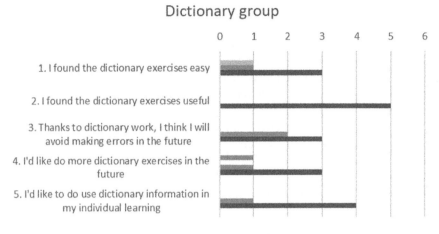

FIGURE 8.3 Questionnaire results in the dictionary group ($N = 5$)

exercises in the future. The majority of learners in this group (80 per cent) also stated that they intended to use dictionaries in their own learning.

Crucially, informal conversations with the teachers confirmed the difficulty of promoting more student-centred formats of teaching. In their view, the main obstacle in implementing DDL was the relatively low proficiency of the students, as well as their deep familiarity with more deductive and explicit ways of receiving new information. The teachers also stressed the role of national, end-of-school exams as a key motivator shaping the expectations of learners in terms of what their language classes should focus on.

Discussion

The aim of this study was to investigate the learning of non-transparent phraseology by secondary school learners of L2 English in the context of two treatments: DDL and a dictionary-based approach. Determining the conditions in which DDL can enhance L2 formulaic competence constitutes a major goal for SLA theory and practice, particularly when it comes to the effective use of corpora by lower-level learners, an area of research which so far has received little attention. The statistical findings indicated that DDL in the form of paper-based concordancing enhanced participants' knowledge of the target phrases, albeit their absolute gains were admittedly small. Specifically, the DDL group improved its performance on both the phrasal test of meaning recognition and the translation test of meaning recall, outperforming the control group and thereby confirming the beneficial effects of DDL. This is in line with previous research which has concluded that DDL is particularly effective in promoting the knowledge of vocabulary, phraseology, and lexicogrammar (Lee et al., 2018; Boulton & Cobb, 2017; Li, 2017). As regards the dictionary group, its post-test results, while descriptively higher after the treatment, did not differ statistically from the pre-test scores, suggesting that this approach did not seem effective in enhancing the knowledge of the target phraseology. This pattern was found on both tests, with the meaning recall result being particularly low and amounting to only 1.6 (out of 15) phrases.

While somewhat disappointing, such results are valuable from a theoretical point of view. Firstly, they show that recall knowledge is more difficult to develop than recognition knowledge, concurring with previous research into the acquisition of L2 vocabulary (see Schmitt, 2010 for details). Secondly, they also underline the importance of including multiple measures of lexical knowledge that tap into different components of this multi-faceted construct. Specifically, the translation test of meaning recall proved to be more challenging for the learners and, indeed, when contrasted statistically, their scores on this test were significantly lower than their performance on the phrasal test of meaning recognition. Interestingly, in a recent study, Gonzalez-Fernandez and Schmitt (2019) found a clear order in the acquisition of different word knowledge components in which recall knowledge was consistently more difficult to acquire than recognition knowledge. Finding a similar pattern in the current study seems to suggest that conceptualizing L2 lexical knowledge in terms of the recall/recognition distinction might also be useful for operationalizing the knowledge of formulaic sequences.

In relation to the effectiveness of the proposed treatments, the study found that the introduction of new phrases by means of paper-based DDL, where learners sift through authentic sentences in order to infer the meaning of unknown phrases, appears more beneficial than reading dictionary definitions and using L1-L2 translations. Having said that, the phraseological gains of the DDL group need to be regarded as small if considered from the perspective of the actual growth in L2 knowledge. To be precise, when the learners' pre-test scores were subtracted from the post-test scores, the average absolute gains amounted to 1.4 phrases (13 per cent) on the phrasal test and 0.8 phrases (6 per cent) on the translation test for the dictionary group, while for the DDL group these values were 2.2 (24 per cent) and 2.4 (19 per cent) phrases, respectively. Thus, it can be concluded that the average gain of the DDL group was just over two phrases on each of the tests.

Such findings are in line with a growing body of work reporting positive effects of DDL on improving a range of L2 features (Boulton & Cobb, 2017). However, what is particularly important about the current study is that it lends support to Boulton's (2010) claim that corpus analysis can be successfully applied with learners of lower-proficiency. His experiment found that paper-based DDL introduced to university-level students of English heightened their linguistic awareness and improved their knowledge of difficult L2 features. The current study extends these findings by providing insights into the use of DDL in secondary education. To reiterate, a three-week treatment involving paper-based DDL led to learners' gains in L2 phraseology, with the introduction of concordancing constituting a new learning opportunity.

With regard to the learners' perceptions of the experimental treatments, it is worth emphasizing the qualitative findings of the study. As revealed by the questionnaire data, participants in the DDL group expressed largely positive attitudes towards the use of corpus-based exercises, with the majority of students confirming the facilitative effects of the treatment, and pointing to the usefulness of corpus consultation in language learning more broadly. From the perspective of learning English, the corpus-based exercises were useful in promoting the new phraseology but also helped learners to avoid errors. Encouragingly, some participants expressed willingness to include more corpus-based exercises in future classes. These are promising findings which align with previous research that has reported L2 learners' positive feelings about the use of DDL (e.g. Yoon & Hirvela, 2004), as well as the benefits of introducing it at lower proficiency levels (e.g. Boulton, 2010 or Vyatkina, 2016). Most importantly perhaps, they demonstrate that DDL can be successfully integrated into secondary school classes and facilitate the process of L2 learning.

Nevertheless, it should not be forgotten that the questionnaire data also showed that the dictionary group expressed similarly positive attitudes towards the more traditional dictionary-based treatment. To be exact, although the group did not make significant gains in the target phrases, the qualitative data suggested that the learners favoured the use of dictionaries as an important learning resource and were keen on using them in the future. This is an interesting finding that can be explained by referring to a number of context-specific features of the study.

Firstly, as revealed by the VLT test, the participants represented a relatively low level of English proficiency; therefore, it is hardly surprising that many of them felt comfortable following the dictionary-based treatment, in which the new phrases were presented in a more deductive way and the use of translation was allowed. With the popularity of the presentation-practice-production model in language teaching practice (Wicher, this volume), it is fair to say that many lower-level classes in Poland (and likely many other EFL contexts as well) tend to follow a teacher-centred style, with the instructor situated in the centre of the didactic process and learners functioning as passive receivers of information. Indeed, informal conversations with both teachers confirmed that one of the biggest obstacles faced during this experiment was overcoming the novelty effect of DDL and fostering a more autonomous behaviour among the students.

Secondly, it is important to remember that the study was conducted in a highly homogenous context, where both the learners and the teachers shared the same mother tongue. It is understandable that in such conditions many participants employed translation as a key strategy for dealing with the new input, treating L1 equivalents as the most efficient way of decoding the unknown meanings of the target phrases. Given research findings that confirm the facilitative role of contrastive analysis and cross-linguistic comparisons (e.g. Laufer & Girsai, 2008), it is important that translation is also considered as a potentially beneficial approach.

The final point concerns the role of exams and curricular requirements as key factors that appeared to have affected the learners' attitudes. As argued by Braun

(2007, p. 306), one of the potential difficulties in incorporating corpus analysis into secondary education is aligning them with "the overall language curriculum". The present study revealed a similar tendency, with both teachers stressing the problem of an exam-oriented curriculum having a considerable impact on learners' behaviour. Focused primarily on passing the end-of-school exams, some participants may have been less willing to invest time in developing corpus literacy skills, leading them to question how this novel treatment benefitted their overall learning goals.

Practical implications

Given the previously mentioned considerations, it is vital to discuss several practical implications of the study. First of all, it demonstrated that formal language instruction in secondary school can include some form of corpus analysis, with the results of the DDL group showing that paper-based concordancing can enhance lower-level L2 learners' knowledge of phraseology. While in absolute terms the learners' gains were modest, no such improvement was observed in the dictionary group, suggesting that corpus-based materials may be a more appropriate way for introducing new phrases and raising learners' awareness of formulaic language as a whole.

Having said that, the study also revealed that many learners in the dictionary group attributed a lot of value to the role of translation and dictionaries in their learning of English. In light of this finding, as well as research indicating the effectiveness of dictionaries in promoting L2 collocational competence (e.g. Dziemianko, 2017), it transpires that more deductive pedagogies should not be necessarily dismissed. Rather, these findings suggest that DDL should have its uses alongside other pedagogical approaches, expanding the teacher's repertoire of instructional treatments. In the case of this experiment, the treatment involved paper-based concordancing, but, as Mukherjee (2006, p. 12) rightly argues, DDL designs can be "plotted on a cline of learner autonomy, ranging from teacher-led and relatively closed concordance-based activities to entirely learner-centered corpus-browsing projects". For instance, with recent advances in technology, computer-assisted language learning (CALL) becomes an increasingly attractive option; and, as stated by Cobb (2019, p. 199), a specific form of CALL-like concordancing – one that "keeps records, includes game elements, incorporates considerations of motivation and context of learning" – might be precisely what is needed to succeed in enhancing L2 formulaic competence. Further, while more research is needed, projects such as ColloCaid (Frankenberg-Garcia, 2018) offer evidence of how corpus data can be successfully employed to inform the development of a new generation of technology-enhanced language learning tools (Meunier, this volume, for a useful discussion of DDL-izing as a way of including more multimodal elements into DDL).

Finally, the study underlines the importance of pedagogical considerations in implementing DDL at lower proficiency levels. Specifically, the results support Vyatkina and Boulton's (2017, p. 2) observation that the effectiveness of DDL "seems to be considerably moderated by a variety of context-related, participant-related, and linguistic variables". As the qualitative analysis revealed, the learners' limited English proficiency and history of exposure to deductive forms of teaching proved to be the main challenges in introducing concordancing as a new form of language work. This points to the role of the didactic processing of DDL, that is, contextualizing it in such a way that it fits the local classroom conditions and corresponds to the overall learning needs of a given group of students (Wicher, this volume).

Limitations and future research

It is important to acknowledge some limitations of the experiment. Firstly, the sample size was small, limiting the generalizability of the findings. The study should be replicated using more learners, ideally representing a range of age groups and L1 backgrounds. Secondly, given that only short-term effects of DDL were measured, another fruitful avenue of inquiry would be to track learners' phraseological development over time and investigate longer-term benefits, such as autonomous learning, accuracy rates in a given language skill, or a heightened awareness of register- and genre-specific variation. Some initial evidence from a two-year longitudinal study into advanced university-level EFL learners (Szudarski, 2018b) suggests that their receptive collocational knowledge improved over time alongside their growing proficiency, but it remains to be seen whether DDL can assist this process even further. Lastly, while Martinez (2011) presents that the phrasal test is a valid measure of phrasal knowledge, meaning recall was measured by a pen-and-paper test developed specifically for the purposes of this study. There is a clear need for more research into different ways of testing the knowledge of formulaic sequences, for there might be other formats that are better suited to tap into this aspect of L2 knowledge.

Conclusions

The aim of the study was to investigate the effects of paper-based DDL and dictionary-based teaching on facilitating the acquisition of phraseology by secondary school EFL learners. Findings revealed that DDL was more effective in enhancing learners' phraseological competence, resulting in improvement at the level of meaning recall and meaning recognition. However, the relatively modest gains pointed to the difficulty of developing phraseological competence by lower-level EFL learners. Furthermore, by investigating participants' perceptions, the study also revealed positive attitudes towards the use of more traditional forms of teaching based on dictionaries, highlighting the importance of the local context as a key factor in the successful integration of DDL into secondary school language education.

Acknowledgements

I would like to express my gratitude to two anonymous teachers, without whose support this research would not have been possible.

References

Bardovi-Harlig, K., Mossman, S., & Vellenga, H. E. (2015). The effect of instruction on pragmatic routines in academic discussion. *Language Teaching Research, 19*, 324–350.

Boulton, A. (2008). Looking for empirical evidence for DDL at lower levels. In B. Lewandowska-Tomaszczyk (Ed.), *Corpus linguistics, computer tools and applications: State of the art* (pp. 581–598). Frankfurt: Peter Lang.

Boulton, A. (2010). Data-driven learning: Taking the computer out of equation. *Language Learning, 60*(3), 534–572.

Boulton, A., & Cobb, T. (2017). Corpus use in language learning: A meta-analysis. *Language Learning, 67*(2), 348–393.

Braun, S. (2007). Integrating corpus work into secondary education: From data-driven learning to needs-driven corpora. *ReCALL, 19*(3), 307–328.

Charles, M. (2012). Proper vocabulary and juicy collocations: EAP students evaluate do-it-yourself corpus-building. *English for Specific Purposes, 31*(2), 93–102.

Cobb, T. (2019). From corpus to CALL: The use of technology in teaching and learning formulaic language. In A. Siyanova-Chanturia & A. Pellicer-Sanchez (Eds.), *Understanding formulaic language: A second language acquisition perspective* (pp. 192–210). London and New York: Routledge.

Davies, M. (2004). *The British National Corpus (BNC)*. Retrieved from http://corpus.byu.edu.

Dziemianko, A. (2017). Paper or electronic? The role of dictionary form in language reception, production and the retention of meaning and collocations. *International Journal of Lexicography, 23*(3), 257–273.

Frankenberg-Garcia, A. (2018). Combining user needs, lexicographic data and digital writing environments. *Language Teaching*, First View, 1–15.

Geluso, J. and Yamaguchi, A. (2014). Discovering formulaic language through data-driven learning: Student attitudes and efficacy. *ReCALL, 26*(2), 225–242.

Gilquin, G., & Granger, S. (2010). How can data-driven learning be used in language teaching. In A. O'Keeffe & M. McCarthy (Eds.), *The Routledge handbook of corpus linguistics* (pp. 359–370). London and New York: Routledge.

Gonzalez-Fernandez, B., & Schmitt, N. (2019). Word knowledge: Exploring the relationships and order of acquisition of vocabulary knowledge components. *Applied Linguistics*, Advance view, 1–29.

Granger, S., & Meunier, F. (2008). Phraseology in language learning and teaching: Where to from here?. In S. Granger & F. Meunier (Eds.), *Phraseology in foreign language learning and teaching* (pp. 247–252). Amsterdam: John Benjamins.

Huang, Z. (2014). The effects of paper-based DDL on the acquisition of lexico-grammatical patterns in L2 writing. *ReCALL, 26*(2), 163–183.

Johns, T. (1997). Contexts: The background, development and trialling of a concordance-based CALL program. In A. Wuchmann, S. Fligelstone, T. McEnery, & G. Knowles (Eds.), *Teaching and learning corpora* (pp. 100–115). London: Longman.

Kennedy, C. and Miceli, T. (2010). Corpus-assisted creative writing: Introducing intermediate Italian students to a corpus as a reference resource. *Language Learning & Technology, 14*(1), 28–44.

Laufer, B., & Girsai, N. (2008). Form-focused instruction in the second language vocabulary learning: A case for contrastive analysis and translation. *Applied Linguistics, 29*(4), 694–716.

Lee, H., Warschauer, M., & Lee, J. H. (2018). The effects of corpus use on second language vocabulary learning: A multilevel meta-analysis. *Applied Linguistics*. Advanced access, 1–44.

Li, S. (2017). Using corpora to develop learners' collocational competence. *Language Learning & Technology, 21*(3), 153–171.

Martinez, R. (2011). *The development of a corpus-informed list of formulaic sequences for language pedagogy* (Unpublished PhD thesis). University of Nottingham.

Martinez, R., & Schmitt, N. (2012). A phrasal expressions lists. *Applied Linguistics, 33*(3), 299–320.

Milton, J. (2013). Measuring the contribution of vocabulary knowledge to proficiency in the four skills. In C. Bardel, C. Lindqvist, & B. Laufer (Eds.), *L2 vocabulary acquisition, knowledge and use: New perspectives on assessment and corpus analysis* (pp. 57–78). Amsterdam: Eurosla.

Moon, S., & Oh, S. -Y. (2018). Unlearning overgenerated be through data-driven learning in the EFL classroom. *ReCALL, 30*(1), 48–67.

Mukherjee, J. (2006). Corpus linguistics and language pedagogy: The state of the art and beyond. In S. Braun, K. Kohn, & J. Mukherjee (Eds.), *Corpus technology and language pedagogy: New resources, new tools, new methods* (pp. 5–24). Frankfurt: Peter Lang.

Northbrook, J., & Conklin, K. (2018). Is what you put in what you get out? Textbook-derived lexical bundle processing in beginner English learners. *Applied Linguistics*, Advance view, 1–19.

Plonsky, L., & Oswald, F. L. (2014). How big is "big"? Interpreting effect sizes in L2 research. *Language Learning, 64*(4), 878–912.

Schmitt, N. (2010). *Researching vocabulary: A vocabulary research manual*. Basingstoke: Palgrave Macmillan.

Schmitt, N., Dornyei, Z., Adolphs, S., & Durow, V. (2004). Knowledge and acquisition of formulaic sequences: A longitudinal study. In N. Schmitt (Ed.), *Formulaic sequences: Acquisition, processing and use* (pp. 55–86). Amsterdam and Philadelphia: John Benjamins.

Schmitt, N., Schmitt, D., & Clapham, C. (2001). Developing and exploring the behavior of two versions of the vocabulary levels test. *Language Testing, 18*(1), 55–88.

Smart, J. (2014). The role of guided induction in paper-based data-driven learning. *ReCALL, 26*(2), 184–201.

Szudarski, P. (2017). Learning and teaching L2 collocations: Insights from research. *TESL Canada Journal, 34*(3), 205–216.

Szudarski, P. (2018a). *Corpus linguistics for vocabulary: A research guide*. London and New York: Routledge.

Szudarski, P (2018b). *The phraseological development of EFL learners*. Paper presented at BAAL Vocabulary SIG Conference. London: University College London.

Vyatkina, N. (2016). Data-driven learning for beginners: The case of German verb-preposition collocations. *ReCALL, 28*(2), 207–226.

Vyatkina, N., & Boulton, A. (2017). Corpora in language learning and teaching. *Language Learning & Technology, 21*(3), 1–8.

Wolter, B., & Gyllstad, H. (2011). Collocational links in the L2 mental lexicon and the influence of L1 intralexical knowledge. *Applied Linguistics, 32*(4), 430–449.

Wray, A. (2002). *Formulaic language and the lexicon*. Cambridge: Cambridge University Press.

Yoon, H., & Hirvela, A. (2004). ESL student attitudes towards corpus use in L2 writing. *Journal of Second Language Writing, 13*(4), 257–283.

9

"IT HELPS ME GET IDEAS ON HOW TO USE MY WORDS"

Primary school students' initial reactions to corpus use in a private tutoring setting

Peter Crosthwaite and Annita Stell

Introduction

This chapter explores the implementation of DDL for improving the writing of L1 English-speaking upper-grade primary school students in a private tutoring setting in Australia. While the number of studies on DDL in secondary education contexts is relatively small compared with that of tertiary contexts, the number of researchers conducting DDL research with primary-age students can probably be counted on one hand. In addition, while we know DDL works well in second language (L2) contexts, the affordances of DDL for first language (L1) primary literacy development are less well known. In the Australian context, literacy is one of the "general capabilities" of the Australian F-10 curriculum. Success in literacy entails development of "the knowledge, skills and dispositions to interpret and use language confidently for learning and communicating" (Australian Curriculum, 2018a). Students in Primary grades 1–6 need to comprehend and produce a range of texts, which requires knowledge of "text structures", "grammar structures", and "the ability to develop strategies and skills for acquiring a wide topic vocabulary". Primary school teachers also "need a clear understanding of the literacy demands and opportunities of their learning area/s" (ibid.). Alongside basic literacy, another "general capability" is that of literacy in information and communication technology (ICT), which involves "students learning to make the most of the digital technologies available to them [and] adapting to new ways of doing things as technologies evolve", achieved through the completion of tasks that develop skills in "information access and management, information creation and presentation, problem-solving, decision-making, communication, creative expression and empirical reasoning" (Australian Curriculum, 2018b).

Given what we know about the affordances of DDL for these goals in other learning contexts (Boulton & Cobb, 2017), if one is to connect the dots, addressing the literacy needs of primary-age learners through the adoption of DDL technologies and pedagogical innovations into the school curriculum should be a *no-brainer*. DDL provides the conditions that allow primary school students (and their teachers) to draw informed, objective, data-driven conclusions about language for the purposes of teaching and learning. This knowledge is an essential part of what it is to be "literate", making fully explicit the (often implicit) knowledge about which words and structures "go together" and the genres and contexts in which such words and structures are commonly found. Engagement with corpora also improves digital and ICT literacy through self-guided manipulation and analysis of digital data in a range of visual formats. However, it would appear that, up to now, an entire sector of the education industry appears to have missed out on the benefits that DDL has to offer.

The lack of empirical DDL research involving primary-age learners is even more frustrating given that the findings of the little research that has been done have generally been positive. Among the most notable contributions at this level, the studies conducted by Sealey and Thompson (2004, 2007) in the United Kingdom are essential reading. This research involved the use of a small subsection of the British National Corpus containing 40 children's texts (the CLLIP corpus, Sealey & Thompson, 2004), with the choice of texts intended to represent the type of texts such students would be expected to read (Sealey & Thompson, 2007). These early DDL studies focused on presenting color-coded concordances from this small corpus via Wordsmith Tools to children ages 8 to 10 years old for the purposes of learning grammar and vocabulary. Sealey and Thompson (2004) suggest that, despite semantic definitions (e.g. a verb is a "doing word") being more typically used for vocabulary and grammar instruction in primary contexts, "there may be more potential [for DDL] for identifying the patterns in language than has been recognised to date" (p. 90). This is a significant claim if applied to the Australian context, where most work on primary literacy has been built around Systemic Functional Linguistics-based approaches, such as *Reading to Learn* (Rose & Martin, 2012), which make heavy use of top-down semantic categorisations of language, function, and genre for teaching and learning. This potential is explored further in Sealey and Thompson (2007), who examined the benefits of DDL for developing metalinguistic awareness in the same group of children. Qualitative interaction data showed that, despite children knowing of the terms for parts of speech (e.g. "noun", "verb") and their general semantic function, children were still unsure of how to label individual words. However, interaction with corpora resulted in children combining their intuitions about language with the visual evidence presented to them as corpus output, allowing them to draw data-driven conclusions about language through empirical support. Moreover, the children themselves went beyond the expectations of the researchers in using the corpus software in ways that they had not been explicitly trained for (see Crosthwaite, Wong, & Cheung, 2019 for similar findings in tertiary education) and often answered both the questions of the researchers and the questions about language raised by the students themselves.

One of the only other contributors of DDL research at the primary school level is Eri Hirata, in the Japanese context. Her PhD (Hirata, 2012) highlighted a range of potential benefits from the incorporation of a corpus-influenced syllabus for primary school L2 English literacy development, while Hirata (2016) developed a multimodal corpus tool for L2 English DDL in a Japanese primary school, noting that young children's increasing exposure and engagement with digital media "affects how they frame early literacy" (p. 22, see also Burnett & Daniels, 2015). Hirata (2018) stressed the need for primary school teacher training in DDL for L1 Japanese-speaking teachers who could benefit from improved metalinguistic knowledge of their L1 and the L2. Hirata (this volume) put this plan into practice, reporting on trainee teachers' generally positive appraisal of the use of a multimodal corpus to support L2 English education at the primary school level. Another notable study at the primary school level is found in Leray and Tyne (2016), who used DDL to improve L1 French spelling, noting longer-lasting improvements for an experimental DDL group over a non-DDL control group. Finally, a very recent study conducted in the Korean primary context (Kim, 2019) used corpus-based concordance materials to teach prepositions, with positive perceptions of this approach from both students and teachers.

Despite these positive steps, Hirata (and many others) notes that primary school teachers already have a great deal of other pre- and in-service training to get through for other non-language subjects and may be unwilling to take on further training in what is still considered (rightly so) a largely untested pedagogical approach at the primary school level. While Römer (2009) suggests it is the task of corpus researchers to "spread the word" about corpora, our own attempts to secure funding and teacher participation for DDL studies at primary schools have so far proven fruitless, and primary school principals in Australia generally complain they have enough of a job keeping smart devices *out* of the classroom rather than allowing them *in*. In addition, securing permission to access primary schools as research sites is always difficult, typically requiring extensive ethical and criminal background procedures that may span multiple administrative bodies.

These difficulties preclude a need for an alternative research context within which to explore primary school students' uptake of DDL pedagogy, addressed in this chapter through the initial introduction of DDL within the context of one-on-one private tutoring sessions conducted at the tutor's home. To the best of our knowledge, there have been very few – if any – DDL studies conducted in private tutoring contexts, and we are certainly not aware of any study that has yet investigated DDL for primary-age students in tutoring settings. In Australia, private tutoring, which is defined as "the extra coaching in examinable, academic subjects provided to students outside school hours", is in itself a generally under-researched section of the education industry, although one that is experiencing exponential growth in the primary education sector in Australia and other Western countries, largely as the result of East Asian immigration (Sriprakash, Proctor, & Hu, 2016, p. 427). Increasingly, the focus of such tutoring is on high school examinations (even as the students are still at primary school) and often involves (among other subjects) formal instruction in the argumentative essay genre. However, many primary school students will have had little experience of reading or writing full argumentative essays within the F-10 primary literacy curriculum given the curriculum's central focus on narrative exposition at earlier grades. The explicit instruction in essay structure provided by private tutors therefore often results in essays that bear the structural hallmarks of the essay genre but that contain the lexis and phraseology of a wide range of non-essay genres. This problem results in reduced self-efficacy for primary school students as they struggle to maintain an appropriate academic stance and voice in their argumentative essay attempts (Pajares, Johnson, & Usher, 2007) without really understanding the reason why.

Given this, we wished to test the utility of providing explicit training in the direct use of two corpus interfaces for DDL (*Sketch Engine for Language Learning*, Baisa & Suchomel, 2014) and the British Academic Written English Corpus (BAWE, Alsop & Nesi, 2009) within the "open" version of Sketch Engine), with L1 primary school students preparing to write argumentative essays across multiple drafts in a private tutoring setting. The focus of this particular chapter was to document students' initial reactions to corpus use, while the larger goal of this project was to determine whether continued use of corpora and engagement with DDL produces the kind of conditions that, according to Bandura's (1986) social cognition theory, help boost students' self-efficacy as they develop their lexical knowledge and problem-solving skills through DDL. This, in turn, would show that DDL has the potential to positively mediate the beliefs that children develop about their academic capabilities in general (Pajares, Miller, & Johnson, 1999), encouraging them to maintain a positive attitude towards their performance and their learning.

Method

Participants

Two Year 5 primary school students (age 10) studying in Australian primary schools were invited to participate. They were current students of the private tutor, a PhD candidate and holder of an MA in applied linguistics, who is also the second author. William and Ivan (pseudonyms) are both Australian citizens of Mandarin Chinese heritage, speak English as an L1 and Mandarin as a heritage language, and have attended Australian primary schools since first grade. The students had been studying argumentative essay writing with the tutor for over six months, and neither student had previously been exposed to corpora.

Despite their similar language and cultural background, the tutor anecdotally reported individual variation in their general learning preferences and ICT experience at school. William tends to be a "visual-dominant" learner (by the tutor's informal appraisal) who "prefers to see examples and observe others before he tries anything new". He is working on improving his knowledge of essay structure and completing full essays independently without assistance. William sees the tutor on weekends for 90 minutes. His school has access to computer labs, although personal smart devices are not allowed. William's ICT skills are measured annually through a standardized test known, the *ICAS Digital Technology*. Based on his test score, he is considered to have an "intermediate" level of ICT competence and is familiar with the basic functions of iPads and laptops. Ivan, according to his tutor, has "a kinesthetic learning style" and "prefers to be more hands-on with new activities". His tutoring sessions focus on improving his lexical choices and sentence structures for argumentative essays. Ivan's ICT skills are considered by the tutor to be higher than William's, as it is compulsory to bring an iPad to complete in-class worksheets at Ivan's school. Ivan sees the tutor twice a week for a total of three hours. Ivan has more experience writing essays with the tutor, having studied with the tutor for almost three years, while William has attended tutorials only for a year. Tutoring sessions are conducted at the tutor's home.

Procedure

In a typical tutoring session, the tutor helps the students with their basic academic and creative writing skills by giving them an essay topic to plan and write about. Writing spans multiple drafts with multiple rounds of written corrective feedback. Tutoring sessions also feature a range of spelling, grammar, and punctuation exercises, as well as online games. The writing and feedback are typically completed before each session, with the tutor discussing these in person during the actual sessions.

We aimed to introduce corpora for revising lexical issues in each students' drafts for a period of 15 minutes before their regular tutorial sessions. Sketch Engine for Language Learning (SkELL) and the British Academic Corpus of Written English (BAWE) contained in the open version of Sketch Engine were selected for this purpose as they are free and fast to access, have a user-friendly interface, contain a high frequency of academic texts (among other types) suitable for the target register, and have a range of built-in corpus functions including "thesaurus" and "word sketch" that allow users to query these corpora in a number of ways without extensive knowledge of regular expressions. These platforms were accessed via a laptop computer positioned in front of both the tutor and student.

Once ethical approval was arranged, each student completed an initial training session involving SkELL. The instructions for this session were designed by the first author, who has extensive experience in developing DDL materials. Each student was introduced to the basic functions of SkELL by exploring the basic concordance interface (labelled "examples" on SkELL) and the "word sketch" and "similar words" (thesaurus) functions. For example, students were encouraged to query nouns such as *essay* and *exam*, reading the resulting concordances before exploring other corpus functions with these same target terms. Each student was then asked to search for a word or phrase of his own related to any writing he was currently doing. The lecturer provided the following instructions to the tutor for this purpose.

> The first session should be a general introduction to SKELL, where you will explore the different functions of this platform with the students.
>
> Choose a couple of example nouns or verbs that you think they would be interested in reading some concordances for (e.g. 'essay', 'exam', 'introduction', 'writing') as well as some 2–3 word expressions. For a couple of the single word expressions, use the 'word sketch' function to explore some of the different combinations you can get. Choose 'essay' for example, you will see the different modifiers and verbs with 'essay' as a subject, etc. Let them play around with this by clicking on the various results. You can also try the 'similar words' function. Then, get them to choose their own words.
>
> Try to spend no more than 10 minutes on this on this initial session.

Following the initial training session, students were asked to submit the first drafts of their upcoming tutorial essays to the tutor. The first author analysed these for examples of inappropriate lexis or phrasing that were considered amenable to treatment through SkELL or the BAWE. In total, three essays were completed across five DDL sessions, with generic essay topics including "whether students should use iPads or laptops at school" and "whether students should have longer holidays". Between 4 and 5 issues with word choice or collocation were highlighted for each draft, and the first author generated potential corpus query strings for use in SkELL that the tutor could ask the students to use. The following sample shows a redacted paragraph from one of the students' essays with the errors underlined and with the accompanying advice given by the lecturer for resolution.

> Additionally, if school holidays are longer, we can get a break from stress. After nine months of hard labour such as completing assessment tasks and finish boring worksheets [. . .] Did you know that you can actually die from over work?
>
> 1) Try 'get a break from stress', then '.* stress' or just 'stress' with the word sketch function in SKELL to find verbs other than 'break' that can be appropriately used with stress.
> 2) Search for 'over work' vs 'overwork', then search for 'over stress' and 'overstress'. What does he notice?

The tutor first encouraged the students to query the corpus for the highlighted issues on their own, before referring to the lecturer's suggested query syntax if there was time. The tutor also provided scaffolded help when the student required some form of assistance through prompting, repeating, or demonstrating through different examples, depending on the situation. Occasionally, the tutor would also ask questions or remind them that they could use one of the online corpora if they tended to resolve the highlighted errors without them. The tutor took observational notes and screenshots of students' corpus queries and search results and noted whether a student made a revision with or without using a corpus, highlighting the former in green and the latter in blue. Both students were also interviewed by the tutor for a short time after each session, with questions related to the learners' attitudes towards corpora and how they were influencing the revision process. The tutor noted more assistance was given during the revision of the first essay in comparison with that given during the revision of the second and third essays. In the final session, the tutor used previous interview responses and screenshots to encourage the students to recall and reflect on their thoughts about the DDL process.

Results

We now discuss the students' initial thoughts about corpus use and document DDL experiences for each child individually.

William: initial reaction to corpus use

During the initial DDL training session, William's reaction to the corpus was considered as "reserved" by his tutor, with William spending time observing the tutor's corpus use and trying to follow the training instructions. William did not make any comments during this process; instead, he nodded and said he understood what he had to do. He was more interested in asking questions about his homework essay task than in asking about the corpus.

First revision session

The first essay topic was "should students use iPads or laptops at school?" William wrote only a single body paragraph for his first written submission, and during the DDL revision session William attempted to resolve the highlighted errors on his own without the use of any corpora, despite being prompted to do so. While many of his revisions were appropriate, the tutor continued to prompt him to use the corpora to find more examples of different words or phrases that could be used following the lecturer's recommended query strings. In the end, William instead spent time observing how the tutor used SkELL or the BAWE rather than attempting to use it on his own. However, the examples the tutor presented from the corpora appeared to help William make decisions about the appropriacy of the words and phrases he had used in his submission. For example, the tutor entered the student's expression "*a small amount of screen*" in SkELL, garnering zero results, before the tutor entered the wildcard query "*small amount of **" in the BAWE via Sketch Engine (Figure 9.1).

After reading the concordances, William mentioned his construction was "wrong" and modified his expression to "*a smaller screen*". We should note

"It helps me get ideas on how to use my words" **157**

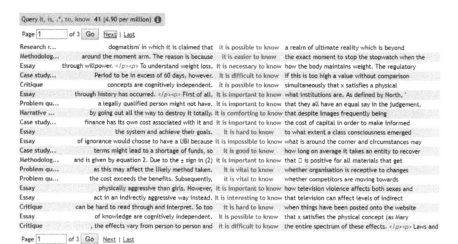

FIGURE 9.1 Example of William's first query in Sketch Engine

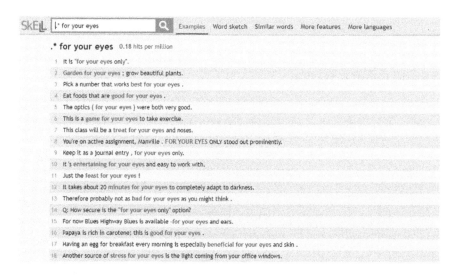

FIGURE 9.2 Example of William's attempt to use SkELL

here that BAWE was not consulted by William any further from this point onwards.

This process was repeated for the poor collocation "*unhealthy for your eyes*", where the tutor queried SkELL for ".* *for your eyes*". William read through the 40 concordances and found that Example 13, "*bad for your eyes*", and Example 18, "*stress for your eyes*", (Figure 9.2) were suitable for his essay, so he modified his expression ("less stressful").

> "The laptop screens can <u>create less stressful</u> for your eyes. "

William's observed initial lack of confidence in using corpora was discussed in the interview following this first revision session. When the tutor asked whether William he would use SkELL or Sketch Engine by himself, he responded:

> *"Not all the time, because sometimes I might not figure out what to enter there, and then if it keeps going as error* [sic] *then I have to find out another way to say it"*

When asked what a corpus could be used for, William responded by commenting on the function of concordances:

> *"It's for sentences that have . . . um . . . so like so . . . for example you write in um . . . fish and it comes up with different combinations of sentences with fish in it"*

At the end of this session, William was encouraged to continue writing his essay for homework so that he could gain extra feedback on his writing in the next session.

Second revision session

Before the second session, William had completed the first full essay independently. The tutor started the session by asking him to recall how SkELL was used in the last session. He replied by simply saying it was used to "find examples". William again needed reminding to consult SkELL at the beginning of the revision session as he continued to resolve the highlighted issues by himself without consulting the corpus. He eventually used SkELL to find words to replace "work" in the sentence *"you can easily find <u>work</u> in documents because it is more convenient to access files"*, where "find work" triggered a sense of finding employment (we believe he intended to write "find your work"). At first, he searched for the full phrase several times, which resulted in zero hits each time. Following this, the tutor then prompted him to use the wildcard (.*) in SkELL for the construction "find. * in documents" so as to find alternatives for "work" (Figure 9.3).

William considered the concordance output for several minutes before the tutor asked him what was wrong. He explained that none of the results matched what he was trying to say – *"they all talk about something very different* [sic]*"*. After a long pause, William asked the tutor if he could change the words around the highlighted phrase. When the tutor nodded, he changed *"work"* to *"classwork"* and *"documents"* to *"your files"*, before writing the following passage via tracked changes without consulting the corpus.

"It helps me get ideas on how to use my words" 159

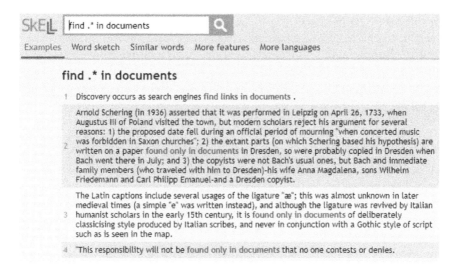

FIGURE 9.3   Example of William's search during session 2

> "You can easily find classwork in your files because it is more convenient to access later if you need it."

Even though William did not eventually make revisions with data found in the concordances, the tutor noted that the process of thinking about the error, consulting the corpus, and making the revisions took a total of around five minutes, which was the longest William had thought about how to resolve an error in any previous session. When interviewed at the end of the session, William was a lot more responsive about SkELL than previously seen:

> "[SKELL] gives you more ideas on what to write and um . . . ideas and more convenient sentences to use in your work."

William revealed he had attempted to use SkELL outside the tutoring session for a language issue in his school homework (although he had forgotten what the issue was). However, he was disappointed by his efforts *"because I couldn't find anything that fit with it [sic]"*. William then discussed difficulties positioning the wildcard in corpus queries:

> "*Sometimes I would just enter "find work", but I don't really know about the dot star [.*] thingy? I think it means, like, if you want to put any word between any other words.*"

Despite these complaints, the tutor was encouraged that William had begun to query the corpus with less prompting than was previously required and that he had used the corpus under his own initiative outside the tutoring sessions. That said, the final revised draft did not contain any revisions using data present in the concordance output, and he was yet to fully explore any of the other functions offered by SkELL.

Third revision session

The topic for the second essay was "whether students should have longer holidays or not". The tutor's goal for this third revision session was to encourage William to consult SkELL independently – without prompting or assistance. William was asked to edit his essay by himself using his notebook PC, while a laptop was positioned next to him with the SkELL platform site left open for him to use if required. William queried SkELL 11 times, making a number of revisions based on the corpus output for the first time. For example, William made the error "no body" in the sentence "*no body would stress about going back to school*". He queried the concordance output for "no body", "no one", and "nobody" to see which was most suitable for the given context and then proceeded to query these terms using wildcards, albeit struggling to position the wildcard appropriately (Figure 9.4). The tutor intervened by prompting him to replace "nobody" with the wildcard (".* would stress") instead (Figure 9.5).

However, the list of concordances caused William to eventually replace "nobody" with "we" in the following sentence:

> We would stress about going back to school.

While William had obviously failed to resolve the error by using the target replacement the tutor had in mind, his revision was made under his own initiative after having consulted the corpus data. When asked why he made this revision, he replied "*because a lot of people used 'we' as well*". He also now understood how the wildcard should be positioned: "*the star dot thingy was used as the word – not before or after word*".

FIGURE 9.4 Failed wildcard attempt

> 6   First, we would stress the immense size of the resource.
> 7   This would stress the country's deficit and also increase general price level.
> 8   As always I would stress the importance of staying tuned to forecast updates.
> 9   I would stress that there is no definitive statement on the timescale.
> 10 In both instances I would stress the importancy of your mum receiving physio treatment.
> 11 However, I would stress that this is not my preferred course of action.
> 12 Finally, we would stress that in vocal music we should concentrate on creating musical values.
> 13 But I would stress, I think we have 59 EBAs in our company.
> 14 We would stress that all these possible developments are at a very early stage of thinking.
> 15 I would stress that we are not talking about millionaires and rich people getting a benefit.

FIGURE 9.5   Results for ".* would stress"

Final revision session

By the fourth revision session, William needed no prompting to use the corpus to make revisions for his third essay topic, which was about "whether people should recycle or not". Most of the errors were revised with terms that were taken directly from concordance results but were at least made after consulting the corpus. During this process, William tended to verbalise his thoughts a lot more than during previous sessions. For example, William had produced the sentence *"if we don't recycle then all the trees and plants will have <u>unclear water</u>"*, with "unclear water" as an error of collocation. Before he searched for example concordances, he told the tutor that he would *"type in the dot and star thingy and the second word"* into SkELL to find a better adjective for water and entered ".* water". It was noted that SkELL took a significantly long time to load in this session, especially when a wildcard was used (this is common for SkELL). While waiting, William stated that *"if it takes this long, it means it's wrong . . . last time, I searched for something, it just came up with no searches* [sic]*"*. After the results finally appeared, he scrolled through the list of examples and said that the word "contaminated" (Example 25) could be used in his sentence (Figure 9.6).

At the end of the session, William's initial description of what a corpus was used for (the "fish" example) was presented back to him by his tutor. His response to his own definition was *"it was wrong"*, before redefining his definition:

> *"It's for if you need a word (. . .) that doesn't fit in your sentence. You can search up* [sic] *SKELL and use a different word. You can do the dot star thingy then write the next word in the search box."*

1	Then run under cold water before peeling.
2	About 200 000 solar water heaters are used.
3	A separate water park offers family fun.
4	Job shower area once cardiovascular physical workout. Water baby showers is recurrent tub areas.
5	Another factor helping inversion layers form is relatively cold water temperatures.
6	I easily slept through those overnight open water crossings.
7	There are many water sport activities including wind surfing.
8	Note lava rock under water left foreground.
9	Their white waters tumble down steep slopes.
10	This enclosed water tank was likely built around 1910.
11	The result is absolute clean drinking water.
12	The printed name is "water".
13	Maintaining pristine water conditions is very important.
14	Particularly important changes among water beetles are known.
15	The water temperature is another independent variable.
16	A typical canned diet is ~79 % water.
17	The water is once again getting darker.
18	The average water temperature is 54 degrees.
19	The fish used is primarily fresh water fish.
20	The longest border line measures 670 meters ! Water temperature is usually around 25 degrees.
21	Add water until chicken is completely covered.
22	They live along waters since ancient times.
23	Another helpful tip is drinking lemon water.
24	Such units are called boiling water reactors.
25	Possible environmental reservoirs include contaminated water sources.

FIGURE 9.6 William's search results for ".* water" for Essay 3 via SkELL

William also revealed he had started to use SkELL at home to help with his tutoring homework:

> "*I used it with the dot star and the next word, but it didn't come with many answers, but I still found something that was suitable for it. I forgot [the word] but it was in the essay*" [William begins searching through the document]. "*I think it was convenient because I already used it twice and was trying to find another word I could put there instead*"

William was also now beginning to gain confidence in using SkELL to assist him with other homework tasks not set by the tutor:

> "*I did [use SKELL] because I wanted to be more used to it and at least try and use it whenever I can. I use it with a star symbol at the front, then I type the word/ phrase in the search box and hope to see some sentences I could be aware of or even use in my writing. Now, I think that SKELL is useful*"

It had taken William only one month to transition from observing the tutor using the corpus in the initial session to using the corpus autonomously both within and outside the tutoring sessions, as revealed in the final session. William closed this final session by insisting he would continue to use the corpus to help with a range of writing tasks he was asked to complete at school.

Ivan: initial reaction to corpus use

Ivan showed a strong interest in querying the corpus himself right from the outset during the initial training session, with the tutor noticing his keen interest while observing him using the Word Sketch function of SkELL for the term "essay". Ivan then browsed through both the BAWE and the SkELL platforms by himself while the tutor gave him instructions, and he spent much time clicking through the output data to refine the results. However, like William, Ivan did not verbalise his thoughts much at this stage.

First revision session

Like William, Ivan had written only a single body paragraph for this first revision session. However, in contrast with William, Ivan was very keen to start working with the corpora and regularly asked the tutor if he could enter his own corpus queries from the outset. Given the time constraint and to allow Ivan to explore the range of functions with some guidance, the tutor restricted his queries to those of the lecturer's suggested query syntax for each highlighted error but did let him enter these queries into the corpus by himself.

Ivan started the session by listening to the tutor's instructions for the underlined poor lexical choice in the sentence "*imagine animals' habitats being destroyed and animals murdering each other to live!*" Ivan was instructed to try to use the wildcard function in the BAWE through Sketch Engine, using the query syntax "*Animals * each other*". This resulted in only one hit (Figure 9.7).

Ivan noticed that this hit was taken from an essay and amended his original formulation to "killing" from "murdering", commenting that using the corpus here "*was a very easy way to check*". For the second highlighted issue ("*Additionally, we will have a clean environment if we recycle*"), Ivan used wildcards again, erroneously typing in "**a clean environment*" into BAWE / Sketch Engine (there should be a space after the wildcard), but this provided a single hit from an essay (Figure 9.8).

He then modified his original error ("*we will have a cleaner environment*"), as well as another occurrence later in his work ("*Therefore, not recycling can effect us*

Query animals, .*, each, other 1 (0.12 per million)

Essay in the first two plays rather appears as wild animals killing each other , the dominant image in the third play is the

FIGURE 9.7 BAWE results for "animals* each other"

164 Peter Crosthwaite and Annita Stell

> Query .*, a, clean, environment 1 (0.12 per million)
> Essay voluntarily to contribute to a better society and a cleaner environment ". An alternate description is that corporate

FIGURE 9.8 Results for "*a clean environment"

[sic] from having a healthy, cleaner and welcome environment"). However, after reading his revisions, he mentioned that he did not think that the second sentence he had revised was correct, so he wanted to consult the corpus again "*to get an idea on what to write*". He queried the corpus and revised this passage to read:

> "Therefore, recycling can make protecting the environment an easier job."
> (Paragraph 3)

During the post-session discussion, Ivan mentioned that he was particularly impressed with the wildcard function:

> "*I like SketchEngine more cos you can use the wildcard function to see how the words are used in a sentence*"

When asked to define what a corpus is used for, Ivan explained that it was:

> "*For when my wording [isn't] too good. It can show me how I can use different words to make my grade higher*"

Revision session 2

During the second session, Ivan asked to edit his essay independently on the word processor with both SkELL and BAWE open in a Web browser. He began editing the highlighted errors without the corpus, so the tutor prompted him to search the corpus to find alternatives to the verb "fix" to revise his usage for the passage ". . . *while some people are trying to fix this tragic problem*". This initially met with little resistance as Ivan was happy with the attempted revision, yet after querying the BAWE he remarked how "*there were a lot of verbs I could replace 'fix' with*". By referring back to previous examples (e.g. "fix"), Ivan showed he was able to apply past query techniques to new contexts while working on different errors across multiple essays. After looking through the results in BAWE, he picked "tackled" because "*It [was] used a lot by Fatty and Mr Goon [in the Mystery of the Burnt Cottage]*", referring to a novel he was reading at the time; seeing the word in BAWE triggered this recollection for him.

He continued to emphasise his satisfaction with the different examples he could choose when using BAWE / Sketch Engine, using it again to revise his construction "*it is critical to know*" within the sentence "*it is critical to know that we will have a clearer environment if we recycle*", which was marked as erroneous. Before

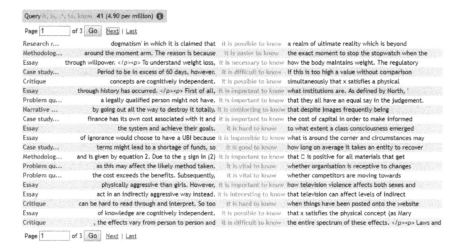

FIGURE 9.9 "*It is * to know*" in BAWE / Sketch Engine

he searched, the tutor asked him why he wanted to use BAWE / Sketch Engine instead of SkELL, to which he responded, "*SKELL is alright but Sketchengine is a little more straightforward*". Figure 9.9 shows how he managed to use the wildcard in the query "*it is * to know*" to find a replacement for "critical".

While reading the concordances, Ivan asked "*which ones are from essays?*" and then read all the examples from essays out loud. He claimed he had found a suitable concordance ("*It is essential to know. . .* ") on page 2 of the results after noticing that many of the phrases either used "*difficult*", "*hard*", or "*important*". He explained while he was reading that ". . . *'difficult' or 'hard' isn't really what I'm looking for. I need something more like 'important' but better*". The use of concordances to look for alternative vocabulary was mentioned again during the post-revision discussion

> "*Yeah! it was pretty good . . . helpful because like if . . . um . . . if my wording wasn't too good, it can show me how I can use different words to make my grade higher.*"

Revision session 3

As with William, the tutor signalled in Ivan's third session that he was to complete revisions with no guidance. Ivan went on to query SkELL 29 times (for some reason making a switch from BAWE to SkELL), and it was noted that a number of revisions made to his document were not those that were highlighted as erroneous by the lecturer. Rather, Ivan revised the essay as a whole, using SkELL frequently as he did so. It was also observed that he managed to use multiple functions of SkELL to resolve single highlighted errors without being prompted. For example, he managed to search for a word to replace "complicated" in the sentence "*this is because downloading new apps in the laptop is far more <u>complicated</u>*", where the intention was to convey something along the lines of "more complex" (and so better). This issue was not in fact highlighted as erroneous in his text, yet he used the *thesaurus / similar words* function of SkELL, finding the word "*sophisticated*" before using it in the following revised passage:

> This is because downloading new apps in the laptop, is far more sophisticated.

Ivan also used a combination of concordance, *word sketch* and *similar words* functions to examine how "amuse" could be replaced within the sentence "*these apps can teach, educate, entertain, amuse, intrigue and all sorts of other helpful things*", which again was not highlighted as erroneous. For example, Ivan used the *similar words* function for "amuse" and clicked on the result "irritate", looking through the concordance results and *word sketch* results for this word before returning to the *similar words* function to find other examples.

It was also observed that Ivan frequently entered complete phrases into the corpus marked as erroneous in his writing, e.g. "*panting under the weight*" and "*then comes in*" to determine if these were valid constructions, and if so, how they could be used in a sentence. The tutor asked him about this approach during the post-session discussion. For the example "*panting under the weight*", Ivan responded that "*it just didn't work and I couldn't find anything for it*", which confirmed his intuitions that the expression was in fact erroneous.

Ivan also noted how he might use the corpus to prepare for his upcoming standardised tests, e.g.:

> "*I would use it* [corpora] *in some occasions . . . just before NAPLAN, ICAS or some other assessment task, so I can get into the mood and get used to doing it . . . . I mean, get used to writing persuasive texts and get a better mark*"

Final revision session

During the last revision session, Ivan was now confident to use the full range of functions within SkELL without issue, switching between concordances, *similar words*, and *word sketch* freely. Ivan had made the error "to succes" in his draft, which he queried in SkELL. This actually led to four hits in the corpus (Figure 9.10).

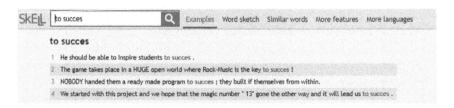

FIGURE 9.10 Concordances of "to succes" in SkELL

Ivan was able to determine from the low frequency of these results that four results *"isn't enough"*, before realising "succeed" should have been used. However, Ivan had issues with using Microsoft Word in this session, resulting in his spending less time using the corpus.

When Ivan was prompted to redefine his understanding of what a corpus was used for following this final session, he stated his definition had not changed much (*"It was the same idea* [sic]"). Ivan commented again that corpora could be a good replacement for and accompaniment to dictionaries for resolving lexical issues:

> *"I think SKELL is for practising how to write an essay. It helps me get ideas on how to use my words – words properly like 'over stress'"*

Discussion

This study explored two L1 primary school students' initial reactions to corpus use for essay writing in a private tutoring setting. Overall, both students reacted positively towards corpora as a tool that could help them resolve lexical issues in their writing, and both reported higher general self-efficacy as a result of their new-found language problem-solving skills after just five short sessions with corpora. We are particularly encouraged by the speed with which both learners took to corpora as a reference resource, which while also found in studies on tertiary learners (e.g. Crosthwaite, 2017), has been replicated here for much younger learners in a shorter timeframe (approx. one hour of training versus five hours of training in Crosthwaite, 2017). This is further emphasised if we contrast the relatively hands-off approach taken in this study to the more-prescribed teacher-led activities described for tertiary learners in Crosthwaite (2017) and Crosthwaite, Wong, and Cheung (2019). While the DDL expert provided suggested corpus queries, these were often not used; together with intermittent tutor scaffolding, William and Ivan took the opportunity to progress through the DDL training and revisions at their own pace.

This success is despite a high degree of divergence in students' initial reactions to corpora, the extent of overall corpus use of and willingness to experiment with the various corpus functions. William's initial reluctance to use the corpus (preferring instead to observe the tutor) and his unwillingness to experiment with different corpus functions stand in contrast with Ivan's enthusiastic adoption of "all things corpusy". This suggests that young learners' general ICT ability is likely a very strong factor in their initial uptake of corpora for DDL. This is presumably less of an issue for older learners who will generally all have some degree of competence in general ICT (either through education or at least through smartphone use), yet this remains an important factor to consider for younger learners, who may not yet have developed general ICT competence or whose schools may lack ICT resources. However, weaker general ICT skills did not appear to be a barrier to entry for William's eventual adoption of corpora for both his tutoring work and other school assignments, which is greatly encouraging especially given the short turnaround from being a reluctant observer to a (secret) self-guided corpus adoptee. The students' perceptions of SkELL as a writing tool also influenced how they approached the activities. William's initial understanding of SkELL is reflected in his focus on searching for specific words or phrases ("pattern defining", Kennedy & Micele, 2010), while his later perception of corpora saw a change in usage to finding alternatives with the wildcard function ("pattern refining", ibid.). On the other hand, Ivan saw SkELL as a tool to help improve writing from the beginning, reflected in his use of multiple corpus functions throughout the sessions.

If significant differences in corpus "aptitude" are found in students, this is where the role of the tutor in providing scaffolding makes an enormous difference. This is reflected in how both students learned to use the wildcard function in SkELL. After William had attempted to use the wildcard independently (and failed), the tutor's example in session 3 made a significant impact on how William used the wildcard in session 4, as he mentioned twice in the session that *"it has to be the dot star thingy plus the second word"*. Each session helped strengthen William's understanding of how the wildcard could be used effectively to find alternative words or phrases to use in a given context. In contrast, Ivan initially relied on constant reminders from the tutor but was soon able to apply the technique without any further assistance. In making the decision to provide more scaffolding at key junctures and concomitantly allowing stronger students the autonomy to proceed on their own, success in using the wildcard function for DDL was possible for both parties.

Obviously, the children and the tutor in this study benefitted enormously from having an expert in DDL looking through the written submissions to find issues that were amenable to corpus consultation and providing the relevant corpus query syntax to facilitate the revision process. This, on the face of it at least, would not be the case in a normal tutoring situation. However, most tutors will generally have a relevant degree (in the case of L1 instruction) or some kind of TESOL certification/experience (for L2 instruction). As DDL increases in popularity, it is not inconceivable that training in corpus consultation at some stage of a tutor's professional development could produce similar benefits. If training in corpus consultation was embedded into more degree programmes or TESOL programmes, graduates of such programmes would be likely to "spread the word" (Römer, 2009) to their own students in similar situations. Following the experimental period, the tutor reported wanting to continue using the corpus with other students, and we are now preparing a paper to report on those findings. We also believe that William and Ivan themselves are now likely to share their own experiences of corpus use with their classmates, who may then go on to "spread the word" themselves. Given what we know about the intense competition between students who attend private tutoring sessions (at least, between their parents!), anything that can be seen as providing an advantage for learning is likely to be very quickly seized upon by others once it is known. We do not consider this a bad thing at all. That said, we aim to continue in our efforts to take DDL beyond private tutoring and into mainstream primary education, as long as someone will give us the opportunity.

References

Alsop, S., & Nesi, H. (2009). Issues in the development of the British Academic Written English (BAWE) corpus. *Corpora*, 4(1), 71–83.

Australian Curriculum (2018a) www.australiancurriculum.edu.au/f-10-curriculum/general-capabilities/literacy/learning-continuum/ (accessed April 2019).

Australian Curriculum (2018b) www.australiancurriculum.edu.au/f-10-curriculum/general-capabilities/information-and-communication-technology-ict-capability/ (accessed April 2019).

Baisa, V., & Suchomel, V. (2014). SkELL: Web interface for english language learning. In *Eighth workshop on recent advances in slavonic natural language processing* (pp. 63–70). Brno: Tribun EU.

Bandura, A. (1986). *Social foundations of thought and action: A social cognitive theory*. Englewood Cliffs, NJ: Prentice-Hall.

Boulton, A., & Cobb, T. (2017). Corpus use in language learning: A meta-analysis. *Language Learning*, 67(2), 348–393.

Burnett, C., & Daniels, K. (2015). Technology and literacy in the early years: Framing young children's meaning-making with new technologies. In S. Garvis & N. Lemon (Eds.), *Understanding digital technologies and young children* (pp. 18–27). Oxon: Routledge.

Crosthwaite, P. (2017). Retesting the limits of data-driven learning: Feedback and error correction. *Computer-Assisted Language Learning*, 30(6), 447–473. doi: 10.1080/09588221.2017.1312462.

Crosthwaite, P., Wong, L. L. C., & Cheung, J. (2019). Characterising postgraduate students' corpus query and usage patterns for disciplinary data-driven Learning. *ReCALL*, online ahead of print. doi: 10.1017/S0958344019000077.

Hirata, E. (2012). *An investigation into the potential of a corpus-influenced syllabus for primary English literacy education in Japan* (Doctoral dissertation, University of Birmingham).

Hirata, E. (2016). The development of multi-modal corpus tool for teaching English to young learners. *Fukuoka Jo Gakuin University Bulletin, Faculty of International Career Department*, 2, 19–32.

Hirata, E. (2018). Teacher education for Teaching English to Young Learners (TEYL): The scope for the integration of data-driven learning. *Fukuoka Jo Gakuin University Bulletin, Faculty of International Career Development*, 4, 127–143.

Kennedy, C., & Miceli, T. (2010). Corpus-assisted creative writing: Introducing intermediate Italian learners to a corpus as a reference resource. *Language Learning & Technology*, 14(1), 28–44.

Kim, H. (2019). The perception of teachers and learners towards an exploratory corpus-based grammar instruction in a Korean EFL primary school context. *Primary English Education*, 25(1), 123–152.

Leray, M., & Tyne, H. (2016). Homophonie et maîtrise du français écrit: apport de l'apprentissage sur corpus. *Linguistik Online*, 78(4). https://doi.org/10.13092/lo.78.2954.

Pajares, F., Johnson, M. J., & Usher, E. L. (2007). Sources of writing self-efficacy beliefs of elementary, middle, and high school students. *Research in the Teaching of English*, 42, 104–120.

Pajares, F., Miller, M. D., & Johnson, M. J. (1999). Gender differences in writing self-beliefs of elementary school students. *Journal of Educational Psychology*, 91, 50–61.

Römer, U. (2009). Corpus research and practice: What help do teachers need and what can we offer? In K. Aijmer (Ed.), *Corpora and language teaching* (pp. 83–98). Amsterdam: John Benjamins.

Rose, D., & Martin, J. R. (2012). *Learning to write, reading to learn: Genre, knowledge and pedagogy in the Sydney school.* London: Equinox.

Sealey, A., & Thompson, P. (2004). ' "What do you call the dull words?": Primary school children using corpus-based approaches to learn about language', *English in Education, 38*(1), 80–91.

Sealey, A., & Thompson, P. (2007). Corpus, concordance, classification: Young learners in the L1 classroom. *Language Awareness, 16*(3), 208–223.

Sriprakash, A., Proctor, H., & Hu, B. (2016). Visible pedagogic work: Parenting, private tutoring and educational advantage in Australia. *Discourse: Studies in the Cultural Politics of Education, 37*(3), 426–441. doi: 10.1080/01596306.2015.1061976.

10
TEACHING FRENCH TO YOUNG LEARNERS THROUGH DDL

Sonia Di Vito

Introduction

Within the context of broader research (*Les Langues Modernes*, 3/2018; Hamez & Pereiro, eds., 2018) on the topicality of grammar teaching, the question of whether the DDL approach for the study of syntactic, morphological, and grammatical phenomena could be successfully applied to younger learners of French as a foreign language (FLE) still requires an answer. Aware of DDL's potential for adult learners of FLE, having already used it as a teaching methodology with university students (see Di Vito, 2013) and in middle school, I report in this chapter how the DDL approach could be introduced successfully as a teaching methodology to arouse the interest of young learners in grammar and to increase learner autonomy and their ability to analyse data and generate hypotheses. To test this, I organised a DDL experiment with middle school students who were studying elements of the French grammar system. The first area of questioning regards whether younger pupils are able to observe grammatical regularities of the French language system through the analysis of concordances. If so, which type of corpus is best suited to them? Can they be exposed to and draw analyses from a large amount of data? Can they use corpus software themselves for this purpose? The second area of questioning is related to the role of the teacher and his or her involvement in the creation of an *ad hoc* corpus and teaching materials based on the DDL approach and whether this presents suitable opportunities for effective language learning and teaching. A brief description of the history of the teaching methodologies used in FLE classrooms in the last two decades is necessary to contextualise this experimentation, as is a basic understanding of FLE in Italy. I then present an outline of DDL studies both on L1 French learners and for FLE.

Foreign language teaching in Europe post-CEFR

The publication of the *Common European Framework of Reference for Languages* (henceforth CEFR) highlighted key principles on which the teaching of foreign languages is increasingly based and where the teaching of foreign languages is linked to the communicative needs of the learners. The CEFR iterates that learning should now be considered an active process in which the teacher is a "counsellor" who guides students through "authentic" language in use rather than that conceived exclusively as teaching material for foreign language courses. After the publication of the CEFR, concepts such as the functional approach (*français fonctionnel*) and instrumental French (*français instrumental*) from the 1970s were re-interpreted for their suitability in favour of the communicative approach as developed in France under the name of *approche actionnelle* (action-oriented approach) (Mourlhon-Dallies, 2008; Carras, Tolas, Kohler, & Szilagyi, 2007; Mangiante et al., 2004; Lions-Olivieri & Liria, 2003). According to the promoters of this didactic approach, a language should not be explicitly taught by the teacher but rather learned through the realisation of tasks that are part of a global training project. The learner is a "social agent" who carries out actions in real circumstances and environments; the foreign language is no longer the explicit goal of learning but a means by which students communicate with other participants to learn how to do things. Learners' needs are at the heart of current teaching practices; consequently, different needs correspond to different goals (first pragmatic and then linguistic).[1] In addition, over the last 15 years, the so-called teaching of multilingualism has developed in accordance with the directives of the Council of Europe, which calls for the multilingual training of its citizens. A team of scholars has been active in analysing and promoting so-called "pluralistic approaches", namely teaching methods that involve the learning of several languages at the same time. In particular, there are four pluralistic approaches identified in the *Framework of Reference for pluralistic approaches to languages and cultures*, which includes the "awakening" to languages – the intercomprehension between related languages, the intercultural approach, and the integrated didactic approach.[2] From the point of view of foreign language teaching, Caon (2012, p. 31 *et seq*.) emphasises that both the attention to the student in their emotional, relational, and cognitive components and their centrality in the process of teaching/learning are widely shared dimensions. However, in teaching practice, supported by manuals, the protagonism of pupils emerges less frequently than that of language teachers, now called "facilitators of language learning".

French L2 in Italy

Until the mid-1990s, French, a language of culture (Caon, 2012, p. 21), was taught in Italy as the first foreign language in middle and high school classes. Since the second half of the 1990s, French has been explicitly downgraded in the curriculum, mainly thanks to the strategy of the "three 'Is'" in Italian – *Informatica, Impresa, Inglese* (computer science, business, English) – that the government of the time included in its educational programme. At the beginning of the 2000s, following calls from the European Commission, the introduction of a second compulsory foreign language (after English) was launched in Italy. Initially, the compulsory second foreign language was French, but it was soon joined by Spanish, leaving fewer students taking up L2 French than before.

In 2018, a volume of the magazine *Synergies Italie* was dedicated to the study of the declinations of the action-oriented approach and FLE in secondary and university education in Italy (Kottelat & Dapavo, 2018). Alongside discussion on theoretical perspectives regarding teacher training, the learning of metalexical notions by learners and various teaching practices of FLE were also up for debate. In particular, Favata's (2018) contribution on new technologies now mentions practices such as the flipped classroom, m-learning, and intercomprehension on the *Miriadi*[3] and *Galanet*[4] platforms as valid tools to help pupils, even beginners, to develop skills in understanding the French language and to discover the common points between Italian and French (Favata, 2018, p. 65).

DDL for French as a foreign language

While DDL's educational applications have developed exponentially for the English language, only in recent years have they found their way into academic circles looking at FLE. In a 2008 article (p. 37), Boulton stated there was a considerable delay in the direct use of corpora in FLE classes, given it was difficult to accept an approach that was mainly descriptive of the use of language and that subverted, among other things, the traditional role of the teacher. In 2008, out of 39 studies carried out on the impact of the DDL approach in language teaching, only three concerned French language learning and the use of corpora (Boulton, 2008, pp. 39–40). Today, the situation has changed: since 2010, quantitative and qualitative studies of the teaching of French as a foreign language through corpora have been developed in various disciplinary fields. In 2010, Chambers conducted a study on the pedagogical use of a corpus of scientific articles for FLE. This study showed that students can benefit from corpora when improving their written production. Also in 2010, Giuliani *et al.* proposed to students of *Didactique du FLE*[5] the analysis of linguistic phenomena (the difference between *quant* and *quand* and *très* and *trop*) to discover the potential of corpus analysis for educational purposes. In 2011, Kamber highlighted how the direct analysis of linguistic corpora could help students in an FLE class to extend their vocabulary, highlighting how the analysis of concordances gives much more information than a simple dictionary and allows students not only to observe the keyword itself but to recognise a broader expression related to it. He ends by saying that this type of activity proposed to students is within everyone's reach and requires only a minimum of training and information.

In other research, Di Vito (2013) evaluated activities carried out in class with university students between level B1 and B1+ of the CEFR, highlighting how the analysis of concordances can be decisive in the learning of syntactic patterns, lexical elements, or sectorial lexicon and in the capacity to disambiguate parasynonyms. Also in 2013, number 97 of the *Bulletin suisse de linguistique appliquée*, coordinated by Henry Tyne, was titled *Apprentissage sur corpus: théories, méthodes, applications et perspectives* and devoted various articles to the learning of linguistic phenomena of French through the consultation of corpora. In it we find, among others, the studies of Kerr (2013, pp. 17–39) and Chambers (2013, pp. 41–58), which show didactic applications of the DDL approach to study linguistic phenomena such as the polysemy of the verb *projeter*, the difference between *sentir* and *se sentir*, the French subjunctive, etc. The studies of the LIDILEM team in Grenoble (among others Tran, Tutin, & Cavalla, 2016; Yan, Tutin, & Tran, 2018; Cavalla, 2009, 2015a, 2015b) have also demonstrated the usefulness of linguistic corpora in the teaching of FLE to university students – for example, for learning discourse markers or verbal expressions at the centre of enunciation and argumentation in academic writing, phraseology related to university writings, or the lexicon of emotions. Finally, André (2018) describes the FLEURON learning platform, a free access multimedia corpus with data covering communicative situations that foreign students are likely to experience once they arrive in France, as produced by speakers acting in multiple contexts.

However, these studies mainly focus on university students (age 19 and over). The only study conducted on young learners of French is that presented by Leray and Tyne (2016), in which the authors highlight the effectiveness of corpora to overcome the spelling difficulties of young learners of L1 French during the transition from oral to written language. The authors conclude that the adoption of DDL practice for young learners of French L1 may offer many benefits, although it is not easy to determine which aspects of the DDL approach had a greater impact on the learning of these pupils.

The "ASC: Apprentissage Sur Corpus" project[6]

Convinced that corpus learning is a stimulating process for younger learners, I decided to experiment with it in middle school FLE classes. This was made possible thanks to the willingness of teachers at the G. Conte College Middle School (*Scuola Secondaria di Primo grado, ex scuola media*), part of the *Istituto comprensivo Cassino 2*.[7]

Participants

A total of 127 students (between 12 and 13 years old) from year eight (*seconda media*) who had already studied FLE in year seven (*prima media*) took part in the study, divided into six mixed-ability classes (all the pupils of year eight attending classes in that school). The students had no previous experience of using concordances in classroom, nor did they know the meaning of the word "corpus".

French is taught as the second compulsory foreign language at this school and is timetabled for two hours of lessons per week. The results of the second-year entrance tests for French[8] showed a good understanding of oral and written language, good written and oral production skills, and good knowledge and use of language structures and functions by these participants. Based on CEFR criteria, the students had fully reached an A1 level in the second year of study of the French language, therefore far exceeding the thresholds required by the MIUR (Italian Ministry of Education) guidelines (MIUR, 2012, p. 49).[9] In fact, they are supposed to have established a level of knowledge equal to A1 for the second foreign language by the end of secondary school. However, in the FLE manuals used in this course of study, the subjects covered in the first and second year already go beyond the level envisaged by the Ministry during the first two years of secondary school.[10]

Compiling our corpora

Regarding the composition of the corpus for the experimentation, the first concern was whether or not to use corpora already available online. After researching the grammatical targets for analysis, we realised that the language of the literature or press on the *Complete Lexical Tutor* website (www.lextutor.ca) was too complex for the work we wanted to do with middle school pupils. The size of a corpus is another important aspect to consider when deciding whether to use it for DDL. As Boulton (2014, p. 131) states, there is no minimum size for a language corpus because the size depends primarily on the purpose for which that corpus was created. Moreover, he argues that if one wants to study a precise variety of language, a small corpus can be used. In addition, as stated by Gilquin and Granger (2010, p. 366), students are at risk of getting lost when faced with large numbers of concordances.

To overcome these potential difficulties, a decision was made to create an *ad hoc* corpus, containing documents written for French speakers of about the same age as our students (pre-adolescents and adolescents): texts easily grasped by pupils thanks to the lexicon and the syntactic structures used. We downloaded from the Internet texts of articles written between October and December 2017 from the magazine *Geo Ados*,[11] written for 10- to 15-year-olds, which covers topics from middle school curricula such as nature, peoples, history, the human body, cinema, games, literature, etc., and *Le Monde des Ados*,[12] which presents news stories, pictures and dossiers on specific important topics for young people. These documents were purged of all images, hypertext links, and any other information not necessary for our experimentation, and saved in txt format to be treated with corpus software for the extraction of concordances (in this case, AntConc).[13] The *Corpus Junior Fr* used in this first phase of experimentation[14] consists of 23 articles amounting to about 10,000 words. I then decided to create another corpus, *Junior Corpus It*, in order to have a resource for making comparisons between the language being learned and the students' mother tongue. The comparative process, as stated by Pinto (2015), presupposes an ability to reflect on the two languages and contributes to increasing the students' metalinguistic awareness. This second corpus currently comprises 22 articles downloaded from the Internet from *Focus Junior*,[15] a monthly magazine for children ages 8 to 13 that deals with science, technology, animal behaviour, and current topics of interest in school life. This corpus was also approximately 10,000 words in size. Our corpora can be considered as *pedagogic corpora* (Pérez-Paradez, this volume), which are created for teaching purposes and differ from available corpora in size (they may be smaller than large corpora), contents (related to the interests of the students with whom they are intended to be used), and text typology (they may contain only one).

Procedure

The "ASC: Apprentissage Sur Corpus" project began in November 2017 with preliminary meetings with the French teachers of the classes involved; the purpose of these meetings was to present the learning method by using it with practical activities for teachers. The teachers had no previous experience with corpora and corpus use in teaching French, so some activities were prepared to introduce them to linguistic analysis through corpora. Three teachers were asked to conduct research on an online corpus (www.lextutor.ca) on grammar points that they felt deserved to be explored and were immediately struck by the potential of this teaching/learning approach for their classrooms. The preliminary meetings also allowed us to establish the grammatical topics that would be presented to students in the following months: *loro, mettre, quel, ce, très,* and *beaucoup*. Our course covered three hours of classes, from December 2017 to January 2018, for each of the six classes, for a total of 18 hours of activity and observation.

The teachers gave me full teaching autonomy in the classes involved, including preparation of materials and planning of activities. In line with the considerations of many scholars (including Gabrielatos, 2005; Boulton, 2009), I chose to present the concordances on paper, with the keyword and the cotext on the right and left highlighted with the colours blue, red, and green, respectively. Each time, the topic of the activity was introduced by writing the title, in French, on the blackboard, with expressions such as "today we will discover. . . ". Then, the concordances on paper were distributed to the students, who were asked to observe the keywords and the cotext on the right and the left. The words on the right and the left were analysed together, and the most opaque terms were translated into Italian; depending on the topic analysed, pupils were asked to observe the grammatical categories of the keyword collocations, their gender, and their number. Students worked in groups of two to four; during the activity they could help each other, make hypotheses, and propose them to the other members of their group. At the end of this activity, the pupils guided the teacher, who had to fill in a grid on the blackboard with the results of the observation, before they proposed the formulation of the relevant rule. To systematise and internalise the discovered rule, I proposed gap-filling exercises or sentence creation exercises on the phenomena analysed.

During the experimentation, besides being teacher/guide to the observation of the concordances, I also played the role of the observer of the students' attitudes and of their possible difficulties, taking notes of what happened during the lessons. As the purpose of this first phase of experimentation was to observe the students' reaction to this new didactic approach to grammar and their commitment to discovering the rules underlying the use of the elements chosen, we administered a questionnaire at the end of the course to obtain their feedback on the activities carried out.

Results

This section explores how the lessons were carried out, concordance use training in L1 (Italian), the activities proposed to the pupils in L2 French, and the results of the questionnaire given to pupils at the end of the experimentation.

Classroom concordance use

To help pupils understand what kind of observation we wanted them to make, we asked them firstly to observe a linguistic phenomenon in their first language, namely the use of the word *loro*, which has multiple functions in Italian, including being a possessive adjective or pronoun, an object pronoun, and a subject pronoun in spoken Italian. Looking at the concordances of *loro* (Figure 10.1), we found all the functions mentioned.

FIGURE 10.1 Concordance lines for *loro*

Pupils were first asked to look at the context to the left and right of this word and to read those words out loud. The second step involved asking them about the grammatical category (articles, prepositions, nouns, verbs) to which the words to the right of *loro* belonged and to group them on the basis of the same category: prepositions (*al, con, della, nella, per, tra*), articles (*il, la*), and verbs (*porterà, sono*) to the left; nouns (*risveglio, casa, inno, incolumità*, etc.), articles (*un, il*), prepositions (*a*), and adverbs (*fuori*) to the right. The third step was to ask them to insert these elements into a table (which allowed us to schematise their uses and to associate the function of the word *loro* with the different collocations), respecting their "position" within the concordances. This activity gave us the following scheme:

1 article + *loro* + noun   *il loro mestiere*
2 preposition + article + *loro* + noun   *nella loro vita*
3 preposition + *loro* + adverb   *per loro fuori*
4 verb + *loro* + noun   *porterà loro cioccolato*
5 noun + *loro*   *colpa loro*

In the fourth step, pupils were asked to reflect on the correlation between the syntactic structure and the grammatical function of the word: In which examples (and in which syntactic structure) does the word indicate possession, or is it a personal pronoun? It was evident to the pupils that in the first two structures it was a possessive adjective and that in the last three structures it was a personal pronoun. The fifth passage served to draw up the two rules of use.

If this activity was thought of as a warm-up activity used to accustom pupils to observing the concordances of an element they had already mastered, one can imagine the potential of such an activity when dealing with the same subject in French. In fact, the element *loro* corresponds, in its various functions, to the French word *leur(s)*. The difficulty for Italian-speaking pupils (and probably also for French-speaking pupils) is the distinction between the pronoun function (invariable) and the possessive adjective function (declinable in the plural) because of the difficulties in the passage from the only oral form [lFR] to the double written form *leur/leurs*. Observing the occurrences of *leur* in the *Corpus Junior Fr*, one immediately notices that *leur* is declined in the plural when it is followed by a noun, while in the only occurrence[16] in which it is preceded by the verb, it is singular. The study of these lines of concordance would also have allowed us to discover the different position of the two elements in the two languages, corresponding to the different functions:

leur + noun (without article) = adjective function (declinable in plural)
leur + verb = pronoun function (not declinable in the plural).

The second case concerns the conjugation of the present indicative of the verb *mettre* (put). The challenge for Italian students is to identify the correspondence

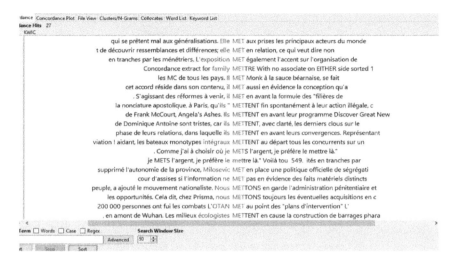

FIGURE 10.2 Concordance lines for *met**

between the subject's personal pronouns and endings. The activity was designed to avoid reducing the discovery of this verb to a simple transcription on the blackboard by the teacher, or even worse, to an observation of it in the textbook. These were the concordances[17] that were distributed in class (Figure 10.2).

Scaffolding was provided before and during the observation of the concordances. In fact, the starting point for the reflection on the conjugation of the verb was to remind the students that in French the personal pronoun subject of the verb is generally always expressed and that the verb agrees with the subject. Secondly, we asked them to include in the table the various forms of the subject personal pronouns and then to observe the various forms of the target word. The pupils found the following forms, listed in order of appearance: *met, mettre, mettent, mets, mettons*. In the next step, they were asked to look for the correspondences between the endings of the verb and the subject pronoun that precedes it and to insert them in the following scheme:

Subject	Verb
je	*mets*
tu	
il	*met*
nous	*mettons*
vous	
ils	*mettent*

Using their previous knowledge of the endings for which no occurrences were found, they also filled in the boxes of the second person singular and plural (*tu mets, vous mettez*). In addition to the discovery of conjugation and its transcription,

> fait régulièrement le portrait d'aventurières). Quelle attitude face à la pornographie ? Le Présid
> 1 4 déjà à parler d'un « brevet 2018 ». Alors, quel brevet allez-vous passer cette année ? Des
> laisser les autres pays se débrouiller seuls. Quelles conséquences ? Depuis à peu près 70 ans, l
> 02 9 la façon de vivre est si différente ! » Quel effet ça fait de quitter les siens ? «
> fiques. Impressionnant ! Et bientôt, devine dans quel magazine ? Et puis, sus des glaces ! Dallol,
> 101 13 assure, ce n'était pas n'importe quel poisson clown, c'était Nemo !! XD Près

FIGURE 10.3 Concordance lines for *quel**

we asked them to carry out a gap-filling exercise with the various forms of the verb. This activity also lends itself to further considerations regarding the use of such concordances not only with foreign students but also with L1 French students since, just as for *leur*, the passage from oral to written production of this verb poses many problems of correspondence in the number of pronounced sounds and transcribed letters (for example, *(je) mets*, four graphemes; [mè], two phonemes). The same procedure was followed for the other grammar topics that were part of the trial.

It is worth noting how this methodology can promote student autonomy. During one lesson, there were some students who worked individually, not in groups. As they had done the required activity more quickly than the other groups, I decided to test their capacity for absolute autonomy, giving them the concordances of the word *quel* (Figure 10.3).[18]

From this small list we asked the two students to tell us in which contexts the word was used and how. After a few minutes of observation, they had worked out the following scheme themselves:

quel magazine	→	*quel* + singular masculine noun
quelle attitude	→	*quelle* + singular feminine noun
quelles conséquences	→	*quelles* + plural feminine noun

They also pointed out that in four of five occurrences the word was used in questioning sentences. This example, perhaps even more so than the others, highlights how the use of concordances in FLE classes can foster the student's autonomy in discovering the language.

Feedback from the questionnaire

At the end of the experimentation, the students were asked to fill in a questionnaire to obtain feedback on the DDL activities. A total of 101 questionnaires were completed. The questionnaire comprised eight open questions, with the first question referring to the number of classes the pupil attended during the period of experimentation.

The second question ("What were the topics you dealt with?") was asked to identify whether pupils remembered the contents of the DDL lessons after more than a month. Over half the pupils (56 per cent) managed to remember all the contents dealt with during the lessons (that is, the verb *mettre*; the demonstrative adjectives; the Italian word *loro*; and, in the classes in which we managed to deal with it, the difference in use of *très*, *beaucoup*, and *beaucoup de*). Just over a quarter of pupils (27 per cent) recalled at least one of the topics dealt with, while 17 per cent had great difficulty in recalling the specific contents dealt with during the lessons.

The third question was intended to direct respondents towards the description of the various phases implemented to analyse the proposed linguistic phenomena. We thought it appropriate to ask this question because the DDL approach is based on the ability of the "researcher" (linguist or student) to observe and find regularity in the system. This meta-cognitive reflection was difficult for many students, who were unable to explain the description of the activities.[19] However, almost half (47.52 per cent) clearly explained the methods of analysis of the occurrences, even among the pupils who had problems in remembering the topics. These pupils cited some of the phases described ("analysing the occurrences", "filling in the table", "deducing the rule", "giving examples", "doing the exercises") and used phrases such as "keyword in the middle" and "seeing what preceded and what followed".

The fourth question was divided into two parts: "Were the instructions that the teacher gave you to analyse the occurrences during the group work clear? Did they allow you to carry out the required activities?" The reason for division was to find out whether the procedures described were understood by the pupils in a clear and effective manner and also to receive feedback on our teaching style. Almost all respondents (94 per cent) answered that the instructions were either "sufficiently" clear to enable them to do the activities or "very" clear.

The fifth question asked pupils if they thought that the proposed activities were difficult, and why. Over 90 per cent of pupils replied that they were not, mainly thanks to the instructions given for completing the activities, while some pupils also pointed out that the "ease" of the exercise was due to working in a group ("working together, things seemed easier to me", "we faced each other in a group and therefore we felt we had more help", "it was not a difficult job at all because we were all together"). Commenting on this question, some found that this activity was "relaxing", "new", and "different to the traditional one". As far as negative feedback is concerned, the difficulty of the activities was attributed to the novelty of the topics; to the fact that the rule had to be deduced on its own; and, in just one example only, to the novelty of the methodology.

Answers to question six – "Did you like this method of learning French grammar? Why/Why not?" – showed that the majority of pupils involved appreciated this "new method of learning". The reasons for such a high level of appreciation (98 per cent) were varied. First of all, it was a different teaching method from the traditional one, which aroused more interest in the topics covered; this method also appeared "less heavy-going" and more entertaining and captured the pupils' attention ("we were not bored"). Some pupils stressed the fact that they managed to learn the content more quickly, while others talked about the progressive advancement of learning (observation, schematisation, deduction and explanation of the rule in groups, and application of it in exercises). Some also appreciated this methodology because "it made me reason with my head" or "it was I who worked out the rule". The fact that it was a lesson full of interaction (pupil–teacher and pupil–pupil) in which everyone was encouraged to participate was also appreciated. Finally, many of them highlighted the positive nature of teamwork, which enabled them to compare ideas, help each other, and remember the contents better.

The remaining two questions asked about any suggested improvements to the activities. The majority of respondents confirmed the activities did not require any modification, whether improvements or omissions. Thirteen per cent of pupils suggested some changes: the duration of the lesson ("it should last longer"), talking more in French, changing phrases that were not clear, more exercises, and a recap of the content covered in the previous lesson. One pupil judged the activities too easy, while another highlighted their difficulty in working in groups and proposed more individual work.

Discussion

In this chapter, I have presented an experiment to test the validity of DDL methodology with younger Italian learners of FLE. Based on suggestions from the French teachers of the school, the pupils analysed some grammatical and syntactical elements as part of DDL-based lessons.

According to the observations made in class, the pupils were able to find the regularity for the proposed elements. One can deduce that the DDL approach has great potential for this and other areas of language even with students of this age. However, individual variation was noted in relation to the speed of observations, reflections, rule formulation, etc.: It seems that for some groups, the activities were really very simple to complete, while for others they took longer. Furthermore, this type of work was not suitable for all types of linguistic phenomena, and the observations and reflections to be made may be too complex for some young people: For example, the analysis of *articles partitifs* will have resulted in a number of ambiguities because their forms (*du/de la/des*) are not only partitives. Hence, teachers should carefully choose which elements to study with DDL.

Regarding the type of corpus best suited for DDL with younger FLE learners, the best corpus is one containing language suitable for the age of the students, since other types of corpora, such as those available online, are less easily understandable by young pupils (to use Pérez-Paradez's words, language that makes "sense to young learners" (Pérez-Paradez's chapter in this volume). As argued by Aston (2002, p. 9), "Home-made corpora may be more appropriate for learning purposes than pre-compiled ones, insofar as they can be specifically targeted to the learner's knowledge and concern".

Regarding whether young learners can deal with exposure to a large amount of data, we noticed a certain difficulty in analysing results with large numbers of concordances. In fact, for some analyses (e.g. *loro* or *très/beaucoup*), we had to guide the students' observations step by step. As argued by Gavioli and Aston (2001, p. 244), learners could start with smaller corpora "which are more limited and manageable" and then move "to others which are richer and more varied" in order to develop autonomy progressively. Therefore, for some types of activity we can expect completely autonomous student performance, although for others, the process requires significant scaffolding. For example, Wicher (this volume) proposes input enhancements, variable assignments, and the manipulation of concordance lines to provide scaffolding.

The numerous advantages of this DDL activity were confirmed by the answers to the questionnaire. Firstly, learners acquired a method to observe the keyword systematically: analysing the left and right cotext, expressing their hypotheses out loud, filling in the grid, making an outline of the uses, and finally formulating the "grammatical rule" on their own. Secondly, pupils showed an increased ability to systematise rules and content: As some pupils responded in the questionnaire, they greatly appreciated the fact that they used schemes that made the results of their observations clearer. Thirdly, they played a very active role during the activities, responding to requests and actively participating in the formulation of the rule; moreover, there were no lulls in activity where they could become bored. Fourthly, their active participation and responses to the questionnaire (in particular the answers to questions five through eight) showed their enthusiasm for the way in which these lessons were conducted, citing teamwork and their status as "observers/researchers (i.e. as protagonists) rather than just "auditors" and requesting more time be devoted to this type of activity. All these factors undoubtedly fuelled their motivation. Lastly, if in the first session the pupils were shy and fearful in answering and participating animatedly in the lesson, in subsequent lessons, having understood the mode of interaction required, they overcame their fears and gained more self-confidence.

However, some disadvantages were observed for FLE teachers. First of all, it takes a great deal of time to prepare this type of activity because one needs to compile the corpus and then extract the concordances, edit, and print them; for this reason, using concordance software directly could save time because keywords and their collocations would be highlighted on the screen, although this would require additional training. Moreover, with regard to classroom work, additional time needs to be allocated since activities of observation, reflection, and formulation of the rule are more time-consuming than an explanation in which the teacher transmits his or her knowledge to the pupils orally. For example, in the activity for *mettre*, the teacher would certainly have spent less time if they had simply written on the blackboard or had pupils observe the conjugation of this verb in the book and asked them to do the exercises. Instead, this activity took 20 minutes (between observation, filling the table, and carrying out the exercises), which may affect the learning of other content in tight teaching schedules.

Conclusion

Clearly, learning languages with corpora is not a panacea, especially because different learning styles must be taken into account (e.g. Flowerdew, 2015); the corpus approach, if used exclusively, can be demotivating if it becomes too mechanical. However, one can consider DDL an appropriate style of teaching because it has induced in the students a feeling of success, progress, and responsibility. We can assimilate this to what Kolb (1984) defines as "experiential learning", divided into four stages: 1) concrete experience (the concordances of the language actually used by French speakers), 2) observation with reflection (the observation of concordances), 3) conceptualisation (realization of schemes to visualise the rule), and 4) experimentation (putting the rule into practice through exercises). Hopefully, this chapter has shown that the corpus approach can successfully provide excellent material for specific language content for younger learners and develop in these learners a range of learning methods in order to complement and enrich existing approaches.

Notes

1. For example, the linguistic needs of someone working in the medical profession who has to know how to speak French are different from the course content and study duration needs of a student who "chooses" to learn French as a second foreign language.
2. For more details on the pluralistic approaches to languages and cultures, see https://carap.ecml.at/Keyconcepts/tabid/2681/language/en-GB/Default.aspx (accessed April 2019).
3. Miriadi is the acronym of "Mutualisation et Innovation pour un Réseau de 'Intercompréhension à Distance" ("Cooperation and Innovation for an Online Intercomprehension Network") and is a working platform (www.miriadi.net/en/what-miriadi [accessed April 2019]) where a wide-ranging audience can learn various related languages by participating in online educational projects established by a network of teachers working on intercomprehension. Miriadi is also a network of people and other entities (such as universities, schools, associations, and so on) who meet virtually on the platform and organise online training projects for foreign language learners and for teachers who want to become experts in intercomprehension methodology of teaching.
4. Galanet was a platform for the online learning of intercomprehension. Designed for an academic audience, the Galanet sessions [. . .] were used at university and high school to train students and pupils in intercomprehension. However, the tasks of the Galanet sessions are not suitable for a younger audience. Today, all materials designed for Galanet are embedded in the platform Miriadi (www.miriadi.net/en/projects [accessed April 2019]).
5. The "Didactics of Languages" master's degree is aimed at future professionals and specialists in languages and cultures, in particular future teachers of French as a foreign language and second language.
6. In English it corresponds to "Learning with corpus".
7. www.iccassino2.edu.it (accessed February 2019); for further details about the school setting and the French curriculum, see Di Vito (2018), pp. 54–55.
8. This information was provided by the teachers participating in the experiment.
9. www.indicazioninazionali.it/wp-content/uploads/2018/08/Indicazioni_Annali_Definitivo.pdf (accessed April 2019)
10. For example, an A1 level pupil is usually not required to talk about events in the past, yet the topic is included in the various manuals of FLE for year eight.
11. www.geoado.com (accessed February 2019)
12. www.lemondedesados.fr (accessed March 2019)
13. Anthony, L. (2014). AntConc (Version 3.4.2) [Computer Software]. Tokyo, Japan: Waseda University. (retrieved from www.laurenceanthony.net/software)

14 A new phase of experimentation is planned with the students of this school in the school year 2019–2020 to help teachers deal with all the grammar topics planned through the analysis of concordances.
15 www.focusjunior.it (accessed April 2019)
16 The fact that we found just a single occurrence in which *leur* has the value of a personal pronoun leads us to think that the size of our corpus is still too small and therefore not yet adequate to allow an analysis of all the uses of a word.
17 In fact, the concordances used for this activity were not extracted from the *Corpus Junior Fr*, because there were not enough occurrences to be analysed. Given the very technical nature of the activity, we decided to use the concordances of *mettre* extracted from the corpus Lextutor. Also, this lack of sufficient occurrences for our analysis pushes us to continue to extend the size of our corpus.
18 Again, we did not obtain all the variants of *quel* – only the masculine singular and the feminine singular and plural.
19 The reason for this difficulty could be explained by the fact that, in order to be able to do this kind of reflection, the student must acquire an active, responsible, and conscious attitude towards learning; to be able to develop this competence, he or she must be educated to do so.

References

André, V. (2018). Nouvelles actions didactiques: faire de la sociolinguistique de corpus pour enseigner et apprendre à interagir en français langue étrangère. *Action Didactique*, *1*, 71–88.

Aston, G. (2002). The learner as corpus designer. In B. Kettemann & G. Marko (Eds.), *Teaching and learning by doing corpus analysis* (pp. 9–25). Amsterdam: Rodopi.

Boulton, A. (2008). Esprit de corpus: Promouvoir l'exploitation de corpus en apprentissage des langues. *Texte et corpus*, *3*, 37–46.

Boulton, A. (2009). Data-driven learning: On paper, in practice. In T. Harris & M. M. Jaén (Eds.), *Corpus linguistics in language teaching* (pp. 1–37). Berne: Peter Lang.

Boulton, A., & Tyne, H. (2014). *Des documents authentiques aux corpus*. Paris: Didier.

Candelier, M. (2007). *CARAP: Framework of references for pluralistic approaches to languages and cultures*. https://carap.ecml.at/Keyconcepts/tabid/2681/language/en-GB/Default.aspx (accessed April 2019).

Caon, F. (2012). *Aimes-tu le français? Percezione dello studio obbligatorio del francese nella scuola media*. Venezia: Edizioni Ca' Foscari.

Carras, C., Tolas, J., Kohler P., & Szilagyi, E. (Eds.). (2007). *Le français sur Objectifs Spécifiques et la classe de langue*. Paris: CLE International.

Cavalla, C. (2009). La phraséologie en classe de FLE. *Les Langues Modernes*, *1*, 1–12.

Cavalla, C. (2015a). L'enseignement des affects en FLE: Essai autour des collocatifs d'intensité. In F. Baider, G. Cislaru, & S. Coffey (Eds.), *Le Langage et L'homme* (pp. 117–130). Belgium: EME.

Cavalla, C. (2015b). Collocations transdisciplinaires dans les écrits de doctorants FLS/FLE. *Linx*, *72*, 95–110.

Chambers, A. (2010). L'apprentissage de l'écriture en langue seconde à l'aide d'un corpus spécialisé. *Revue française de linguistique appliquée 2*, *XV*, 9–20.

Chambers, A. (2013). Learning and teaching the subjunctive in French: The contribution of corpus data. *Bulletin suisse de linguistique appliquée*, *97*, 41–58.

Council of Europe. (2001). *Common European framework of reference for languages: Learning, teaching, assessment*. Cambridge: Cambridge University Press.

Di Vito, S. (2013). L'utilisation des corpus dans l'analyse linguistique et dans l'apprentissage du FLE. *Linx*, *68–69*, 159–176.

Di Vito, S. (2018). Apprendre le FLE à partir d'un corpus. *Les Langues Modernes*, *3*, 52–60.

Favata, G. (2018). Les technologies en aide aux professeurs de langues étrangères: enseigner le français à l'ère de l'Internet. *Synergies Italie, 14*, 55–67.

Flowerdew, L. (2015). Data-driven learning and language learning theories: Wither the twain shall meet. In A. Len ko-Szyman ska & A. Boulton (Eds.), *Multiple affordances of language corpora for data-driven learning* (pp. 15–36) (Studies in Corpus Linguistics, 69). Amsterdam: John Benjamins.

Gabrielatos, C. (2005). Corpora and language teaching: Just a flying or wedding bells? *TESL-EJ, 8*(4). https://files.eric.ed.gov/fulltext/EJ1068106.pdf (accessed February 2019).

Gavioli, L., & Aston, G. (2001). Enriching reality: Language corpora in language pedagogy. *ELT Journal, 55*(3), 238–246.

Gilquin, G., & Granger, S. (2010). How can data driven learning be used in language teaching? In A. O'Keefe & M. McCarthy (Eds.), *The Routledge handbook of corpus linguistics* (pp. 359–370). London: Routledge.

Giuliani, D., & Hannachi, R. (2010). Linguistique de corpus et didactique du F.L.E.: Une exploitation du corpus IntUne. *Cahiers de praxématique, 54–55*, 145–160.

Hamez, M. -P., & Pereiro, M. (Eds.). (2018). *Grammaire?Vous avez dit grammaire? Représentations et pratiques enseignantes. Les Langues Modernes, 3.*

Kamber, A. (2011). Contexte et sens: utilisation d'un corpus écrit dans l'enseignement/apprentissage du FLE. *Travaux neuchâtelois de linguistique, 55*, 199–218.

Kerr, B. (2013). Grammatical description and classroom application: Theory and practice in data-driven learning. *Bulletin suisse de linguistique appliquée, 97*, 17–39.

Kolb, D. (1984). *Experiential learning: Experience as the source of learning and development.* Englewood Cliffs: Prentice Hall.

Kottelat, P., & Dapavo, R. (2018). Perspective actionnelle et français langue étrangère en Italie: états des lieux, questionnements, perspectives. *Synergies Italie, 14.*

Leray, M., & Tyne, H. (2016). Homophonie et maitrise du français écrit: apport de l'apprentissage sur corpus. *Linguistik Online, Corpus, grammaire et français langue étrangère: une concordance nécessaire, 78*(4), 131–148.

Lions-Olivieri, M. -L., & Liria, Ph. (2003). *L'approche actionnelle dans l'enseignement des langues.* Paris: Editions Maison des Langues.

MIUR [Ministero dell'Istruzione, dell'Università e della Ricerca]. (2012). *Annali della Pubblica Istruzione. Indicazioni Nazionali per il curricolo della scuola dell'infanzia e del primo ciclo d'istruzione*, Anno LXXXVIII. Firenze: Le Monnier. Retrieved from http://www.indicazioninazionali.it/wp-content/uploads/2018/08/Indicazioni_Annali_Definitivo.pdf (accessed April 2019).

Mourlhon-Dallies, F. (2008). *Enseigner une langue à des fins professionnelles.* Paris: Didier.

Pinto, M. A. (2015). *La Consapevolezza metalinguistica: Concetti e strumenti di misurazione in lingua italiana e tedesca.* Conference held in Rome, Sapienza University, 4 September 2015. Retrieved from https://www.pintomatel.com/wp-content/uploads/2018/08/48.CML_SCHWEIZER_SCHULE.pdf (accessed April 2019).

Tran, T. T. H., Tutin, A., & Cavalla, C. (2016). Pour un enseignement systématique des marqueurs discursifs à l'aide de corpus en classe de FLE: l'exemple des marqueurs de reformulation. *Linguistik online, 78*(14/16), 114–128. DOI: 10.13092/lo.78.2953 (accessed April 2019).

Tyne, H. (ed.). (2013). Apprentissage sur corpus: théories, méthodes, applications et perspectives. *Bulletin suisse de linguistique appliquée, 97.*

Yan, R., Tutin, A., & Tran, T. T. H. (2018). Routines verbales pour le français langue étrangère: des corpus d'experts aux corpus d'apprenants. *Lidil, 58*, 1–20, http://journals.openedition.org/lidil/5411 (accessed April 2019).

11
DATA-DRIVEN LEARNING IN A GREEK SECONDARY EDUCATION SETTING

The implementation of a blended approach

Vasiliki Papaioannou, Marina Mattheoudakis, and Eleni Agathopoulou

Introduction

Despite growing interest in DDL over the past 20 years, the majority of studies on corpus-driven language learning have been carried out in tertiary education environments with adult and (most often) quite advanced second language (L2) students (Boulton & Cobb, 2017). Studies with younger and low/mid-level L2 proficiency students are less prominent in the literature. Why then might DDL be suitable for younger L2 learners? DDL is a computer-based methodology. Adolescents are well acquainted with forming queries on the general Internet (although not always competent, see Gatto, this volume), and both computers and the Internet are an essential part of their everyday lives. In addition, adolescents desire control over any aspect of their lives, including their own approach to learning. For modern students, being passive recipients of knowledge is a demotivator. This requires a learning environment that allows them to "have a go" and take responsibility for learning. Given what we know about DDL so far in this volume, it seems the ideal methodology to provide adolescents with such an environment.

In a DDL lesson, the teacher is not the expert or the source of all knowledge; he or she is rather the facilitator of learning (Johns, 1991), who stands by the students and provides guidance and support whenever necessary. In DDL, rather than being spoon-fed, students learn by discovering. It is essentially an inductive approach to language learning, and the focus lies in the learner: The learner is the agent who investigates language, finds clues about the meaning and relations between linguistic items, and generate hypotheses regarding meaning and rules. Activities involving concordance lines can be used as consciousness-raising activities, providing learners with opportunities to discover language before (hopefully) producing it. This makes DDL particularly attractive to high school students as it provides them with a sense of autonomy that mirrors their general struggles for autonomy elsewhere in life. Allowing students to make their own choices and offering them the chance to take the initiative actively engages them in learning, motivates them, and addresses their need to demonstrate independence (Wilson & Horch, 2002). Concordancing activities in the hands of capable teachers can also be seen as fun or amusing for adolescents (Lamy & Mortensen, 2017).

That said, considering a lack of previous research on the actual application of DDL in mixed-level secondary education settings, this study investigates how a DDL methodology can be applied for the teaching of L2 English modal auxiliary verbs in a senior high school setting in Greece. Modal auxiliary verbs are a challenging grammatical phenomenon to acquire for L2 learners, as even native speakers find it difficult to successfully interpret their possible meanings (Bald, 1991, as cited in Klages & Römer, 2002). This makes acquiring modals "particularly troublesome" for learners of English (Palmer, 2003, p. 1). This is compounded for learners who are taught English in primary and secondary education, because of such learners' "limited access to the cultural values encoded in the descriptive labels used in traditional paraphrases" (Klages & Römer, 2002, p. 201). These observations reflect the findings of similar research on the acquisition of English modals conducted in the Greek context (e.g. Kostaki-Psoma, 2015; Manika, 2009). For example, Kostaki-Psoma (2015) investigated the acquisition of "can" and "could" by Greek learners of English, noting that the multiple meanings and functions of the two modals may confuse them.

Much of this may be due to the sometimes misleading and inaccurate descriptions of lexicogrammatical phenomena in traditional EFL course books. Teachers' intuitions or the examples given in available textbooks only account for a limited range of the different instances of modal auxiliary verbs as they are used by native English speakers in different settings. All students who enter senior high school in Greece have had nine years of English classes. English is a compulsory subject in all three years of general high school, with two 45-minute lessons per week. Rather than focusing on vocabulary and grammar competence, the curriculum lists various instances of communication that a learner should be able to cope with. However, in practice, Greek state school teachers rely heavily on prescribed text books, which are used as reference grammar books and include practice activities on modal verbs. A cursory examination of six different textbook series used in Greek senior high schools revealed each adopts the same methodology for grammar teaching: explicit presentation of the grammatical rule followed by intensive, systematic drilling and controlled, guided activities.

Learners' source language is also a factor affecting acquisition. Manika (2009) investigated the learning and use of modal verbs by Greek EFL students in state schools, finding that learners face difficulties in making appropriate associations between modal verbs and their corresponding notions in authentic communicative contexts. This results in learners' tendency to mentally translate English modals into their Greek equivalents. Learners then face the dilemma of which modal verb to choose for each instance of communication, since there is no one-to-one semantic/pragmatic equivalence with corresponding verbs in Greek. Students' common complaints that "modal verbs seem to mean the same thing" is indicative of their frustration in acquiring them. To overcome this difficulty, Manika (2009) suggests to describe – and thus teach – modality not as distinct lexicogrammatical elements but rather as interrelated parts of specific speech acts. The pragmatics of modal verbs in use should not therefore be neglected, and the correct "form-meaning connections" (Manika, 2009, p. 309) should be the aim if learning the appropriate sense and use for each modal is to be achieved. This can be achieved, as Kostaki-Psoma (2015) suggests, if learners receive sufficient exposure to authentic samples of language, presentation of forms in context, and contextualized meaningful practice.

DDL is therefore an ideal methodology for the teaching and learning of modal auxiliary verbs, as this approach facilitates the provision of an abundance of "relevant, authentic, and interesting examples as opposed to made-up traditional 'grammar examples'" (Lamy & Mortensen, 2017, p. 11). DDL materials represent the kind of authentic language use that encourages learners to engage more with the language of cross-cultural communication than might be the case when using traditional classroom pedagogies (Meunier, 2002). Concordances tend to focus on meaning rather than rules; by this, we mean the learner can use instances of language in use contained in corpora as the starting point to make inferences about grammatical rules (Boulton, 2011). Concordances are also claimed to expand knowledge about grammatical structures that the learner is already familiar with (Hunston, 2002). Finally, previous research in the Greek secondary context claims that learners in Greece favour metacognitive, affective, and compensation strategies over memory strategies (Platsidou & Sipitanou, 2014). The DDL methodology seems to suit learners who employ the aforementioned strategies since it encourages and enhances cooperation, initiative, and "intelligent guessing".

But is DDL suitable for all high school students? In upper secondary education in Greece, learners' English language proficiency ranges from level A2 to C1 of the CEFR, with the majority of these at the lower end of the scale (Mattheoudakis & Nikolaidis, 2005). DDL studies, however, have primarily focused on more advanced L2 learners. For example, Davis and Russell-Pinson (2004, p. 260) justify working with advanced students as doing so shows "a more complete picture of the different ways in which students can use large corpora to study and analyze the grammar of the second language". However, DDL has been claimed to be suitable for learners of various proficiency levels (Nugraha, Miftakh, & Wachyudi, 2017) as the degree of "purity" or directness of the approach can be adjusted to the needs of the target class. For example, teachers may choose to adopt a paper-based approach to DDL in which concordances are hand-picked and edited so as to be less intimidating for classroom use, or they may adopt a "pure" hands-on approach in which learners query the corpora themselves. The former suits lower proficiency learners, whilst the latter is more appropriate for relatively advanced students. Given that high school classes are generally of mixed L2 proficiency levels, incorporating a "flexible design" (Wicher, this volume) to DDL lessons, including *both* paper-based and hands-on corpus consultation, could appeal to a more diverse range of students. This diversity also brings about ideal conditions for language learning, as in a DDL lesson students often share a computer and are usually encouraged to share their query findings with classmates and assist one another in performing tasks, with plentiful opportunities for negotiation for meaning and scaffolding (Ellis, 2003). Such interaction has also been shown to lead to successful peer relations and academic achievement, which may raise students' interest and enjoyment in their school work as well as greater expectancy for success at school (Ryan & Patrick, 2001). Eager to see if we can reap the benefits of DDL methodology, we aimed to study the results of its application in a diverse Greek senior high school setting. Our main focus was whether DDL is suitable for the acquisition of modal auxiliaries through appropriate adaptation of existing textbook materials.

Method

Participants

This study was conducted in the Second Senior High school of Orestiada, a small town of around 20,000 residents at the northeastern borders of Greece. The participants in our study were 64 students (35 girls and 29 boys) who were all second grade students (ages 15 to 16) belonging to three classes. The two experimental groups (1 and 2) consisted of 24 and 20 students (classes B1 and B2 respectively), while the control group consisted of 20 students (class B3). The choice of these particular classes as experimental and control groups was made based on the schedule of their English language classes and the availability of the computer lab. According to the results from the Oxford Placement Test (U.C.L.E., 2001), learners were distributed across CEFR levels as follows: A1 = 9 per cent, A2 = 5 per cent, B1 = 59 per cent, B2 = 22 per cent, and C1 = 5 per cent. All classes had learners of all five levels.

Corpora and tools

Two corpora were employed for the creation of DDL activities: (a) the English Coursebooks Corpus (ECCo), a pedagogic corpus consisting of material (reading sections only) from four different coursebooks at CEFR B1+ level approved by the Ministry of Education for use in Greek senior high schools; and (b) the Corpus of American Contemporary English (COCA, Davies, 2008). ECCo contains 104,238 tokens and 8,664 types in total and, since the course books which provided the texts for its creation were not available electronically, we digitized them using optical character recognition software. ECCo was found to contain 1,363 tokens of modal verbs, including the modal verbs "will", "would", "could", "should", "may", and "might", which we taught in our DDL lessons. The compilation of ECCo provided the data for the creation of pedagogically appropriate teaching materials that would be both comprehensible and relevant to the materials used for the control group, namely the textbook *Take Off! B1+ Course Book* (Jones, 2013). WordSmith Tools (Scott, 2012) was used to create concordances of the ECCo corpus for use with the printed teaching materials. As a complement to ECCo, we decided to use COCA as a platform for students' direct corpus queries. COCA is one of the largest available free corpora of English (containing 520 million words); it can also be accessed freely, has a user-friendly interface, and provides an abundance of naturally occurring English from various genres.

Procedure

In this section, we present the procedure of our training sessions and the DDL lessons. Our approach had the following characteristics:

a   It was a *blended approach* (Ebeling, 2009, p. 67) since it combined data-driven materials with face-to-face in-class teaching.
b   It involved both "pure" hands-on corpus consultation by students and teacher-tailored learning materials in the form of handouts containing pre-selected concordance output.
c   It employed both in-house pedagogic (ECCo) and general online (COCA) corpora.

The different access configurations to the data resources provided are illustrated in Figure 11.1.

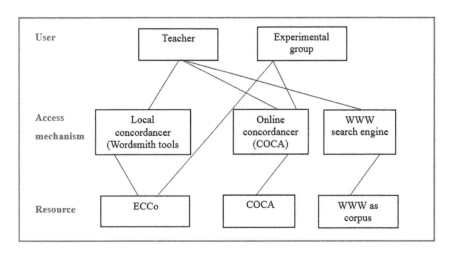

FIGURE 11.1 Configurations of access to the data resources used in DDL lessons

Source: (adapted from Lew, 2009, p. 298)

DDL training

Previous studies (e.g. Hatzitheodorou & Mattheoudakis, 2007) have stressed the need for appropriate DDL training when implementing DDL in schools since the majority of students are not familiar with DDL methodology. In the present study, DDL training materials were developed by the researchers, who were also the teachers of the classes in question. None of the students who participated had any previous experience in using corpora. For this reason, it was necessary that they become accustomed to being "learning detectives" (Johns, 1991).

To this aim, all students who belonged to the two experimental groups took training on how to query a corpus and interpret the results. Four DDL training sessions were organized, with activities designed following the typology of induction exercises for introducing students to corpora provided by Lee and Swales (2006). This includes guessing the meaning of words by studying concordances and looking at similar and commonly confused lexical items, among other activities that are described in more detail in the following.

Training session 1

The first training session had two main aims – to introduce students to KWIC (Key Word in Context) corpus queries in a non-intimidating way and to provide the students with their first "hands-on" activity using COCA. To "gently" initiate students into corpus queries, we first took "the 'KWIC' term out of the equation" Boulton (2010, p. 534) by using Google as a corpus. All students worked in pairs on one of the school lab's PCs with Internet access. The first activity of this session involved finding the meaning of an unknown phrase, namely *"swirl of innuendo"*, after encountering it in an article previously presented in class. The first step was to Google the word "innuendo" and get students to try to guess its meaning by consulting the output data. The second step was to consult an online English dictionary[1] and see the description of the word's meaning as well as the examples that complement each entry. This simple activity was actually very important as it was easy for all students to engage in and thus gave them the confidence required to proceed to query the corpus in the next step. The third step involved students querying COCA for the word "innuendo" and checking the KWIC output. They were asked to examine the first ten concordances and to choose and discuss in class one of the concordance lines containing the target word.

After the first training session was over, students discussed their experiences. All students stated they had used Google in the past, and the majority had consulted online dictionaries, but no one was previously familiar with corpora. All students, however, agreed on the usefulness of using a computer to find the meaning of an unknown word, and that they wouldn't mind working on corpora again. As one student stated: "This is just another tool the internet offers us to learn new words".

Training session 2

The second training session exclusively focused on the COCA concordancer. The aim was for the students to familiarize themselves with raw concordance output and take two further steps into querying the corpus; the first step involved producing more refined queries, while the second involved querying for chunks rather than single words.

At the beginning of the session, the phrase "swirl of innuendo" was written on the board. By then, the students knew the meaning of "innuendo" but not that of "swirl". They were once again guided to enter the COCA platform and query the word "swirl". However, they were advised to narrow down the query output by choosing to investigate only "spoken", "magazines", and "newspaper" subcorpora. The rationale was that the "academic" and "fiction" subcorpora would be more likely to contain either specialized terminology or dated vocabulary, while "spoken", "newspaper", and "magazines" subcorpora were expected to provide mostly everyday language.

The students were then asked to focus in more detail on the information that can be drawn from each concordance line. They paid attention to the fact that different parts of speech are highlighted in different colours, which helped them to draw their own conclusions as to which words usually precede and follow the node word "swirl". In keeping with previous studies (cf. O'Keeffe, McCarthy, & Carter, 2007) which stress the importance of acquiring new vocabulary and grammatical structures through chunks, the students were asked to perform a query of the chunk "swirl of" rather than the single lexical item. Conducting this query was slightly more difficult that querying for a single word, as evidenced by more students asking for the teacher's assistance than in the previous session. However, as students worked in pairs on each computer, all pairs produced results through cooperation with no student left behind. When asked for their impressions on querying for chunks rather than single words, they admitted it was slightly more difficult, but almost all students declared they would rather learn chunks or phrases rather than single words since this makes them "remember vocabulary" and "understand the way English is used better". Finally, they were again guided to extract a full sentence from a concordance line and to share their findings with the rest of the class.

Training session 3

The third DDL training session was intended to consolidate knowledge acquired in the second session, with a focus on clarifying the meaning and distinguishing the use of words that can be easily confused, which, according to Higgins (1991), is one of the basic objectives of classroom concordancing. Pairs of commonly confused words were selected from the Oxford English Dictionary, including "affect/ effect", "adverse/averse", "born/ borne", and "complement/ compliment". Students were asked to query these in COCA, but this time they were allowed to choose what to investigate among the choices provided. The students were also given a worksheet to fill out with the findings of their investigation.

Training session 4

The fourth training session involved the pedagogic corpus ECCo, with students working individually on a printed handout with edited concordances. These lines were produced by the teacher using WordSmith Tools and included only full sentences containing instances of verbs in past simple and past continuous forms. The purpose of this session was to use queries for grammatical structures as a means for assisting students to discover grammatical rules (Higgins, 1991). This was the students' first attempt to revise certain grammatical structures using an indirect DDL approach, in this case using concordances focusing on past simple and past continuous tenses. Students were asked to investigate sentences contained in the worksheet for any repeated words/structures, using the findings to make generalizations and form their own rules regarding the formation of each tense.

DDL training on modal verbs

Following the DDL training sessions, learners were familiar with concordances and making their own queries. The next lessons focused on the main senses of modal verbs, their grammatical properties, and the use of the pairs "will/would", "could/ should", and "may/might".

Lesson 1: the main senses of modal verbs

The first lesson's primary objective was to provide an introduction to the main senses of modal auxiliaries by looking closely at popular quotes and investigating their meaning. The usefulness of exploiting quotations in language learning has been discussed in Partington (1998), while Munoz and Towner (2009) have discussed the benefits of using quotations for educational purposes for teenagers as quotations are common in Facebook language and young people are accustomed to seeing and understanding them. The use of quotes also provided students with the gentlest re-introduction into concordancing since several weeks had intervened between training and DDL sessions. At the beginning of this 45-minute lesson, students were presented with six different popular quotes in the following list, each containing a modal auxiliary.

Words can be powerful, inspirational, funny...

1. Believe you can, and you're halfway there (T. Roosevelt)
2. When I let go of what I am, I become what I might be (Lao Tzu)
3. You may be disappointed if you fail, but you're doomed if you don't try (B. Sills)
4. Tension is who you think you should be. Relaxation is what you are (Chinese proverb)
5. People will forget what you said, people will forget what you did, but they will never forget how you made them feel (M. Angelou)

6   W: If I were married to you, I would put poison in your coffee.
    M: If I were married to you, I would drink it (1900s joke)

The lesson can very loosely be called "a DDL lesson" as the list of quotes is intended to *resemble* concordances, though they are not strictly presented as such. After reading the quotes, students were asked to comment on the use of modals and were able to conclude that each quote contained modal auxiliaries, which were used to express beliefs, attitudes, opinions, and hopes. The use of well-known quotes made this lesson enjoyable even for students who had claimed that they do not enjoy grammar learning, commenting they enjoyed the lesson because they "love quotes" and "it was like Facebook", while subtly learning about grammar as well.

Lesson 2: the grammatical properties of modal verbs

The second lesson was an introduction to the main grammatical properties of modal auxiliaries. Students worked in pairs in the school's computer lab and were asked to access the COCA interface to search through the KWIC results of "will", "would", "should", "could", "may", or "might", paying attention to the node word and its surrounding items. In this lesson we chose a "guided-inductive" approach to corpus consultation (Johansson, 2009), which involves assisting students in discovering the main rules concerning the usage of modal verbs by asking them to answer such questions as *"Are modal verbs followed by 'to'/take an ' – ing'?"* or *"How do modals form the interrogative/negative form?"* These questions focused on the NICE properties of modal verbs, these being "negation", "inversion", "code", and "emphasis". Each student was given a worksheet to record the answers to each question before they discussed their findings and formed generalisations concerning the grammatical properties of modal verbs. One of their first findings was that their search word was not a modal in all sentences and the results were colour coded accordingly; for instance, the word "May" in the sentence *"Well, like the whole world back in April, May and June, I was watching in horror"* is highlighted grey, while the word "may" in the sentences *"It is tax day as you may already know"* and *"Is it true that low fat milk may be 2 percent but regular milk is 4 percent?"* is purple. This way they learned how to recognize modal auxiliary verbs and disregard non-modal usages.

Students' suggested this session was quite demanding as compared with previous sessions as they had to query the corpus and then fill in the handout; they also commented that the activity required concentration, cooperation, and accuracy in order to be able to complete the tasks within 45 minutes. Nevertheless, the majority answered all questions and claimed that they liked that the language examples were highlighted, even though some students complained about not knowing the meaning of certain vocabulary in the concordances.

Lesson 3: "will" and "would"

The third DDL lesson focused on the usage of the modal verbs "will" and "would". Here we followed an indirect approach to DDL, in which the students worked

---

Will you join us?

1. Look at the following sentences. Can you identify any grammatical structures that 'will' and 'would' often appear next to?

    a   Today's recipe will serve 4 (people).
    b   The factory has been fined and will be shut until a filtering system has been installed.
    c   . . . you are going to have a difficult day because other buskers will have taken the best pitchers.
    d   . . . in the future automatic flying cars will be operating without human pilots.
    e   George: Hey . . . try some of our food!
         John: Sounds great, George. I definitely will.
    f   . . . if I say I can't go, my friend will ask someone else. . .

FIGURE 11.2

Will you join us?

'Would' is used to express **willingness** and **prediction**.
What do the following express?

    a   A lot of animals would have become extinct by now without zoos to protect them!
    b   I couldn't understand why anyone would do it.
    c   Building a sports centre would be really expensive too.

FIGURE 11.3

from a worksheet. The first activity was created with selected concordances from ECCo (see Figure 11.2), each containing an instance of "will" or "would".

This approach was used so as to gently initiate the DDL lesson as adapted DDL materials have been claimed to be more appropriate for lower level students (Bennett, 2010). Here, the students were asked to investigate the concordance lines for grammatical properties by paying particular attention to the words that preceded and followed the modal verb. There were also three activities which prompted the students to investigate the senses of "will" and "would", in which we offer the senses of modals, with students asked to match them with examples of use taken from the corpora (see Figure 11.3). Two of these tasks gave them a very limited choice of three examples taken from ECCo, while the third one asked them to search through a separate handout which contained 30 concordance lines taken from COCA. In this way, they were given the chance to work both with text book language and naturally occurring language.

The next three activities involved induction; the learners were asked to look closely at the ten concordance lines included in one of the activities and to examine the text for repeated structures in the cotext of "would" (Figures 11.4 and

> *Will you join us?*
>
> **Can you tell if the underlined phrases refer to the <u>present or the past</u>?**
>
> 1 First of all <u>would you say</u> that unemployment was a factor in the rise in crime?
> 2 It said that she needed to get away for a few days <u>and would come back</u> later in the week.
> 3 A surfer's greatest disappointment <u>would be missing the opportunity</u> to surf in the best weather conditions.
> 4 Lizzie: I <u>would have been shouting</u> at them from day one!
> 5 . . . <u>it would be better</u> if young people learnt about first aid in their free time.
> 6 I was nervous at first and I'm glad I speak English or <u>it could have been very difficult.</u>
> 7 Let me tell you, if I had known <u>it would really hurt me.</u> I would never have bought it!
> 8 Mrs A: <u>Would that mean</u> that we wouldn't have to pay at all?
> 9 Interviewer: I see. Now, if you were to be offered a post, <u>would you be able to start</u> straight away?
> 10 If I had known I couldn't do those things here, <u>I would have taken advantage</u> of my last days in the city.

FIGURE 11.4

> *Will you join us?*
>
> • Read the sentences (5), (7), (9), (10) again and find <u>one</u> feature they have <u>in common</u> as far as the context in which 'would' is used is concerned.
>
> ....
>
> • Now, look carefully at sentences (7) and (9) and say how they are<u>different</u>? Can you explain the difference?
>
> ....

FIGURE 11.5

11.5). Their observations led them to understand the formation and use of the second conditional and third conditional.

This lesson also included production exercises in which the students were able to practice their newly acquired knowledge (Figure 11.6).

We checked their understanding by asking them to use the patterns they had just learned to create a few sentences of their own. These involved using fragments of concordance lines taken from COCA in order to form full sentences (Figure 11.7).

Will you join us?

Form full sentences out of the following words taken from CBS, CNN, and ABC TV networks respectively using 'will'.

a   The president/ address/ nation/ from/Oval Office/ at 8am eastern time.
b   Bashar Assad/tell Time magazine/ this week/ Syria/ withdraw/ from Lebanon/ this summer.
c   LISA McRee: You/ come/ back/ and/talk/ to /us?

FIGURE 11.6

Will you join us?

Form full sentences out of the following words taken from ABC, CNN and ABC TV channels respectively, using 'would'

a   If/ you/ can/ see/your wife/ what/you/say/to her?
b   KING: if/you/ be/ a prosecutor now,/ you/ be/ down?
c   I realize/ it/ be/sloppy/ of you/to be/ too/specific.

FIGURE 11.7

The last activity included in the lesson was a gap-filling activity assigned as homework (Figure 11.8). This activity was created with six edited concordance lines from ECCo, and its objective was to consolidate the newly acquired knowledge on modals "will" and "would".

Students reported increased confidence in doing these activities since they did not have to make queries online. All students worked on their own handout; however, they were encouraged to cooperate, discuss their choices, and exchange opinions and impressions on the activities. Most were able to finish the activities on time, and their answers suggested they had grasped the different uses of "will" and "would".

Lesson 4: "could" and "should"

The fourth DDL lesson covered the use of modal verbs "could" and "should". As with the previous lesson, we began with carefully chosen concordance lines from ECCo, which the students had to investigate in order to discover how "could" and "should" are used in English and to formulate relevant grammatical rules. The first activity required them to look through 11 concordances to try to figure out which modals they would be working with (Figure 11.9).

The second question asked students to search for any similarities between the two lexical items, while the third and the fourth tasks guided them to discover the

Will you join us?

HOMEWORK

Let's try the following activity!

Fill in the following gaps with
a   will/would, and
b   the verb provided in the appropriate form

a   I was wondering if you could answer a few of my queries. I . . . . (be) very grateful.
b   When Frank . . . . (not) (wake up) Ann got some help from the family dog.
c   How . . . . (get) to the theatre? My car broke down and it's in the shop.
d   If I hadn't taken the holiday, I suppose I . . . . (become) a successful university lecturer, but fate had other plans.
e   Tom: I thought it was a fair punishment, although I . . . . (be) very embarrassed if it had been me.
f   Due to the train strike, we'll be going by coach. It . . . . (wait) for us here in the morning.

FIGURE 11.8

You can do it!

Look at the following sentences.
Which are the modal verbs that you can see?

1   Amazing! Could you tell us something about some of the 1980 eruption?
2   I could feel eyes staring at me and could hear unusual noises all around.
3   The newspapers are predicting that Becky could be the richest woman in England.
4   Instead of going skiing, they could do something less adventurous.
5   If these improvements were made, we could all be very proud of our block of flats.
6   The whole class could hear my stomach rumbling in the afternoon!
7   Could I have your passport and ticket, please?
8   Those with tickets for Manchester and North should change at Crewe station.
9   Furthermore, parents should set limits to the hours their children watch TV.
10 It's a four-hour flight, so they should get in around three thirty.
11 If a stranger approaches, they should go to the nearest safe place.

FIGURE 11.9

senses of "could" and "should" by offering those senses and asking them to match them with each sentence (Figure 11.10).

Students then performed another awareness raising task which made them realize that "could" and "should" can also be found in the second and third conditional. Then, they completed a gap-filling task in which they could practice what they had learned in the previous steps (Figure 11.11).

> *You can do it!*
>
> o   What is <u>common</u> between 'could' and 'should'?
>
>   ....
>
> o   'Could' may express <u>past ability, formal request, formal permission, general possibility or opportunity.</u>
>   Which sentence shows each of the above senses?
>
>   ....
>
> o   'Should' may express <u>advice/suggestion, obligation or deduction</u>.
>   Which sentence shows each of the above senses?
>
>   ....
>
> o   What is common between sentences 5 and 11?
>   What do they both express?
>
>   ....

FIGURE 11.10

> *You can do it!*
>
> **Look at the following sentences. Fill in either 'could' or 'should'**
>
> 1 I think she. . . . . be allowed to skate.
> 2 They claim to show just how greedy Shelly. . . . . be
> 3 Critics insist the private sector. . . . . bring about changes must sooner.
> 4 Simon: And we. . . . . mention the book opens with your amazing preview.
> 5 Flatow:. . . . . you describe the paintings for us?
> 6 Mr Doxiadis: First I. . . . . say, first of all, my co-author is Christos Papadimitriou.

FIGURE 11.11

In the next two activities, students used fragments of concordances from COCA selected by the teacher. Those included affirmative, interrogative, and negative forms of those two modal verbs. The final activity was assigned for homework and aimed to help them consolidate their knowledge and give them time to reflect on what they had learned in class (Figure 11.12).

Students commented that they enjoyed discovering grammar rules rather than reading about them from the course book appendix, a practice that seems to be boring and tiresome. Another comment was that the lesson would be even better if they were given the chance to make their own online queries again.

> ### *You can do it!*
>
> **Form full sentences out of the following words taken from ABC, CNN and ABC TV channels respectively, using 'should'**
>
> a   Nutley resident: People/ be/ responsible /for their actions.
> b   The law proposed is not right. It /be/ voted down.
> c   I don't know what the moral is. Or how the song/ end.

FIGURE 11.12

> ### *Shoot for the moon; you might get there!*
>
> - **Have a look at the following sentences.**
>   **Which are the modal verbs that today's lesson focuses on?**
>
>   a   ..and I'd like, if I may, to give a few handy tips..
>   b   May you have a long a healthy life!
>   c   Dr Porentz: Can I answer?
>   King: You may.
>   d   Thank you, God bless you, and may God bless the United States of America.
>   e   Female 1: Hi, I'm from a local radio station and Jill thought you might be able to talk to me about your work. . .
>   f   When you administer it to human patients, you might as well call it patient necrosis factor.
>   g   Senator: Well, if I might say, I want to repeat . . . the turtle eggs may be accidentally crushed by tourists. . .
>   h   Doctor: If you give in to phobia, then you may let it rule your life.
>   i   Excuse me miss, I'm Julia Marquez for WRSB, may I ask your name and what are you doing in this line?

FIGURE 11.13

Lesson 5: "may" and "might"

In the final DDL lesson, students were once again presented with concordance lines from ECCo, and were asked a series of questions that helped them to identify and generalize the rules that govern the usage of 'may' and 'might' (Figures 11.13 & 11.14).

There were also two activities whose goal was to practice the rules the learners had "discovered" through the previous questions. The first activity involved matching the two halves of concordances which had been taken from ECCo (Figure 11.15).

The second activity was the now familiar production of sentences with fragments taken from COCA's spoken section. Finally, there was a consolidation activity in the form of a gap-filling task to be done at home.

> *Shoot for the moon; you might get there!*
>
> ➤ 'May' is a modal auxiliary verb commonly found in English.
>   What does it refer to *past, present or future*?
>
> ➤ 'Might' is a modal auxiliary verb commonly found in English.
>   What does it refer to the *past, present or future*?
>
> ➤ 'May' is used to express specific functions.
>   Can you identify what do the sentences above express?
>
>   - *general truth*
>   - *wish*
>   - *permission*
>   - *possibility*

FIGURE 11.14

> *Shoot for the moon; you might get there!*
>
> **Match the fragments to make full sentences**
>
> 1. It is important to stay calm, as panic leads to rash actions which..
> 2. In what ways..
> 3. Indeed, as our understanding of them grows, they..
> 4. James and his family started to worry that they..
> 5. Clouseau is worried that he too..
>
> a ...may result in injury
> b ...might by killed
> c ...may have even bigger part to play in society
> d ...might a job like this help students
> e ...might have a ghost up there

FIGURE 11.15

Student's answers, as well as their participation in class, showed that most of them grasped the different meanings of "may" and "might". In this lesson, teacher guidance and intervention was minimal, since students were now familiar with reading concordances and formulating rules. At the end of the final DDL lesson the students claimed that corpus querying is something that "gets better with time" and also that they wouldn't mind conducting corpus queries in future lessons.

Discussion and conclusion

Regarding the actual application of a DDL methodology in a senior high school class, our study showed that, given the appropriate material, both direct and indirect approaches can be successfully combined. A dual approach is beneficial as indirect DDL can help eliminate any fears or reservations students may have about querying a corpus, while a direct DDL approach allows students to benefit fully from the exposure to and investigation of authentic language, even in medium- to low-level classes such as ours. There were also practical considerations too; the school's computer lab is not always available to the foreign language teacher and Internet access is not always reliable, often necessitating adopting an indirect DDL approach. In the informal interviews which took place after the DDL sessions, the majority of students claimed that making corpus queries was easy, although more than half of them admitted that those queries seemed "awkward". Also, most students described their preference for corpus examples, and more than half of the students claimed that they would choose concordances over textbook rules when learning grammar, even though a number of them claimed that it was sometimes difficult to conduct corpus queries. However, despite the awkwardness of the first contact with the new methodology, the students quickly adapted to it and showed promising progress. Close observation of the work the students did on the DDL material revealed that some students adapted quickly to DDL, demonstrating an ability to notice and interpret patterns in texts and chunks of language, either in printed concordance output or through online concordances. A key to success is that would-be DDL practitioners should improvise and search for the optimum way to provide their students with access to corpora and relevant activities according to their particular learning contexts and student needs.

Another factor in the success of our approach is that the format of the DDL tasks was similar to the ones found in traditional high school course books, e.g. fill-in-the-gap, matching, and multiple-choice exercises. What was different, however, is the lesson design and the order of the previously mentioned tasks; the lesson began with the investigation of corpus-derived examples which illustrated linguistic features; it then proceeded to formulate rules by exchanging opinions in class and, lastly, consolidating the newly found knowledge through activities based on data taken from corpora. However, we felt that if we made use only of printed handouts containing edited concordances, we would water down the "pure" DDL approach to a degree that might be unrecognizable and eventually lose those unique characteristics that are its strength: the motivation it offers the learner to act as a researcher, the degree of autonomy, and the immersion into real "raw" data. Students were not overly intimidated by the novelty of the DDL approach; rather, they seemed well acquainted with computer technology and noted its relevance with "mainstream" learning practices. Students were left with a somewhat familiar, non-intimidating learning experience without compromising the "data-driveness" of our approach.

Taking into account other factors, such as school timetable constraints and availability of equipment, is equally important if DDL is to be successfully integrated into the Greek high school environment. Moreover, in order for any indirect or direct DDL methodology to be applicable in a state school class in Greece, it is crucial that any material, corpora, and activities be carefully adapted so as to conform to the guidelines of the national curriculum (cf. Braun, 2007). We met this requirement through the compilation of our pedagogic corpus, the design of the activities, and the selection of concordances from COCA which were appropriately adapted to match the target features covered by the textbook. It is feasible to adapt the standard language learning procedure in senior high school in order to make it data-driven so as to comply with the directives set by the Ministry of Education and, at the same time, incorporate the unique principles governing DDL. The use of ECCo ensured that students would be taught with the Ministry's approved material, and the use of COCA provided us with abundant authentic examples of language use and a user-friendly interface. Careful design of both the learning activities and the DDL lessons as a whole was also crucial for the successful application of DDL methodology. Since relevant studies in secondary education are scarce, we could only design the DDL lessons the way any novel approach is designed – by trial and error – yet we believe that there is much potential for existing pedagogy to be adapted to incorporate DDL.

The importance of training in corpus use prior to DDL also cannot be overstated in this context. The main benefits of the training sessions were twofold; first and foremost, they helped learners overcome the fear of DDL by providing them with a gentle initiation through relatively easy tasks which they had to take one step at a time. One example of this was the use of Web and Googling as a gentle initiation to corpus search. As far as the Web as corpus approach is concerned, the findings of this study were in line with the observation by Robb (2003) that linguists tend to use the Web as a "quick and dirty" source of language data for everyday concerns, while, at the same time, carefully compiled corpora create a more principled and orderly bank of texts for linguistic analysis. While it is true that none of the students were familiar with KWIC searches or even with the term "corpus", they conducted their first searches for unknown terms with a certain confidence since they were already familiar with querying various search engines. In other words, the Web as corpus approach was crucial in introducing DDL (at least in its "light" version) not as a radical new technique but as a well-trodden path, "demystifying" corpus use (Gabrielatos, 2005). In fact, during the first training sessions, we were impressed by the students' active participation in the learning process. They did not follow blindly the activities dictated in the handout; instead, they questioned the choice of online tools used for the activities, exchanging views and past experiences of searching online for unknown vocabulary and suggesting alternative ways of querying the Web. Secondly, the training offered the students practical skills so as to be able to read concordances and examine the linguistic structures contained in them with the aim to make their own pedagogically useful generalisations. These training sessions triggered the student's ability to "notice" and form hypotheses with regards to the linguistic items they came across at each step of the learning process. In order to become language researchers (the ultimate goal of any DDL approach), they first acted as "trainee" researchers; later on, during the DDL lessons, they became "junior" researchers aided by the guidance of the teacher.

The present study drew its conclusions from in-class observations and informal interviews of the learners. A limitation of the study is that, aside from short interviews, more detailed feedback from the learners at the end of the course was not collected. In addition, the present research comprised a rather small sample of learners. We believe that a larger-scale experimental study with a greater number of learners could validate the positive results attained by our target group. We also believe that a longitudinal study, which would track student performance over a longer period of time, would be of much interest. This could be a way to examine the possible "holistic benefits that can accrue from the regular practice of DDL" (Kerr, 2013, p. 17). Further research could also involve an approach employing a blend of DDL and Grammar Translation, as suggested by Lin and Lee (2015). This could appeal to a wider spectrum of learners' preferences – those who favour the traditional teaching approach and those who are open-minded to novel approaches to language learning; one should not forget that any class includes both types of learners.

It is our belief that the present study's insights on how to implement a DDL approach in the young foreign language classroom could encourage teachers to further explore this methodology. The key is flexibility – the degree of "purity" of the DDL approach taken will depend on learners' age; their level of knowledge of the target language; the process of familiarising students (and teachers) with corpora and corpus queries; and the availability of computers, Internet access, and relevant software in the school computer laboratory.

Note

1 *Cambridge Dictionary*, available free online at https://dictionary.cambridge.org/dictionary

References

Bald, W.-D. (1991). Modal auxiliaries: Form and function in texts. In C. Uhlig & R. Zimmermann (Eds.), *Anglistentag 1990. Proceedings* (pp. 348–361). Tübingen: Niemeyer.

Bennett, G. R. (2010). *Using corpora in the language learning classroom*. Ann Arbor, MI: University of Michigan Press.

Boulton, A. (2010). Data-driven learning: Taking the computer out of the equation. *Language Learning, 60*, 534–572.

Boulton, A. (2011). Data-driven learning: The perpetual enigma. In S. Goźdź- Roszkowski (Ed.), *Explorations across languages and corpora* (pp. 563–580). Frankfurt: Peter Lang.

Boulton, A., & Cobb, T. (2017). Corpus use in language learning: A meta-analysis. *Language Learning, 67*(2), 348–393.

Braun, S. (2007). Integrating corpus work into secondary education: From data-driven learning to needs-driven corpora. *ReCALL, 19*(3), 307–328.

Davies, M. (2008). *The Corpus of Contemporary American English (COCA): 560 million words, 1990-present*. Retrieved from https://corpus.byu.edu/coca/

Davis, B., & Russell-Pinson, L. (2004). Concordancing and corpora for K-12 teachers: Project MORE. *Language and Computers, 52*(1), 147–169.

Ebeling, S. O. (2009). Oslo interactive English corpus-driven exercises on the web. In K. Aijmer (Ed.), *Corpora and language teaching* (pp. 67–82). Amsterdam: John Benjamins.

Ellis, R. (2003). *Task-based language learning and teaching*. Oxford: Oxford University Press.
Gabrielatos, C. (2005). Corpora and language teaching: Just a fling or wedding bells? *TESL-EJ, 8*(4), n4.
Hatzitheodorou, A. M., & Mattheoudakis M. (2007). The projection of stance in the Greek Corpus of Learner English (GRICLE). *Proceedings of Corpus Linguistics*, University of Birmingham, UK, 2007. Retrieved from http://ucrel.lancs.ac.uk/publications/CL2007/paper/86_Paper.pdf
Higgins, J. (1991). Fuel for learning: The neglected element of textbooks and CALL. *CAELL Journal, 2*(2), 3–7.
Hunston, S. (2002). *Corpora in applied linguistics*. Cambridge: Cambridge University Press.
Johansson, S. (2009). Some thoughts on corpora and second-language acquisition. In K. Aijmer (Ed.), *Corpora and language teaching* (pp. 33–44). Amsterdam: John Benjamins.
Johns, T. (1991). From printout to handout: Grammar and vocabulary teaching in the context of data-driven learning. In T. Johns & P. King (Eds.), *Classroom concordancing: English Language Research Journal, 4*, 27–45.
Jones, L. (2013). *Take off! B1+: Coursebook*. Athens: Hillside Press.
Kerr, B. (2013). Grammatical description and classroom application. *Theory and practice in data-driven learning: Bulletin VALS-ASLA, 97*, 17–39.
Klages, M., & Römer, U. (2002). Translating modal meanings in the EFL classroom. In S. Scholz et al. (Eds.), *Language: Context and cognition: Papers in honour of Wolf-Dietrich Bald's 60th birthday* (pp. 201–216). Munich: Langenscheidt-Longman.
Kostaki-Psoma, E. (2015). *Teaching inductively the modal verbs can and could for the function of request to Greek learners*. Cambridge Delta Research papers: GR102. Retrieved from www.academia.edu/31614211/Teaching_inductively_the_modal_verbs_can_and_could_for_the_function_of_request_to_Greek_learners
Lamy, M., & Mortensen, H. J. (2017). *Using concordance programs in the modern foreign language classroom*. Retrieved from www.ict4lt.org/en/index.htm
Lee, D., & Swales, J. (2006). A corpus-based EAP course for NNS doctoral students: Moving from available specialized corpora to self-compiled corpora. *English for Specific Purposes, 25*, 56–75.
Lew, R. (2009). The web as corpus versus traditional corpora: Their relative utility for linguists and language learners. In P. Baker (Ed.), *Contemporary corpus linguistics* (Vol. 16, pp. 289–300). London: Continuum.
Lin, M. H., & Lee, J. Y. (2015). Data-driven learning: Changing the teaching of grammar in EFL classes. *ELT Journal, 69*(3), 264–274.
Manika, E. (2009). Modal verbs in modern Greek and English. In A. Tsangalidis & R. Facchinetti (Eds.), *Studies on English modality: In honour of Frank Palmer* (vol. 111, pp. 307–336). Bern: Peter Lang.
Mattheoudakis, M., & Nikolaidis, K. (2005). Stirring the waters: University INSET in Greece. *European Journal of Teacher Education, 28*(1), 49–66.
Meunier, F. (2002). The pedagogic value of native and learner corpora in EFL grammar teaching. In S. Granger, J. Hung, & S. Petch-Tyson (Eds.), *Computer learner corpora, second language acquisition and foreign language teaching* (pp. 1919–1941). Amsterdam: John Benjamins.
Munoz, C., & Towner, T. (2009). Opening Facebook: How to use Facebook in the college classroom. In I. Gibson, R. Weber, K. McFerrin, R. Carlsen, & D. Willis (Eds.), *Proceedings of society for information technology & teacher education international conference* (pp. 2623–2627). Charleston, SC: AACE.

Nugraha, S. I., Miftakh, F., & Wachyudi, K. (2017). Teaching grammar through data-driven learning (DDL) approach. In *Advances in social science, education and humanities research (ASSEHR)* (pp. 300–303). Paris: Atlantis Press.

O'Keeffe, A., McCarthy, M., & Carter, R. (2007). *From corpus to classroom: Language use and language teaching.* Cambridge, UK: Cambridge University Press.

Palmer, F. R. (2003). Modality in English: Theoretical, descriptive and typological issues. In R. Facchinetti, M. Krug, & F. Palmer (Eds.), *Modality in contemporary English* (pp. 1–17). Berlin & New York: Mouton de Gruyer.

Partington, A. (1998). *Patterns and meanings: Using corpora for English language research and teaching.* Amsterdam: John Benjamins Publishing.

Platsidou, M., & Sipitanou, A. (2014). Exploring relationships with grade level, gender and language proficiency in the foreign language learning strategy use of children and early adolescents. *International Journal of Research Studies in Language Learning, 4*(1), 1–14.

Robb, T. (2003). Google as a quick 'n' dirty corpus tool. *TESL-EJ, 7*(2). www.teslej.org/wordpress/issues/volume7/ej26/ej26int/

Ryan, A. M., & Patrick, H. (2001). The classroom social environment and changes in adolescents' motivation and engagement during middle school. *American Educational Research Journal, 38*(2), 437–460.

Scott, M. (2012). *WordSmith tools version 6.* Stroud: Lexical Analysis software.

U.C.L.E. Syndicate. (2001). *Quick placement test.* Oxford: Oxford University Press.

Wilson, L. M., & Horch, H. W. (2002). Implications of brain research for teaching young adolescents. *Middle School Journal, 34*(1), 57–61.

12
THE EFFECT OF DATA-DRIVEN LEARNING ACTIVITIES ON YOUNG EFL LEARNERS' PROCESSING OF ENGLISH IDIOMS

Trisevgeni Liontou

Idioms & EFL learners

According to Brenner (2013), the English language is rich in idioms, i.e. multiword expressions with a figurative meaning that cannot always be inferred by adding up the meanings of their constituent parts. Native speakers tend to use a diverse set of vocabulary items that do not have a literal meaning because they can better express their feelings and experiences through figurative expressions. For learners of English as a foreign language (EFL), idioms are highly heterogeneous, stretching across a continuum of compositionality. At one end of the spectrum stand transparent idioms, i.e. figurative expressions whose meanings can be effortlessly deduced because of to the clear connection between the literal meanings of individual words and their idiomatic interpretations (Boers & Demecheleer, 2001; Hinkel, 2017). At the other end lie opaque idioms, in which the constituent words do not make a significant contribution towards the decoding of the idiomatic meaning (Abel, 2003; Liontas, 2003). Despite their inherent complexity, idioms are frequently used to give life and richness to language by taking existing words, combining them in a new sense, and creating new meanings (Bulut, 2004; Doroodi & Hashemian, 2011; Simpson & Mendis, 2003). Cooper (1999, p. 259) highlights that "since idiomatic expressions are so frequently encountered in both spoken and written discourse, they require special attention in language programs and should not be relegated to a position of secondary importance in the curriculum". Similarly, Moreno (2011) and Liontas (2015, 2017) support the view that, since idioms are an integral aspect of verbal communication, they should receive special attention in teaching. However, Celce-Murcia and Larsen-Freeman (1999, p. 39) describe idioms as "notoriously difficult" for FL learners, and many foreign language teachers would agree with the idea that even the most advanced learners appear to be afraid of making errors and tend to avoid using idioms for this reason (Irujo, 1986). Nevertheless, idioms are so frequently encountered in native oral and written discourse that their acquisition is extremely important for achieving command of the target language, and learners need to build up a large repertoire of figurative expressions for active usage (Boers, Eyckmans, & Stengers, 2006; Cieslicka, 2006; Sadeghi, Dastjerdi, & Ketabi, 2010). To make the situation more complex, the abundance of L1 studies on idiom comprehension and acquisition (cf. Cain, Oakhill, & Lemmon, 2005; Oakhill et al., 2016) have been accompanied by a regrettable lack of comparable research into the representation and processing of idiomatic expressions by foreign language learners. Moreover, the majority of L2 studies have been primarily descriptive in nature (cf. Grant, 2007; Grant & Nation, 2006; Liu, 2003; Simpson & Mendis, 2003), with only a small minority of researchers addressing the issue of whether and how idioms can cause foreign language learners additional difficulties during the learning process (cf. Cooper, 1999; Doroodi & Hashemian, 2011; Siyanova-Chanturia, Conklin, & Schmitt, 2011).

In a much-cited study, Liontas (2001) demonstrated that idiom interpretation was seriously impaired if there was a lack of context surrounding both matching and non-matching idioms. This corroborates the results found by Irujo (1986), Colombo (1993), Cain *et al.* (2005), and Sadeghi *et al.* (2010), who maintained that context might facilitate the interpretation of figurative language by providing the necessary semantic information for readers to infer the appropriate sense and that a lack of context can seriously reduce the accuracy of idiom interpretation by L2 learners. More recently, Mohamadi-Asl (2013) found that extended contexts had a positive impact on Iranian upper-intermediate EFL learners' processing of idioms in stories, and Xie (2017) reported similar findings as regards sophomore Chinese EFL learners' understanding of English idioms. Other factors in the successful comprehension of idioms for EFL learners include previous lexical knowledge, as shown in Zyzik (2011), who found that target idioms with known constituent parts yielded higher scores on production and recognition tests than idioms with previously unknown lexical items. The L1 also has a strong influence on comprehension of idioms, as shown in Laufer (2000), who suggested avoidance of idioms by L2 learners could be related to the degree of similarity between idiomatic expressions between source and target languages.

However, it should be said here that most empirical studies to date have been conducted in laboratory settings with adult learners and scant attention has been paid to fostering idiomatic competence in younger learners (cf. Beloussova, 2015). Thus, echoing Khonbi and Sadeghi (2017) and Szudarski (2017), establishing the optimal classroom conditions for younger learners learning L2 phrases still remains to be addressed.

DDL & L2 formulaic language processing

Over the past 15 years, an increasing number of researchers have paid special attention to what corpus linguistics has to offer language pedagogy, and the amount of publications on related topics has also increased steadily (cf. Bennett, 2010; Friginal, 2018; Timmis, 2015). While the tools required to query corpora have become relatively easier to use than in the past, DDL has still not been widely implemented in mainstream pedagogical contexts, and Römer (2011) urges interested parties to "look forward to [more] information about language patterns being incorporated in language teaching materials".

Though some DDL studies have already been conducted on various aspects of vocabulary acquisition, collocational competence (Li, 2017), and even the use of formulaic language (Bardovi-Harlig, Mossman, & Vellenga, 2014), idiomaticity for L2 learning has been left largely untouched in the DDL literature. Notable exceptions include Geluso and Yamaguchi (2014), who attempted to implement an EFL curriculum designed around DDL with the aim of improving spoken fluency in an L2 academic context, looking into how effective students were in employing newly discovered set phrases in an appropriate manner. The findings indicated that students believed DDL to be a useful and effective tool in the classroom and strongly felt that such an approach to language learning increased their knowledge of collocations. However, they did note some difficulties for the DDL approach, including confusion when encountering unfamiliar vocabulary and cut-off concordance lines and concerns about students' ability to embed learned phrases in a pragmatically appropriate way. Similarly, Huang (2014) investigated whether and to what extent DDL activities can improve student's use of idioms involving abstract nouns in the L2 English writing of 40 Chinese university students, compared with the performance of a control group. Pre-test, immediate post-test, and delayed post-test written submissions were analyzed, with the results suggesting the experimental group's written submissions contained a higher variety of collocational and colligational patterns and had fewer linguistic errors in using the target abstract nouns as a result of DDL. The post-experiment learning journals and questionnaires administered to the experimental group further confirmed that concordance activities encouraged usage-based learning, helped students notice the lexical collocations and prepositional colligations of the target words, and thus improved accuracy and complexity in their productive language. Despite these positive findings, potential problems of using concordance activities for independent learning were once again reflected in the students' written output and reported in their learning journals.

Despite the reported difficulties, it is important to note that DDL is no longer viewed as a purely discovery-based approach to learning as originally proposed by Johns (1991) – with many researchers acknowledging the usefulness of teacher-prepared corpus materials focusing on known grammatical or lexical rules (Basanta & Martin, 2007; Clifton & Phillips, 2006; Boulton, 2010; Reppen, 2010) – and that DDL is not only limited to studying concordance lines or incomplete sentences that focus on a common word or phrase (Boulton, 2009a; Davies, 2008). In his discussion of what constitutes data-driven learning, Boulton (2011) notes that DDL is "not an all-or-nothing affair: its boundaries are fuzzy, and any identifiable cut-off point will necessarily be arbitrary"

(p. 575). He further argues that, for DDL to reach a wider audience, it needs to be viewed not as a radical or revolutionary practice but as an ordinary practice that could supplement, enhance, and extend everyday teaching practices. Under DDL, students discover facts about the language they are learning by themselves from authentic examples and are, thus, motivated to remember what they have worked to find out (Gavioli, 2001; Hadley, 2002), while DDL has long been hypothesized to improve students' general skills of using context to deduce meaning (Stevens, 1991). A range of small-scale research has been conducted in that direction (cf. Braun, 2007; Cobb & Horst, 2002; Lee, Warschauer, & Lee, 2018). However, as Boulton (2009a) acknowledges, despite the considerable research interest and the multiplicity of resources available, corpus consultation remains rare even in university and research environments (Thompson, 2007) and it appears to have had virtually no impact on "ordinary" learning practices elsewhere. Echoing Boulton, Hirata (in this volume) stresses that corpus-based language learning is still largely limited to adult learners because of the nature of available corpus data and the difficulties that might arise when using available concordance software tools, as other contributors to this volume have also pointed out. In addition, corpus-based language learning is not still recognized amongst teachers of younger learners and, as a result, little is known about the implementation of DDL with younger EFL learners regarding its use with idiomatic expressions. We know that younger EFL learners have difficulty interpreting or decoding phrases with a figurative meaning that cannot always be inferred by adding up the meanings of their constituent parts. However, because of the facilitating effect appropriate context can have on such a decoding process, the use of corpus-based activities to aid the learning of idioms seems like an obvious choice, as corpora provide plentiful examples of idiomatic phrases in authentic contexts alongside data on their frequency of use.

Aims

The present study followed an experimental approach in order to investigate whether young EFL learners' ability to process idiomatic expressions could be improved when studying corpus data in the form of examples, concordance lines, and extended sentences. The rationale for the study is taken from an informal survey of 118 in-service English language teachers, which brought to light a number of teaching "difficulties" Greek EFL teachers reported facing when teaching younger learners, such as the need for inclusion of more authentic examples in coursebooks along with support in creating up-to-date materials which expose students to everyday language through topics closer to their interests. These issues could be addressed by making more use of corpus-based resources. Focusing specifically on the acquisition of idioms, the present study followed a quasi-experimental design where DDL treatment was administered to one group of EFL learners (experimental group), with their performance compared with that of a control group which learned idioms through textbook samples and activities.

Method

Participants: Learners participating in the current study came from a private secondary school in Athens and had all been taught English as a foreign language as a compulsory school subject for a minimum of five years. A total of 60 students 12 to 15 years old took part in the study. Signed forms of consent from parents for the involvement of students in the project were collected. In order to have a strong quasi-experimental design, a larger number of students was pre-tested to ensure that, after the formation of the two groups, there were no significant language competence differences among the subjects of the experimental and the control group; in this way, internal threats to validity were controlled. The participants were purposefully selected from this larger number of students after administering a calibrated English language test (University of Cambridge ESOL Examinations Preliminary English Test – PET) to ensure that language proficiency was comparable. In order to determine their level of vocabulary knowledge, Nation's (2001) Vocabulary Size Test (VST) was also administered. After being homogenized in terms of language proficiency level, the participants were randomly assigned to one of the two equally sized groups, one of which was considered as the experimental group and the other one as the control group (Table 12.1).

Participants in the present study all reported experiencing their first taste of corpus-based activities without having received any special training beforehand or having any experience of corpora. They all attended an introductory one-hour session to become familiar with the layout and basic features of the two online corpora, the British National Corpus (BNC) and the Corpus of Contemporary American English (COCA), available online at www.english-corpora.org. The "Help" section of the specific platform included within each collection provided a detailed overview of the features of the corpus, with students reacting favourably to the information in the "Using the corpus to teach and learn English" (www.english-corpora.org/coca/help/learners.asp) section that, according to the creators of the platform, was "addressed

TABLE 12.1 L2 proficiency and vocabulary size of groups

GROUP		PET	VST
Experimental Group	Mean	93.40	32.13
	N	30	30
	Std. Deviation	5.876	3.037
Control group	Mean	93.27	32.93
	N	30	30
	Std. Deviation	5.024	2.273
Total	Mean	93.33	32.53
	N	60	60
	Std. Deviation	5.420	2.690

to students and teachers of English". It is worth pointing out that, based on students' informal comments, the platform seemed rather easy for them to explore despite their young age. Some of the students were competent enough to perform advanced searches once familiar with the platform and when asked by the researcher whether such features were difficult for them to use, they commented that similar syntax rules (e.g. wildcards, coding system, etc.) are also used in basic programming lessons they had been exposed to as part of their standard ICT lessons at school.

Selection of target items: There was a total of 80 idioms defined in the assigned coursebook (*Upstream Intermediate* by Evans, 2012) from the "*Idioms & Fixed Phrases*" sections included in each unit of the specific coursebook. By the end of the 16-week treatment, learners had been exposed to 80 idioms in alignment with the contents of their assigned coursebook.

Instruments and procedure: Both groups were taught by the same EFL teacher throughout the school year. The classes were held once a week with each session lasting approximately 90 minutes. Since learners in the control group served as a benchmark, they participated in regular classes using the assigned coursebook with no modifications and completed only the pre-test (week 1) and post-test (week 16). Corpus-informed examples of authentic written and spoken discourse were used as the treatment for the experimental group, in which students could answer questions about idiomatic phrases themselves by studying corpus data in the form of concordance lines and extended (but not simplified) examples. Both inductive and deductive reasoning activities were used, such as cloze and matching exercises, along with extracting data from KWICs and complete sentences, identifying patterns, and grouping information appropriately. Some examples of the designed tasks are presented here:

Key-Word-in-Context Tasks: As can be seen in Figure 12.1, the target idiom was presented in a highlighted mode in the centre of the screen. Special care was taken to include concordances that were relatively simple for intermediate EFL learners to process while providing a sufficient amount of context for them to deduce meaning and analyze real-life use of the target idiomatic phrase. The aim of such tasks was to enhance learners' guessing the meaning of unknown words from context skill while familiarizing themselves with the typical layout of concordance tables.

Idiom "wheels": As an extension activity, students were asked to fill in various "wheels" of idiomatic phrases. This method helps students to visualize idioms in terms of their respective component parts (see Figure 12.2). An idiom-rich topic such as *parts of the body* was chosen. Students were provided with a list of corpus-based examples that included both idiomatic and non-idiomatic usages of each keyword and were asked to trace the idiomatic phrases and add them to the appropriate wheel. For example, "EAR" is used to form a number of idioms, such as "*have nothing between the ears*" or "*be all ears*", while "*ear infection*", despite being a frequent collocation, is not an idiom and thus should not form part of the idiom wheel. As a follow-up activity, wheel posters can be placed on the classroom walls for future reference, or they can be further supplemented with new examples

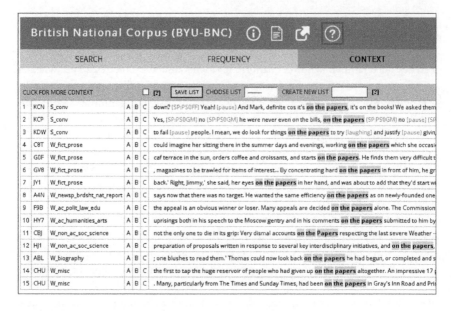

FIGURE 12.1 Sample concordances containing target idiom

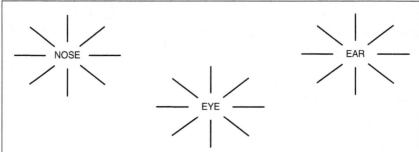

1. I was away from home a lot and ended up collapsing with exhaustion, I got really ill I had a kind of **ear** infection which caused giddiness and I had to come out of the West End play I was appearing in at the time,
2. I don't expect college kids to know everything, even though some think they do. They're **wet behind the ears**. They have no experience in life. But for heaven's sake, they should be learning how to think for themselves in college.
3. He surfed the most savage seas, smiling from **ear to ear** and jumping with joy, and he saved many lives. He was a good man,
4. How about all the other famous women who **have nothing between the ears?** Geez. I doubt seriously that she cares one fig about such things. I am almost positive that she cares about her children's well-being. I hate the media for perpetuating such shallowness.
5. If you can think of a better practical alternative we're **all ears**, it might also be a good idea to insert a little flag or notification somewhere that tells users how to attach their files.

FIGURE 12.2 Idiom "wheel" completion task

Read the following short passages and try to explain the idioms in hold.

1. It was a different town then,. Mick Sprague said. He remembers riding his bicycle as a boy out Six; Mile to the Northville area, where he could enjoy the hiliier terrain. **"Once In a blue moon**. I would see another car" he said." That's how rural it was back then, no cars, no noise . . . You could spend the entire day and come home at suppertime" he said. (COCA)

2. I don't think Badi is a good influence. What did the two of you do last night? A dark bruise covers his eye. "What is this? "I grab his shoulders. "Did Badi hit you? That brat! Your eye is **black and blue!** When I get my hands on him . . . Why did he do this?" Jamal brushes my hand away, "it doesn't hurt". (COHA)

3. I can't **claim to have green fingers**. In fact, every plant I touch seems to take offense and wither! That doesn't mean that t don't appreciate the beauty that, a colorful bloom can provide however. I value the welcome burst of colour in what might otherwise be a somewhat dreary sea of green foliage. The fact that I'm no gardener doesn't mean that my garden has no flowers. Some seem quite capable of growing without any help, but, without interaction they run the risk of being overtaken by weeds (COCA)

4. **Hi I am green** with computers (a pensioner and late starter) but have photos of my two dogs but do not know how to put them on the forum, – any help to do this would be greatly appreciated. Matsho. # hey Matsho, if you go to the reply box and select "go advanced" it will give you the option under where you would input text to "add attachments" click that it will prompt a new screen to open.

FIGURE 12.3 Idioms across genres

written by students themselves (such an approach was not followed in the present study, as student were to be exposed to a specific set of idioms only).

Genre-based tasks: Students were exposed to different text genres since corpus-based data includes extracts from a range of sources, such as newspapers, magazines, novels, history books, forum posts, and even blog comments (Figure 12.3). For example, in the following activity, extract 1 is from an interview, extract 2 is from a soap opera, extract 3 is from a novel, and extract 4 is from an online forum post. Having EFL students exposed to a range of text genres could prove beneficial since the purpose of the communication and the context (including the audience, the topic, and the mode) directly shape the organization and the language of a text (Paltridge, 2001). Using corpora, extracting these different genre examples took a matter of seconds.

Corpus-based domino cards: Instead of using the invented, contrived examples from the coursebook, the game-like task of corpus-based domino cards was frequently employed amongst participants of the experimental group. As can be seen in Figure 12.4, the target idiom was presented in an extended context and students worked in pairs or small groups to match relevant parts. This type of task proved very versatile in the specific teaching context as an easy and entertaining game to practice any set of idioms. Moreover, based on the EFL teacher's informal classroom observation throughout the experimental period, the students seemed to become more confident in searching online corpora for this purpose, using classroom computers to search or cross-check their answers on assigned

Neil Aspden, eight, was beaten by the 12-year-old bullies . . . Neil's mother, Sherie, 28, said:[1] couldn't believe it when I saw him. He was **black and blue** all over and looked half dead.' Neil is now recovering in St James's Hospital after Wednesday's attack.	He was playing alone near his home when he was approached by the boys who wanted him to go shoplifting. When he refused they punched him in the face and dragged him to shops two miles away. After the beating, he was rescued by a motorist.
Perhaps Matthew was in love with Jenny, as much as he could be in love with anyone." But what does your pa say? "He's not pleased, " Jenny said after a small pause." So I haven't been absolutely truthful with him.	I've told a little **white lie** and said that I will only be staying with you for a week or so. You know my feelings about Matthew," Jenny said." They haven't changed. I shall stay as long as the job lasts – or until my situation changes."
As you won't ask the governess's name, I'll tell you myself,' continued St John.' I've got it written down. It's always better to have facts **in black and white**.' And he took out of his wallet a tiny piece of paper, which I recognized as part of my sketch book, and showed it to me.	On it I read, in my own writing,' JANE EYRE', which I must have written without thinking.' The advertisements and Briggs spoke of a Jane Eyre, but I only knew a Jane Elliott,' said St John.' Are you Jane Eyre?" Yes – yes. . .
She was more innocent than clever. Few could say exactly what it was that made her so important, especially to people outside England, except for the fact that one could not take one's eyes off the woman. Yet that was no small thing. Diana was someone one had to look at, and such a person comes alone **once in a blue moon**.	She had a soft heart; that was evident. She had a **knack** for helping people in distress. And all such qualities rose in a face that everyone was simply pleased to see. In a way, she was more royal than the royals. She was the sentimental favourite figurehead.

FIGURE 12.4 Sample corpus-based domino cards

DDL activities and even to create their own domino cards on sets of idioms for classroom use with their classmates.

Corpus-based read-to-write Tasks: As can be seen in Figure 12.5, extended corpus-based examples were provided for students to guess meaning, provide a definition, and write similar examples to swap with their classmates.

Complete the following table.

Idiom in Sentence	Meaning/ Definition	Your example
Sparkster, as always I enjoyed reading your new book. It is interesting **food for thought** within the context of dealing with a parent or spouse with a personality disorder, but I also wonder about this within the context of a larger group of people targeting individuals.		
I have not played the Elemental, but I will be as soon as it's improved to the point where I get to jump right into an enjoyable and balanced game. For now, to **wet my appetite**, I'm wondering for you Master of Magic fans, do you think Elemental has the key aspects of the original MoM that made it such a classic?		
You **made my mouth water** reading your blog. I live in California, so I have access to seafood and having lived in Japan for 25 years since I was born there, I was surrounded by seafood, but never ate uni like you did before.		
To be a successful Beta, a man has to not only **bring home the bacon** and give- his money- away freely and without reservation, he also has to be the equivalent of a comedy channel on cable TV. He must be entertaining, engaging, and eternally fun to be around		

FIGURE 12.5 Use of corpus examples for definition writing task

An extension of this task was the "corpus-based meaning bluff", another game-like task with corpus-based examples. A set of cards, each with one idiomatic phrase in context, was prepared either by the teacher or by the students themselves. Working in groups, students had to guess the meaning of the phrase and write definitions (including false ones). Groups then sat facing each other and in turns read aloud their corpus-based example and definitions to members of the other team, who had to guess which definition was the correct one. Each team was awarded a point every time they managed to fool the other team.

Corpus-based lexical inference: As can be seen in Figure 12.6, students were given a list of examples on a specific word that, among other usages, gave rise to a specific idiom (such as "THIN", which is used to form the idiom "*thin air*") and were asked to trace the idiomatic usage of the keyword in any of the given sentences and guess its meaning based on the surrounding context.

As regards the teaching process itself, the DDL treatment was mainly based on printed handouts for either classroom or homework use. Nevertheless, the more confident students became in reading concordance output, the more frequently they consulted a computer and performed their own searching to design the previously mentioned corpus-based activity cards.

The control group underwent the traditional coursebook-based method of teaching with the same set of idioms presented to them in invented, contrived examples throughout the coursebook, receiving no other treatment but that of completing controlled practice activities, such as gap-filling, underlining, and matching ones provided in their coursebook, with no modifications. Both groups received instruction by the same EFL teacher, and they were both exposed to the same set of idioms a similar number of times throughout the school semester (16 weeks), while special attention was paid to eliminate any additional exposure to the target items by modifying the syllabus accordingly.

1	She was leading the way; very **tall**, very **thin**, very old; skinny old legs stiff as stilts.
2	I used to like the Invisible **Man** as well. He could vanish into **thin air** and nobody could trace him.
3	"You must be properly inside. Where the planes go, the **air** is **thin**." ' i should hope so,' said Gurder, stoutly.' That's why it's air."
4	Julius got the door open, and she followed him inside. As he had said, it was just a couple of rooms, very simply furnished. A **thin layer** of dust covered everything, but Jessamy didn't care.
5	The sharp nose and **thin lips** gave his angular face a harshness which was softened by the neatly trimmed black moustache he had worn since his early twenties.
6	There was water at the bottom covered by a **thin** skin of **ice** and he splashed into it face first. He scrambled frantically out, coughing and spluttering. He tried to climb the other side, but the snow was too deep and soft and he kept sinking into it.

FIGURE 12.6 Use of corpus examples for lexical inference

Pre- and post-test: Students' knowledge of or familiarity with the specific set of idioms was tested twice using a pre-test (to establish their initial knowledge) and a delayed post-test to explore whether and to what extent corpora-based teaching practices had an impact on young EFL learners' overall acquisition of idiomatic phrases. The researcher-developed test consisted of 20 multiple-choice and 20 definition-matching items. The items incorporated knowledge of the specific set of idioms and synonyms of those target items that were taught during the 16-week treatment period. All target items were chosen from the assigned coursebook students were using during the semester (*Upstream Intermediate*). It should be added that including multiple measures of knowledge is commonplace in vocabulary research, enabling researchers to tap into learners' competence at multiple levels and produce richer insights into the multifaceted nature of L2 lexical knowledge (Schmitt, 2010). The test was piloted with a group of language learners similar to those in the main study, and modifications were made based on both participants' comments during the piloting phase and suggestions kindly made by experts in the field who were professors with more than ten years of experience teaching English language–related courses. The reliability of the test was estimated to be .82 using Kuder-Richarson 21 formula (setting the cut-off score per item to .70).

Findings

Table 12.2 shows the pre and post-test results for both the experimental and the control groups. Kolmogorov-Smirnov test results suggest the data was normally distributed for each test (pre/post) for both groups ($p > 0.05$).

In order to check whether a significant relationship between DDL and intermediate EFL learners' improved acquisition of idiomatic phrases did exist, a comparison was made between the pre- and post-test results within each group. A paired-sample t-test revealed a significant increase in the performance of both the experimental group ($t = -50.36$, $df = 29$, $p < .001$) and the control group ($t = -29.41$, $df = 29$, $p < .001$) between the two tests, which is to be expected as both groups received instruction on idiomatic expressions.

When comparing the mean performance in the pre-test and post-test between the two groups, a repeated measures ANOVA (Figure 12.7) revealed a significant difference between experimental/control groups in terms of the change in scores pre- to post-test, with the experimental group experiencing the largest gain in scores with a large effect size ($F (1, 58) = 114.64$, $p < .001$, partial eta

TABLE 12.2 Pre- and post-test scores

Group	Mean (SD) Pre-test	Mean (SD) Post-test
Experimental group ($n = 30$)	16.33 (1.80)	32.23 (2.32)
Control group ($n = 30$)	15.10 (1.32)	26.83 (1.82)

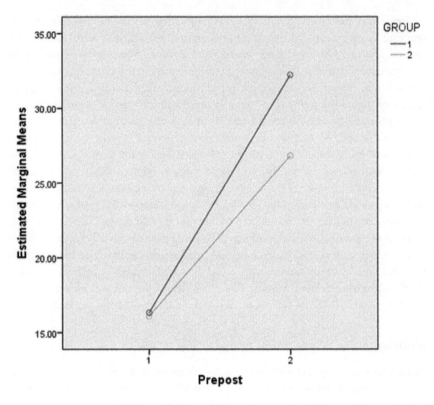

FIGURE 12.7 Estimated marginal means of pre-post test scores between experimental group (1) and control group (2)

squared = .664). Levene's test of equality of error variances was non-significant, suggesting the model accurately represented the degree of variation shown.

Discussion

The aim of the present study was to investigate whether intermediate EFL learners' ability to process idiomatic expressions could be improved when exposed to authentic examples of written and spoken discourse, while setting up situations in which students could answer questions about language themselves by studying corpus data in the form of concordance lines and extended examples. At the same time, the ultimate aim of the study was to add to the very limited database of relevant research on the use of DDL for acquiring idioms and to assist learners with methods that can best facilitate the development of their idiomatic repertoire through DDL. The findings indicated a positive relationship between EFL learners' idiomatic language development and DDL, since learners of the experimental group performed significantly better than the control group in the post-test. This is likely because students were exposed to a wider range of authentic contexts for idioms and took part in a range of corpus-based activities that were considerably more engaging than their traditional coursebook-based English language lessons. These findings are in agreement with previous studies that have shown positive results of the application of DDL to high-level students (e.g. Cobb, 1997; Kennedy & Miceli, 2001; Lenko-Szymanska, 2002) but further add to our present state of knowledge as regards the positive impact of DDL activities on younger learners. Unlike Hunston (2002), Cobb and Horst (2002), and Bernadini's (2000) view that DDL is more beneficial for advanced learners, the empirical results of the present study lend support to the view that corpus-based activities can indeed offer younger, intermediate level students a more complete and diverse picture of frequently used (yet troublesome to learn) idiomatic phrases encountered in everyday discourse. Furthermore, the fact that the participants in the present study were experiencing their first taste of DDL without having received any special training beforehand suggests DDL can lead to immediate learning on par with traditional approaches. This may also be taken to suggest that training and further experience on DDL could give it a distinct advantage over traditional teaching practices, even at lower levels of language competence.

The results of the present study conform to previous studies (Boulton, 2008; Chambers, 2005; Frankenberg-Garcia, 2014; Römer, 2004), which found that a corpus-based data-driven approach to teaching and learning vocabulary in general is more effective than traditional methods, including consultation of a coursebook or reference book, such as a dictionary. Learners in the experimental group outperformed learners in the control group presumably because of the fact that the former had the chance to look beyond the sentence level to patterns found in extended discourse and could further explore the connection between different forms and senses of a word as they analyzed concordance lines and extended examples of each target word. In the present study, an attempt was made to provide students with examples that were not simplified but clearly illustrated the different senses and usage of the target words. At the same time, as Boulton (2009b) suggests, providing printed materials has the substantial advantage of obviating the need for computer laboratories while such material may actually improve the efficiency of the process by reducing some of the difficulties associated with hands-on work, especially the risk of students being "overwhelmed" by the mass of irrelevant and even incomprehensible data. Moreover, in accord with Reppen (2010), picking out certain concordance lines does not reduce the authenticity of the materials; on the contrary, it makes the authentic materials more relevant, appropriate, and meaningful for the learners. In fact, by introducing learners to the output lines of KWICs and extended examples in the form of teacher-prepared printed materials in the classroom and helping them to discover patterns of language use, the participants did not show much difficulty working independently with online corpora at a later stage of the study.

Finally, it is worth highlighting at this point that the data-driven learning activities used in the present study were complementary to other activities included in the assigned coursebook, in which the development of students' communicative competence through skill-based and integrated tasks was also emphasized. Having said that, it might be safe to argue that inductive and exploratory activities for "notoriously difficult" language features could be supplemented with a range of meaning-focused and fluency-building tasks in which learners would attempt to reach a specific communicative purpose. With clear language-learning outcomes in mind, a teacher can create a wide variety of data-driven learning materials for his or her students to use throughout a standard lesson. For instance, corpus-based data could replace made-up examples in the presentation stage of a reading comprehension task or be used as consciousness-raising input before the administration of a writing task. As can be seen from the sample tasks included in the methodology section, the present study did not opt for "dramatic" changes in the ELT classroom but adopted a more practical and manageable within a standard classroom-setting approach that aimed at integrating DDL activities into the assigned coursebook with activities based on authentic discourse from different text types that could supplement, enrich, and extend the ones offered by the designers of the specific coursebook. In the light of these positive results, ELT teachers could consider incorporating DDL activities into the teaching process as an integral part of their teaching agenda in order to facilitate overall language instruction. Initially, training students to search online corpora and concordance lines on their own might be a slow process. Nevertheless, once students develop the habit and online searching becomes automatic, it can yield substantial development in students' language ability as they become more autonomous and independent and they are able to manage their learning and monitor their progress over time. As far as teachers themselves are concerned, one possible response to their wishes for improved teaching materials could be their participation in training seminars during which they could familiarize themselves with available corpora and feel more confident to indulge in designing supplementary material themselves in accord with their students' needs and preferences. At the same time, echoing other researchers, we should sound a note of caution and further stress the fact that teachers who want to use corpora with their students need to have a good understanding of the multifaceted aspects of corpus literacy and carefully consider which groups of learners may profit most from which types of materials for any corpus-based intervention to be successful.

However, the implementation of DDL in the present study presented a number of challenges that it is hoped will be overcome in future research. For instance, as only a specific set of idioms included in the school coursebook were used, the DDL activities inevitably focused on a specific group of words; should the range of idiomatic phrases increase, the generalizability of the present results might be strengthened. Moreover, given that existing research (cf. Doroodi & Hashemian, 2011; Ellis, 2012) has shown that transparent idioms, i.e. figurative expressions whose meanings can be effortlessly deduced because of the clear connection between the literal meanings (i.e. *cover your tracks*), are generally easier to comprehend than opaque ones in which the constituent words do not make a significant contribution towards the decoding of the idiomatic meaning (i.e. *bring home the bacon*); as such, more in-depth research is needed into whether DDL could be particularly beneficial when learning opaque versus transparent idioms. It would also be useful to extend the adopted methodology to EFL learners at both lower and higher grade levels and for conclusions to be drawn from a much more extensive sample of participants. Moreover, the present study did not investigate students' general attitudes and beliefs towards DDL techniques and to what extent these could affect their overall language proficiency, an insight that could help teachers apply such approaches in their teaching context more effectively. From a psycholinguistic perspective, future studies may investigate the psychological factors that come into play when using corpus databases. For example, it might be worthwhile to see how independent corpus searching can influence language learners' feelings of self-efficacy and autonomy. At the same time, following Meunier's suggestion (this volume), the current scope of DDL could be expanded to integrate new tools, new multimodal types of input, and inclusive DDL tasks that are integrated in meaning-focused curricular and extra-curricular activities carried out through freely accessible mobile applications.

To conclude, there is no doubt that corpora can improve pedagogical practice in a number of ways, both indirectly by informing teaching materials and reference works and directly as language learning tools and repositories for the design of data-intensive learning activities (Aston, 2001; Boulton & Cobb, 2017; Green, 2018; Tyler, 2010). As Bernardini (2002, p. 165) artfully states, "Corpora are rich sources of autonomous learning activities of a serendipitous kind" that give each interested learner the opportunity to become a *"traveller* instead of a *researcher"* (Bernardini, 2000, p. 131). However, more research on the impact and learning outcomes of corpus-based methods is needed in order to provide large-scale evidence-based pedagogical guidelines on the types of tasks that could be beneficial for different types of language learners and skills that would benefit most from a corpus-based teaching approach. On the other hand, given the fact that corpus-based practices are not an "end all be all" to language teaching but can facilitate language acquisition, teachers should not feel intimidated or overwhelmed at the thought of working with corpora or use them only for "special" courses or class periods; rather, they could have corpus-influenced materials, corpus-cited texts, and corpus-based activities integrated throughout their syllabus. In a nutshell, echoing Boulton (2009a), for DDL to become *ordinary* practice it should be employed by *ordinary* teachers as *ordinary* practice alongside other *ordinary* activities and materials within any *ordinary* language learning classroom.

References

Abel, B. (2003). English idioms in the first language and second language lexicon: A dual representation approach. *Second Language Research, 19*(4), 329–358.

Aston, G. (2001). *Learning with corpora*. Houston, TX: Athelstan.

Bardovi-Harlig, K., Mossman, S., & Vellenga, H. E. (2015). The effect of instruction on pragmatic routines in academic discussion. *Language Teaching Research, 19*(3), 324–350.

Basanta, C. P., & Martin, M. E. R. (2007). The application of data-driven learning to a small scale corpus: Using film transcripts for teaching conversational skills. *Language and Computers: Studies in Practical Linguistics, 61,* 141–158.

Beloussova, V. (2015). *Idiom learning materials for Estonian Secondary School students* (Unpublished MA thesis). University of Tartu, Estonia.

Bennett, G. (2010). *Using CORPORA in the language learning classroom.* Ann Arbor: University of Michigan Press.

Bernardini, S. (2000). *Competence, capacity, corpora.* Bologna: CLUEB.

Bernardini, S. (2002). Exploring new directions for discovery learning. In B. Kettemann & G. Marko (Eds.), *Teaching and learning by doing corpus analysis* (pp. 165–182). Amsterdam, The Netherlands: Rodopi.

Boers, F., & Demecheleer, M. (2001). Measuring the impact of cross-cultural differences on learners' comprehension of imageable idioms. *ELT Journal, 55*(3), 255–262.

Boers, F., Eyckmans, J., & Stengers, H. (2006). Means of motivating multiword units: Rationale, mnemonic benefits and cognitive-style variables. In S. Foster-Cohen, M. Medved Krajnovic, & J. Mihaljevic Djigunovic (Eds.), *EUROSLA yearbook* 6 (pp. 169–190). Amsterdam and Philadelphia: John Benjamins.

Boulton, A. (2008). DDL: Reaching the parts other teaching can't reach? In A. Frankenberg-Garcia (Ed.), *Proceedings of the 8th teaching and language corpora conference (TaLc8)* (pp. 28–44). Amsterdam: Rodopi.

Boulton, A. (2009a). Testing the limits of data-driven learning: Language proficiency and training. *ReCALL, 21,* 37–54.

Boulton, A. (2009b). Data-driven learning: On paper, in practice. In T. Harris & M. Moreno Jaén (Eds.), *Corpus linguistics in language teaching* (p. XX). Bern: Peter Lang, Linguistic Insights.

Boulton, A. (2010). Data-driven learning: On paper, in practice. In T. Harris & M. Moreno Jaén (Eds.), *Corpus linguistics in language teaching* (pp. 17–52). Bern: Peter Lang.

Boulton, A. (2011). Data-driven learning: The perpetual enigma. In S. Gozdz-Roszkowski (Ed.), *Explorations across languages and corpora* (pp. 563–580). Frankfurt: Peter Lang.

Boulton, A., & Cobb, T. (2017). Corpus use in language learning: A meta-analysis. *Language Learning, 67*(2), 348–393.

Braun, S. (2007). Integrating corpus work into secondary education: From data-driven learning to needs-driven corpora. *ReCALL, 19*(3), 307–328.

Brenner, G. (2013). *Webster's new world American idioms handbook.* New York, NY: Webster's New World.

Bulut, T. (2004). Idiom processing in L2: Through rose-colored glasses. *The Reading Matrix, 4*(2), 105–116.

Cain, K., Oakhill, J., & Lemmon, K. (2005). The relation between children's reading comprehension level and their comprehension of idioms. *Journal of Experimental Child Psychology, 90*(1), 65–87.

Celce-Murcia, M., & Larsen-Freeman, D. (1999). *The grammar book: An ESL/EFL teacher's course* (2nd ed.). Boston: Heinle & Heinle.

Chambers, A. (2005). Integrating corpus consultation in language studies. *Language Learning & Technology, 9,* 111–125.

Cieslicka, A. (2006). Literal salience in on-line processing of idiomatic expressions by second language learners. *Second Language Research, 22*(2), 115–144.

Clifton, J., & Phillips, D. (2006). Ensuring high surrender value for corporate clients and increasing the authority of the language instructor: The dividents of a data-driven lexical approach to ESP. *The Journal of Language for International Business, 17*(2), 72–81.

Cobb, T. (1997). Is there any measurable learning from hands-on concordancing? *System, 25*, 301–315.

Cobb, T., & Horst, M. (2002). *Growing academic vocabulary with a collaborative on-line database.* ERIC Document Reproduction Service No. ED457698.

Colombo, L. (1993). The comprehension of ambiguous idioms in context. In C. Cacciari & P. Tabossi (Eds.), *Idioms: Processing, Structure, and Interpretation* (pp. 163–200). Hillsdale, NJ: Lawrence Erlbaum Associates.

Cooper, T. (1999). Processing of idioms by L2 learners of English. *TESOL Quarterly, 33*(2), 233–262.

Davies, M. (2008). *The Corpus of Contemporary American English (COCA): 400+ million words, 1990-present.* Retrieved from https://www.english-corpora.org/coca/.

Doroodi, S., & Hashemian, M. (2011). The relationship between reading comprehension and figurative competence in L2 learners. *Theory and Practice in Language Studies, 1*(6), 711–717.

Ellis, N. (2012). Formulaic language and second language acquisition: Zipf and the phrasal teddy bear. *Annual Review of Applied Linguistics, 32*, 17–44.

Evans, V. (2012). *Upstream intermediate coursebook.* Berkshire, UK: Express Publishing.

Frankenberg-Garcia, A. (2014). The use of corpus examples for language comprehension and production. *ReCALL, 26*(2), 128–146.

Friginal, E. (2018). *Corpus linguistics for English teachers: New tools, online resources, and classroom activities.* New York: Routledge.

Gavioli, L. (2001). The learner as researcher: Introducing corpus concordancing in the classroom. In G. Aston (Ed.), *Learning with corpora* (pp. 108–137). Houston, TX: Athelstan.

Geluso, J., & Yamaguchi, A. (2014). Discovering formulaic language through data-driven learning: Student attitudes and efficacy. *ReCALL, 26*(2), 225–242.

Grant, L. (2007). In a manner of speaking: Assessing frequent spoken figurative *idioms* to assist ESL/EFL teachers. *System, 35*(2), 169–181.

Grant, L., & Nation, P. (2006). How many idioms are there in English? *International Journal of Applied Linguistics, 15*(1), 1–14.

Green, B. (2018). Corpora in Language Learning. *The TESOL Encyclopedia of English Language Teaching*, 1–9.

Hadley, G. (2002). Sensing the winds of change: An introduction to data-driven learning. *RELC Journal, 33*(2), 99–124.

Hinkel, E. (2017). Teaching idiomatic expressions and phrases: Insights and techniques. *Iranian Journal of Language Teaching Research, 5*(3), 45–59.

Huang, Z. (2014). The effects of paper-based DDL on the acquisition of lexico-grammatical patterns in L2 writing. *ReCALL, 26*, 163–183.

Hunston, S. (2002). *Corpora in applied linguistics.* Cambridge, UK: Cambridge University Press.

Irujo, S. (1986). Don't put your leg in your mouth: Transfer in the acquisition of idioms in a second language. *TESOL Quarterly, 20*(2), 287–304.

Johns, T. F. (1991). Should you be persuaded: Two examples of data-driven learning. In T. Johns & P. King (Eds.), *Classroom concordancing: English Language Research Journal, 4*, 1–16.

Kennedy, G., & Miceli, T. (2001). An evaluation of intermediate students' approaches to corpus investigation. *Language Learning and Technology, 5*(3), 77–90.

Khonbi, Z., & Sadeghi, K. (2017). Improving English language learners' idiomatic competence: Does mode of teaching play a role? *Iranian Journal of Language Teaching Research, 5*(3), 61–79.

Laufer, B. (2000). Avoidance of idioms in a second language: The effect of L1-L2 degree of similarity. *Studia Linguistica, 54*(2), 186–196.

Lee, H., Warschauer, M., & Ho Lee, J. (2018). The effects of corpus use on second language vocabulary learning: A multilevel meta-analysis. *Applied Linguistics, 39*, 1–34.

Lenko-Szymanska, A. (2002). How to trace the growth in learners' active vocabulary? A corpus-based Study. In B. Kettemann & G. Marko (Eds.), *Teaching and learning by doing corpus analysis* (pp. 217–230). Amsterdam: Brill | Rodopi.

Li, S. (2017). Using corpora to develop learners' collocational competence. *Language Learning & Technology, 21*(3), 153–171.

Liontas, J. (2001). That's all Greek to me! The comprehension and interpretation of modern Greek phrasal idioms. *The Reading Matrix, 1*(1), 1–31.

Liontas, J. (2003). Killing two birds with one stone: Understanding Spanish VP idioms in and out of context. *Hispania, 86*(2), 289–301.

Liontas, J. (2015). Developing idiomatic competence in the ESOL classroom: A pragmatic account. *TESOL Journal, 6*(4), 621–658.

Liontas, J. (2017). Why teach idioms? A challenge to the profession. *Iranian Journal of Language Teaching Research, 5*(3), 5–25.

Liu, D. (2003). The most frequently used spoken American English idioms: A corpus analysis and its implications. *TESOL Quarterly, 37*(4), 671–700.

Moreno, E. M. G. (2011). The role of etymology in the teaching of idioms related to colors in an L2. *Porta Linguarum, 16*, 19–32.

Mohamadi-Asl, F. (2013). The impact of context on learning idioms in EFL classes. *MEXTESOL Journal, 37*(1), 1–12.

Nation, I. S. P. (2001). *Learning vocabulary in another language.* Cambridge: Cambridge University Press.

Oakhill, J., Cain, K., & Nesi, B. (2016). Understanding of idiomatic expressions in context in skilled and less skilled comprehenders: Online processing and interpretation. *Scientific Studies of Reading, 20*(2), 124–139.

Paltridge, B. (2001). *Genre and the language learning classroom.* Ann Arbor: University of Michigan Press.

Reppen, R. (2010). *Using corpora in the language classroom.* Cambridge, UK: Cambridge University Press.

Römer, U. (2004). Comparing real and ideal language learner input: The use of an EFL textbook corpus in corpus linguistics and language teaching. In G. Aston, S. Bernardini, & D. Stewart (Eds.), *Corpora and language learners* (pp. 151–168). Amsterdam, The Netherlands: John Benjamins.

Römer, U. (2011). Corpus research applications in second language teaching. *Annual Review of Applied Linguistics, 31*, 205–225.

Sadeghi, B., Dastjerdi, H., & Ketabi, S. (2010). Patterns of Persian EFL learners' comprehension of idiomatic expressions: Reading strategies and cross-cultural mappings in focus. *Asian Social Science, 6*(8), 81–99.

Schmitt, N. (2010). *Researching vocabulary: A vocabulary research manual.* Basingstoke: Palgrave Macmillan.

Simpson, R., & Mendis, D. (2003). A corpus-based study of idioms in academic speech. *TESOL Quarterly, 37*(3), 419–441.

Siyanova-Chanturia, A., Conklin, K., & Schmitt, N. (2011). Adding more fuel to the fire: An eye-tracking study of idiom processing by native and non-native speakers. *Second Language Research, 27*(2), 251–272.

Stevens, V. (1991). Classroom concordancing: Vocabulary materials derived from relevant, authentic text. *English for Special Purposes Journal, 10*, 35–46.

Szudarski, P. (2017). Learning and teaching L2 collocations: Insights from research. *TESL Canada Journal, 34*(3), 205–216.

Thompson, P. (2007). Corpus-based EAP pedagogy. *Journal of English for Academic Purposes, 6*(4), 319–335.

Timmis, I. (2015). *Corpus linguistics for ELT: Research and practice.* New York: Routledge.

Tyler, A. (2010). Usage-based approaches to language and their applications to second language learning. *Annual Review of Applied Linguistics, 30,* 270–291.

Xie, H. (2017). Investigating Chinese EFL learners' comprehension of English idioms. *Journal of Language Teaching and Research, 8*(2), 329–336.

Zyzik, E. (2011). Second language idiom learning: The effects of lexical knowledge and pedagogical sequencing. *Language Teaching Research, 15*(4), 413–433.

AFTERWORD

Peter Crosthwaite

This volume has addressed the dire need for studies exploring the affordances of data-driven learning (DDL) for pre-tertiary learners. The first section outlined a variety of conceptual recommendations and methodological solutions for the implementation of DDL into school curricula, as well as how to overcome potential barriers to its integration. In the second section, a range of new and innovative approaches to corpora and corpus tools that can facilitate DDL for younger learners has been presented, although this represents only the tip of the iceberg going forward. The third section has shown that DDL *can and does work* with primary and secondary learners of both first and second languages in a diverse range of language learning and teaching contexts, while the contributors have provided a variety of practical DDL-focused lesson plans and activities. We hope that the reader comes away from this volume with a sense of excitement – excitement about the potential opportunities that DDL can offer for younger learners and excitement to implement the ideas outlined in this volume in your own classrooms.

However, we are obviously well aware that more work needs to be done if corpora and DDL can even come close to being integrated into pre-tertiary curricula, whether this is for L1 or L2 education or at the primary or secondary levels of education. I end this volume with a call for further research on a number of matters arising from the work conducted in this volume. These are presented in no particular order – rather, one needs to consider each as an equally important piece of the puzzle to be solved if mainstream integration and normalisation of DDL is to occur.

- It is apparent that much more needs to be done to convince teachers of younger learners to adopt DDL in the classroom. While this is not necessarily specific to teachers of younger learners per se, the fact that a number of studies in this volume were set in teacher training contexts is indicative of the current state of progress regarding the integration of DDL in pre-tertiary curricula. There is a great need

- for larger funded projects looking at how DDL can be introduced into pre- or in-sessional teacher training courses. As reported in this volume, it can be a struggle to persuade teachers of the value of corpus consultation for DDL, yet this is where the first battle needs to be won if one is to win the war, so to speak.
- In order to win the hearts and minds of teachers, much work still needs to be done on developing suitable corpora and corpus tools for younger learners. The corpora and tools outlined in this volume are a fantastic step in the right direction – successfully engaging even the youngest learners in querying and manipulating language data for a range of learning outcomes. However, it is telling that, for a number of studies in this volume, the contributors have resorted to the use of printed concordances rather than direct corpus consultation. Obviously, this approach does bring a number of benefits (as outlined in the chapters themselves), and we must consider, as shown in Alex Boulton's foreword to this volume, that DDL comes in many shapes and sizes. Yet going forward, I believe we are still in need of a "killer app" for DDL. As with Hirata (this volume), this app will ideally be multimodal, with access to a range of corpora that are standardised for proficiency level, genre, and audience. In addition (although this is some way off), this "killer app" will be one where the system itself does the work when it comes to querying the corpus data, preferably based on simple oral commands from the end user. At the risk of sounding a little *Star Trek*, we are now nearing a point in technological development where a teacher in a classroom could stand up and say, "Computer, tell me about the use of 'conclude' in essay writing" and have the system provide ten visually appealing concordances, repeating them back to the class orally before providing two or three variants that might be of interest. The technology to do this is already here – it just requires the research community to bring it all together.
- Much of the work in this volume is (necessarily perhaps) exploratory and qualitative, with a smaller range of quantitative studies conducted with one or two class groups of younger learners over a period of less than a year. While this is par for the course in DDL studies generally, there is still an obvious need for larger studies investigating the incorporation of DDL into local or even national curricula, exploring the benefits of this approach with participants numbering in the hundreds or even thousands, and charting the successes (as well as any failures) in the implementation of DDL over extended periods. As Schaeffer-Lacroix (this volume) suggests, innovations take time to be adopted, yet in most cases the DDL ends when the researchers' time is up and the papers arising are published. Will the teachers and students who experienced DDL in this volume still be "language detectives" in a year's time? This remains to be seen.

Despite the challenges raised here, I conclude this afterword with a renewed sense of optimism that the field is heading in the direction necessary to overcome them. The studies presented in this volume are some of the clearest evidence yet that DDL has a place in the pre-tertiary curriculum and that the best is yet to come for DDL with younger learners in the near future.

INDEX

abilities 6, 98, 106, 108
accessible xiv, xvi, 9, 23, 62, 70–71, 90, 101, 112, 233
accuracy 25, 37, 38, 47, 116, 124, 147, 195, 209, 210
acquire 8, 17, 58, 75, 83, 144, 185, 188
acquired 14, 88–89, 183, 193, 197, 198
action 2, 34, 58, 74, 161, 172, 173
active 2, 3, 14, 57, 172, 183, 185, 204, 209
adjective(s) 8, 48, 52, 54, 55, 75, 117, 125, 161, 177, 178, 181
adolescents 106, 175, 187, 188
adult 60, 70, 88, 100, 109, 137, 171, 187
adverbs 54, 75, 79, 178
ages 55, 69, 135, 151, 176, 190
aims 13, 17, 22, 23, 38, 102, 107, 192, 211
alignment 5, 6, 13, 14, 18, 26–27, 213
analyze 17, 34, 36, 136, 139, 210
annotation 36, 51, 71, 72, 75, 76, 77, 80
AntConc 175, 184
appendix 36, 115, 116, 118–120, 124, 200
assessment 4, 5, 6, 13–15, 17, 18, 25–26, 33, 34, 51, 155, 166
assignments 35, 38, 40, 41, 168, 183
assistance 101, 153, 155, 156, 160, 168, 193
attitude 33, 58, 97, 98, 135, 153, 176
audience 60, 61, 77, 92, 100, 211, 215, 229
authenticity 23, 32, 41, 110, 221
autonomous 3, 58, 68, 133, 145, 183, 222, 223
auxiliary 188, 189, 194, 195, 202
availability 112, 133, 190, 203, 205
avoid 6, 43, 113, 139, 142, 145, 179, 208–209

background 17, 32, 57, 69, 83, 89, 107, 115, 147, 152
barriers 6, 47, 48, 54–57, 60, 61, 62, 112, 167, 228
BAWE 8, 153, 154–157, 163–165
beginner 39, 70, 74, 173
behaviour 69, 89, 106, 109, 145
beliefs 5, 6, 48, 95, 153, 195, 205, 223
benefit 22, 40, 67, 68, 97, 102, 134, 190, 223
bilingual x, 125, 139
blackboard xii, 41, 176, 179, 183
blended 8, 187, 191
BNC 19, 24, 70, 76, 77, 88, 111, 118, 128, 135, 138, 212
browser 73, 91, 164
BYU 24, 90, 94, 138

capabilities 6, 108, 150, 153
CEFR 8, 32, 33, 35, 43, 49, 50, 75, 172, 173–174, 175, 189, 190
challenge 38, 43, 69, 79, 80, 134, 178, 222
characteristics 21, 33, 48, 61, 75, 76, 84, 107, 108, 191, 203
child-friendly 6, 31, 103
chunking xiii
chunks 19, 77, 193, 203
click 54, 71, 112, 163, 215
CLIL 119, 127
CoAl 13–16, 25, 27
coca 8, 24, 90, 94, 95, 97, 99, 190, 191–193, 195–197, 200, 201, 204, 212, 215
cognitive 3, 14, 23, 33, 34, 40, 41, 74, 83, 108, 172, 181, 189
collocates 112, 114, 117, 138

Index

collocation 3, 7, 23–25, 43, 77, 110, 114, 116, 117–118, 125, 128, 183
comprehension 8, 40, 74, 89, 90–91, 172, 173, 184, 209, 222
computer-assisted 2, 146
concordancer 5, 51, 52, 58–62, 112–113, 193
conference xii, xv, 15, 47, 64, 82, 167, 204, 224, 242
confidence 22, 97, 99, 106, 109, 112, 158, 162, 192, 198, 204
consciousness-raising xiii, 38, 39, 93, 101, 222
construction 8, 34, 36, 72, 73, 156, 158, 164
consult 3, 38, 100, 158, 160, 164, 192
corpus-assisted x, 133, 135, 136, 140
corpus-driven 187
cotext 36, 40, 42, 43, 113, 176, 183, 196
coursebook 213, 216, 218, 219, 221, 222
courses 17, 44, 58, 106, 114, 172, 219, 223, 229
cross-cultural 189
culture 33, 69, 83, 93, 109, 172

decision 31, 32, 33, 77, 120, 126, 135, 156, 175
deductive 3, 35, 139, 143, 145–147, 213
definition 14, 23, 24, 26, 32, 36, 75, 134, 139, 144, 151, 161, 218, 219
detectives 3, 134, 192, 229
devices 32, 61, 62, 89, 106, 152, 154
dictionaries 7, 115, 139, 143, 145–147, 167, 192
disciplinary 3, 173
discovery 53, 59, 68, 103, 133, 179, 210
domain xiii, 27, 111, 112, 114, 119, 120, 128
dynamic xiii, 77, 106, 112

EAP 70, 190
ECCo 190, 191, 194, 196, 198, 201, 204
engage 6, 8, 15, 26, 33, 38, 72, 109, 113, 134, 189, 192
enhanced 3, 19, 21, 49, 62, 106, 120, 146
error 3, 17, 25, 38, 39, 55, 60, 158,–161, 163, 166, 204, 220
ESL xiv, 96
Europe 5, 14, 22, 32–34, 43–44, 172
exercise 22, 40, 42, 43, 59, 72, 118–120, 125, 128, 180, 181
experiment 8, 127, 137–139, 140, 143–147, 167, 171, 174, 182, 184
exploration 47, 48, 51, 55, 57, 58, 61, 79, 93
exposure 17, 77, 80, 89, 93, 136, 147, 152, 183, 189, 203, 218

feedback 38, 40, 51, 115, 154, 158, 177, 180–182, 205
FLE 171, 173–175, 180, 182–184
fluency 25, 37, 38, 74, 108, 114, 136, 210, 220
focus-on-form 3, 19
formulaic 15, 24, 135–137, 142, 143, 144, 146, 147, 209–211
framework 22, 32, 33, 48, 90, 91, 172

game xvi, 20, 24, 55, 146, 216, 217
gap-filling 59, 176, 180, 198, 199, 201, 218
generation xiv, 67, 108, 113, 146
genre 23, 70, 112, 128, 147, 151, 153, 215, 229
grade 14, 150, 153, 164, 165, 199, 223
guidance 18, 40, 53, 71, 72, 101, 102, 140, 163, 165, 187, 202, 204
guidelines 62, 175, 204, 223

handout 194–196, 198, 204
hands-on xiii –xv, 3, 31, 94, 106, 118, 154, 189–192, 221
homework 1, 24, 52, 81, 156, 158, 159, 162, 198–200, 218
human 43, 74, 88, 110, 175, 196, 210
hypotheses 171, 176, 183, 187, 204

idiom 2, 209, 213, 214, 216–218
idiomatic 9, 37, 208, 209, 211, 213, 218–222
implementation 39, 53, 101, 103, 134, 136, 150, 187, 211, 222, 228, 229
implications 7, 15, 89, 94, 95, 115, 116, 124, 146
impressions 94, 95, 97–99, 193, 198
improvement 9, 146, 147
independent 23, 25, 116, 162, 210, 222, 223
inductive 3, 35, 88, 93, 96, 114, 115, 117, 133, 187, 195, 213, 222
informal 34, 37, 143, 145, 153, 203, 205, 211, 213, 216
innovation 3, 6, 26, 47–49, 60, 61, 109, 184
insights 55, 135, 138, 140, 144, 205, 219
instructions 115, 117, 154, 156, 163, 181
integrate 2, 32, 34, 36, 48, 52, 89, 90, 233
interact 14, 33, 34, 82, 89, 90, 112
intercultural 33, 172
interfaces 19, 47, 71, 73, 133, 153
interpretation 54, 100, 102, 110, 111, 209
intervention 38, 134, 136, 202, 222
interviews xiv, 6, 8, 50, 54, 57, 60, 69, 72, 73, 75, 80, 135, 203, 205
intuition xvi, 108, 117, 120, 121, 125

Japanese 7, 21, 76, 93, 101, 103, 152
journals xiii, xiv, 111, 136, 210
junior 175, 176, 178, 185, 202

keyword 91, 173, 176, 181, 183, 213, 218
key-word-in-context 91, 138, 213
KWIC 36, 37, 40, 42, 43, 73, 91, 92, 113, 192, 195, 204

lexicogrammatical 22–23, 36–39, 43, 44, 136, 188, 189
Lexicography 81, 122, 166
lexicon 174, 175
lexis 3, 77, 153, 155
lextutor 175, 176, 185
limitations 18, 19, 112, 113, 116, 147
limits 23, 43, 54, 199
linguists 2, 68, 71, 74, 84, 110, 113, 204
longitudinal 147, 205
lyricstraining 5, 21, 22, 27

mainstream 5, 7, 9, 47, 103, 169, 203, 210, 228
MALL 2, 84
manipulation 6, 40, 44, 134, 151, 183
matching 17, 111, 113, 139, 201, 203, 209, 218
meaning-focused 22, 26, 222, 223
meaning-making 88–90
meanings 53, 93, 145, 188, 202, 208, 211, 222
media 50, 89–92, 100, 106, 109, 152, 174, 214
mediation 15, 17, 31, 44, 70, 71, 83, 134
meta-analysis 3, 4
metalinguistic 58, 151, 152, 175
mobile 2, 19, 21, 24, 84, 223
modal(s) 8, 76–77, 99, 188–190, 194–196, 198–202
modern 3, 32, 89, 187
motivation 24, 42, 48, 62, 99, 146, 183, 203
multilingual 8, 83, 172
multilingualism 2, 172
multimedia 6, 53, 71, 75, 79, 80, 174
multimodality 13, 19, 20, 21, 22, 89
multiword 15–17, 19, 21, 26, 208

natives 2, 7, 106–109, 114, 117, 120
natural 23, 69, 77, 95, 106, 137
negative 40, 58, 181, 195, 200
non-native 15, 93, 100, 110
noun 23, 42, 43, 55, 57, 111, 151, 178, 180

objective 2, 151, 194, 198
occurrence 41, 53, 83, 111, 115, 118, 163, 185

opaque 43, 176, 208, 222, 223
opinions 50, 60, 95, 97, 195, 198, 205
outcomes 5, 13, 14, 15–17, 25, 26, 93, 222, 223, 229

pairs 51, 68, 125, 128, 139, 192–194, 216
paper-based 18, 136, 137, 143, 144, 146, 147, 189, 190
paradigm 36, 107
parents 108, 168, 199, 212
participation 14, 152, 183, 202, 204, 222
passive 2, 14, 75, 145, 187
pattern 37, 39, 43, 55, 73, 134, 136, 144, 168
perceptions 7, 48, 50, 57, 61, 134, 135, 137, 142, 145, 147, 152, 168
perspectives 5, 173, 174
phrasal 135, 136–144, 147
phraseology 3, 7, 83, 107, 135, 137, 139, 140, 143–147, 153, 174
picture 31, 38, 89, 189, 221
platform 7, 51, 99, 155, 160, 174, 184, 191, 193, 212, 213
playphrase 5, 19, 20, 22
plural 42, 135, 178–180, 185
possessive 8, 177, 178
possibilities 43, 59, 60, 70, 74, 80
post-test 135, 137, 141, 142, 144, 210, 213, 219, 220
practitioners 89, 92, 93, 103, 203
pragmatic 44, 89, 136, 172, 189
preferences 6, 106, 153, 205, 222
preposition 39, 126, 178
pre-tertiary 1, 2, 4, 5, 67, 114, 228, 229
pre-test 137, 141, 144, 210, 213, 219
principles 32, 33, 69, 107, 115, 135, 172, 204
printout 17, 27, 46, 224
problem-solving 3, 108, 134, 150, 153, 167
professional 5, 14, 56, 69, 102, 168
program xv, 57, 139
programme 7, 14, 90, 173
pupils 32, 91, 93, 96, 100, 108, 171–179, 181–184

qualitative 8, 54, 70, 97, 99, 110, 116, 120, 135, 145, 147, 157, 173, 229
quality 13, 71, 93, 102, 136
quantitative 17, 110, 111, 115–118, 124, 173, 229
quasi-experimental 137, 211, 212
questionnaire 7, 50, 94, 95, 115, 137, 142, 143, 145, 177, 180, 183

reaction 8, 156, 163, 177
reality 7, 14, 41, 134
refinement 7, 106, 107, 112, 114, 115, 120, 121, 124, 125

reflection 15, 120, 179, 181, 183–185
register 3, 44, 112, 147, 154
representative 40, 70, 71, 74, 82, 110
representativeness 50, 69, 110
retrieval 7, 27, 106, 107, 109, 111–113
revision 8, 36, 49, 156, 158, 160, 161, 163–166, 168
risk 110, 175, 215, 221, 229
rule 35, 38, 43, 79, 176, 181–184, 188, 201

sample 6, 54, 62, 76, 92, 115, 138, 139, 147, 155, 205, 214, 216, 222, 223
scaffolding 6, 8, 25, 52, 72, 89, 134, 167, 168, 179, 183, 199
scenario 39, 49, 51, 69, 70–72, 80
screen 50, 90–92, 138, 156, 183, 213, 215
self-efficacy 8, 153, 167, 223
semantic 42, 43, 54, 55, 139, 151, 189, 209
senior 188, 190, 202, 204
sequences 135, 136, 142, 144, 147
sketch 8, 24, 50, 51, 53–61, 67, 153–158, 163–166, 216
sketchengine 164, 165
skill 4, 44, 79, 136, 147, 213
SLA 21, 22, 133, 143
social 14, 48, 51, 74, 82, 89, 107, 153, 172
Spanish 21, 25, 32, 71, 173
speech 19, 38, 51, 67, 71, 74, 88, 136, 151, 189, 193
spelling 68, 113, 116, 124, 125, 152, 154, 174
strategies 24, 25, 113, 119, 150, 189
structure 32–39, 41, 44, 77, 153, 178
subjunctive 43, 174
success 9, 69, 126, 134, 135, 150, 167, 168, 184, 190, 203
survey 67, 90, 93, 95, 97, 100–103, 115, 142, 211
syllabus 152, 218, 223
syntactic 35, 171, 174, 175, 178

task-based xiii, 49
TBLT 6, 35–36, 49
teenage 6, 67, 68, 74, 77, 79, 84
tests 7, 14, 17, 18, 24, 140, 141, 144, 166, 175, 209, 219
textbook 3, 6, 8, 74, 95, 96, 179, 188, 190, 191, 203, 204, 211
TEYL 88, 89, 92, 93, 97, 102, 103
theories 6, 14, 32, 81, 82, 174
trainee 7, 35, 47–49, 51, 54, 60, 62, 152, 204
transfer 8, 31, 38, 43
tutoring 8, 150, 152–154, 159, 162, 163, 167, 168, 169
typology 176, 192

units 15, 17, 19, 21, 26, 36, 73, 80, 93, 96, 134–135, 138, 142, 162
uptake 4, 6, 18, 54, 60, 62, 152, 167
usage-based 14, 83, 210
user-friendly 22, 24, 61, 62, 154, 191, 204

value 18, 24, 41, 42, 61, 102, 103, 107, 134, 146, 185, 215, 229
variables 13, 34, 39, 147
variation 8, 22, 44, 112, 136, 139, 147, 153, 182, 220
verbal 50, 56, 89, 174, 208
video 2, 7, 13, 20, 21, 69, 71–73, 82, 91
visual 3, 32, 35, 75, 89, 100, 153

Web-based 84, 133
website 50, 62, 84
wildcard 156, 158–160, 161, 163–165, 168
wording 111, 119, 128, 164, 165
Wordsmith 62, 151, 191, 194
worksheet 54, 116, 117, 193–196
workshop 64, 140, 187